Sell Up an
the Inland W

D1362937

Other titles by the same authors

Sell up and Sail (5th edition)
Watersteps through France
Back Door to Byzantium
A Spell in Wild France
Sail into the Sunset
Watersteps round Europe

Sell Up and Cruise the Inland Waterways

Bill & Laurel Cooper

Adlard Coles Nautical · London

Published by Adlard Coles Nautical
an imprint of A & C Black (Publishers) Ltd
36 Soho Square, London W1D 3QY
www.adlardcoles.com

First published 2010

ISBN 978-0-7136-7988-5

A CIP catalogue record for this book is available from the British Library.

This book is produced using paper that is made from wood grown in managed, sustainable forests. It is natural, renewable and recyclable. The logging and manufacturing processes conform to the environmental regulations of the country of origin.

Designed by Susan McIntyre
Typeset in 10.5 on 13pt FB Californian

Printed and bound in the UK by Martins the Printers

Note: while all reasonable care has been taken in the publication of this edition, the publisher takes no responsibility for the use of the methods or products described in the book.

Contents

Acknowledgements

Our grateful thanks go to all those boat people who have unwittingly contributed to this book over a glass of wine or a dockside chat.

Our thanks also go to the following people and organisations:

Tom, Dick and Barry, craftsmen and friends at Lowestoft.

Kevin of KM Electronics and www.yachtbits.com, a top-class amp chaser.

Carole Edwards, our patient and helpful editor.

Numerous French *bateliers* and the Dutch skippers who have been so helpful to us over the years.

The late Carrie Hoffman whose knowledge and experience on European waterways is greatly missed.

The ophthalmic consultants, staff and management of the Paget University Hospital at Great Yarmouth, who recently saved Bill's eyesight.

Our children, for still not interfering and trusting us out on our own.

Bruges, the Markt.

Introduction

As a couple we have been living aboard boats for over 30 years.
Having both been brought up on the Norfolk Broads, we have always enjoyed sailing and being afloat generally. We started with a National Twelve racing dinghy in our teens, ending up with our present 'old folk's boat', *Faraway*.

Bill's deep interest in river navigation started when he was in the Royal Navy. He found himself navigating ships and boats of various sizes, not only at sea, but also in rivers and canals all over the world.

We have been cruising together for a life-time. Some was spent deep-sea ocean-going, some on the great rivers of the world, and some was ditch-crawling. Why? We like travelling by water. It's a satisfying and healthy life. There is no stress, because you leave it all behind. You see wonderful places, meet wonderful people, and the lifestyle does not have to be expensive.

Anyone interested in boats will at some time contemplate new waters. The experienced may wish to be adventurous, and cruise the Danube, the Shannon, or the Intracoastal Waterway in the USA. Some, perhaps new to waterways, may wish to buy or build, but, knowing that boating mistakes can be expensive, are cautious. We sympathise with those who might like to dip a toe in quiet waters by chartering a self-drive boat for a holiday, as so many enthusiasts started out. All of us have much to learn.

❖ The cruising mindset ❖

In *Sell Up and Sail* we went deeply into the psychology of cruising, and have no space to repeat it here. Read it if you get the chance, as it complements this book. Lest for lack of guidance you end up with all the grief and none of the pleasure (God forbid), we will précis the main points:

There are three important rules that we follow:

- Keep learning.
- Keep an open mind about places, people, food and drink.
- Travel with moderate expectations.

1

We notice that people with an optimistic outlook do better in the contentment department of the cruising lifestyle; the constant 'carpers' do less well. As a bonus you will probably find that the daily problems you will have to solve and the healthy, open-air life should keep you firing on all cylinders into a happy old age.

However, there is more to inland waters than we can impart in one book. We'll try to infect you with our enthusiasm and give a sense of the adventure that you will enjoy. Inland waters are exciting, without the risk of seasickness – a cause of many people giving up sea-going because their partners are susceptible. We can open new vistas for those who wish to sell up and lead a life on the water but with fewer heroic ambitions. The inland waterways beckon.

Nobody knows everything about boats but, over the years, we have picked up a wealth of knowledge (often the hard way) and we are keen to pass on to you as much of this information and practical advice as possible. We are not fans of the bureaucracy which exists on the waterways but have to live with it; we do try to keep a professional attitude and hope that it is reciprocated. Above all we exercise prudence – which often comes from learning by our mistakes.

The nature of the subject means that some chapters will overlap others; we have endeavoured to arrange them in a way which will both inform and entertain. To this end you will find cameos of waterway life, gleaned from our travels. We stop from time to time for a relaxing interlude which will give you an insight into how you will live on the waterways: shopping, eating out, waiting for a lock, doing some maintenance, swapping stories with someone new or visiting some wonderful local sites of interest.

Finally, we hope our book will fire up your interest and give you plenty of inspiration – the cruising life is one of the finest experiences you can have and we can't now imagine living any other way. So make the decision and join us – we don't think you will regret it.

Bill and Laurel Cooper

BEFORE YOU GO

- Pay all debts, moral, social, and financial.
- Learn as much as you can - not just certificates, we mean gain real boating experience.
- Solve all your shoreside problems:
  - Money – make sure you are fully financed.
  - Property – if you are cruising for long periods, ensure your home is safe.
  - Health – get a check-up.
  - Relationships – does your partner want to go?
  - Job – take a sabbatical?

1

Waterway boats in general

We can tell you more about unsuitable boats than we can about suitable ones. Tall masts, deep draughts, and fragile hulls are inadvisable, though we cruised the Intracoastal Waterway happily in a boat with the first two disadvantages. There are fundamental differences between the ideal inland waters boat and the ideal sea-going boat. The criterion is that, while dedicated sea-going boats can sometimes navigate inland, the reverse is not normally true.

Inland boats cost much less to build and run than sea-going craft. One can, for example, sell a semi-detached house in the southern half of England and spend about one third of the proceeds on a good narrowboat, or a second-hand motor cruiser. You'd have plenty of change if you bought a second-hand barge. Our 27m (88ft) barge Hosanna cost us about £100,000 and we sailed her for 22 years. New construction is an open-ended question. We cannot give detailed advice on raising capital and estimating running costs when they depend so much on taste and lifestyle.

There are Arthur Daleys in the boat world too. Be wary of syndicates, even with friends, but especially if the syndicate has a professional manager. Foreign syndicate managers often play by different rules so be sure he is playing the same game as yourself.

Most inland navigations have developed their own characteristic craft, which does not mean that other craft cannot manage these waters. Traditional craft were largely for propulsion by sail, oar, or towing by man or beast. They moved without power as we would know it. We, ourselves, had purchased our sixth boat and were well into middle age before we considered an engine to be necessary; the proliferation of craft on the waterways nowadays has changed that view. Rarely now does one have time and elbow room to sail up to a mooring or anchorage without help from fossil fuels.

Though the coming of the internal combustion engine transformed inland navigation, many traditional boat forms remain unchanged. Devoted adherents will tell you why.

Any good boat is lovable. Provided it meets measurement limits it can 'do' inland waters anywhere you are permitted to take it. This is one of the points we wish to convey in this book. Inland navigation enthusiasts are no longer tied to one system in one country. The cost of transporting a boat from one country to another, and even continents, is now affordable, and the means convenient. Transport of substantial-sized boats by lorry or container ship is often done these days. The horizons of the inland navigator are no longer confined to the view over local reed beds; the world is his fresh-water oyster. A recent Inland Waters meeting in Brussels was called 'From Limerick to Kiev', because you can do just that in your inland waters boat (according to the EU Commissioner, who forgot the Irish and North Seas).

❖ Types and dimensions of boats ❖

Most readers of this book will contemplate living aboard an Inland Waters Boat (call it an IWB) for at least part of the year. How do they visualise this boat? Experienced people will know what they want, but for the remainder we offer some thoughts on boat ownership, so that the reader can see what grabs him. In our younger days we changed boats very frequently, and we are poorer as a result because many of our boats, though giving pleasure at the time, proved to be costly errors. It was not until Bill retired and designed his own boat that we got one we could keep and love: *Fare Well*, a ketch that was a dream come true, in which we and our cat lived and cruised 45,000 miles in 10 years.

This was followed by *Hosanna*, a sailing barge based on a Dutch *luxe-motor* which we converted and proved a happy home for another 28,000 miles over 22 years.

In choosing the right boat for inland waters, size is important. But what type of boat? Considering the wide variety on the waterways of the world, you wonder 'Is it necessary to have so many different types?'

Every waterway has its 'ideal' boat, and local enthusiasts will glorify its virtues with blind faith that goes beyond patriotism, especially if they own an antique example. These designs have evolved to meet local needs, so after several centuries of refinement they are now superb for their task. Historically they are interesting and valuable. We would be culturally the poorer without the narrowboat, the Humber keel, the Thames barge, and the Norfolk wherry before we even step across the Channel or the Pond, to the *tjalks* (pronounced challocks) of Holland, the *péniches* of Flanders, the catboats of the Chesapeake. New World boats followed the types that early settlers remembered from the old home, providing they were fit for the purpose, and even used the same names.

Some designs have stalled, failing to adapt to changing circumstances and improvements in knowledge and materials. Indeed, the enthusiasts resist change in the interests of 'authenticity'. We must take a hard look at what works for the 21st century.

Local craft had to fit the dimensions of locks and bridges and depth of water. A boat might, at times, need to do estuary and coastal work. They needed a propulsion method that suited the geography and the climate, and, for economy, used locally available materials. Thus early boats on the Nile were built of local reeds, and endured for centuries during which time all trade was local. New materials were unavailable or more expensive than the existing ones. Nobody would use reed boats now for transport of cargo or passengers.

In our own region, the Norfolk Broads, the local trading craft was the wherry; it was about 60ft (18.2m) long, the limit for turning in the narrow, winding rivers. It was clinker-built because local craftsmen had always built that way. It was rigged for sailing because there are no towpaths among the reeds and marshes in these windy quasi-tidal waters, and it was shallow-draughted to suit the rivers and Broads. It had a simple, single sail on a counter-balanced mast that could quickly be lowered and raised to shoot bridges, and it could be sailed and tacked by one man. A few old examples of wherries are still lovingly preserved as floating museum pieces. A few people still live aboard wherry yachts, but their navigation under sail nowadays is difficult, involving skills that need more than part-time experience to acquire. The examples still sailing have to move with caution in crowded waters.

We have navigated as many inland waters as most, and find that anything of appropriate size can give pleasure. Some boats have features that are marvellous at sea or in the estuary, which can be maddening in narrow waterways. A few are potentially dangerous away from their home waters.

❖ **What sort of boat do you want?** ❖

Unless you are very clear about this, you may end up with a boat with more or fewer features than you need. The decision is a large and costly one, so do some homework; but make the homework enjoyable. Look at as many boats of various types as possible and put some on a short list; then pause for thought before making an even shorter list. For goodness' sake make it a joint decision; share the blame with your co-owner!

ANSWER THESE 10 QUESTIONS:

1 How much have you got to spend?

2 What type of boat do you want and what are its important features?

3 Which waters do you intend to cruise?

4 What bureaucratic restrictions, rules and inspections will she and/or you have to satisfy before she may navigate?

5 Will you buy new or build?

6 If the latter, will you build her yourself? Or alter an existing boat?

7 Do you know what skills are likely to be involved?

8 Do you have any of those skills? Can you learn them?

9 You will need a high persistence quotient; how do you rate yourself in the matter of determination?

10 Do you enjoy a large measure of spousal, or partner, or family support?

We could write another book on questions 9 and 10, and the various techniques required to engender the above support and consent but have no wish to create familial tensions. This is a subject you must work out for yourself, but we gave advice about it in *Sell Up and Sail*. Obviously the technique of persuading a partner to undergo all the real and imagined discomforts of deep-sea life demands at least a second class degree in manipulation. On inland waters, you will be bringing her/him in roughly at 'A' level. (Or not so roughly: gently is probably best. Don't use Shanghaiing or press gang tactics here.)

Apart from Q7–10, can we solve the above numbered problems for you? The answer is NO! All we can do is make a few comments and suggestions. It is difficult to try to anticipate individual tastes. But there are some aspects that have to override fixed ideas. Unfortunately, Bill missed out when tact was being distributed. So, please be tolerant, even if some of us find it difficult.

We talked about types of boat from a generic and/or locality point of view. Now think of availability and cost. There are quite a few options for you to consider when choosing your boat such as:

- A workboat already converted for cruising.
- A workboat to be converted to your own requirements.
- A reproduction of a traditional workboat type built in modern materials.
- A real working boat in which you can pretend to be a real bargee.
- A new-build, standard motor cruiser of modern design.
- A modern motor cruiser, custom-designed and built to suit you.
- A second-hand motor cruiser that appeals to you.
- A second-hand pleasure-boat, built to a popular design.

We tend to favour the workboat type but during the next few chapters we will look at all the various options.

Whatever the shapely details of your chosen boat, if she gives you happiness, and takes you somewhere, you will grow to love her. Give her a chance; do not expect her to do well in circumstances for which she is completely unsuited. But your boat *must* be strongly built.

Before we talk about boat types and layout, we should consider other aspects of inland boating which might influence boat shape, size, or construction material.

Comfort

This is an important criterion for living aboard. We wrote a lot about living aboard a sea-going craft, where the exigencies of survival at sea in bad weather militate against creature comforts. Inland, you can indulge yourself. The only physical damage your boat will sustain will be due to incompetence, either your own or somebody else's; or something breaking while the boat is being hauled out of the water or put back in; or fire, perhaps. It does happen. If you are sensitive, substitute the word 'accident' for 'incompetence'. Most insurance claim forms say it's not our fault.

Safety

Hydrostatic stability is less important as you are not likely to be heeled over by natural forces in the way that a sea-going boat is by wave motion. In an IWB, the initial stability, as she starts to heel, is often far greater than in a sailing yacht with tonnes of lead on her fin keel. The IWB gets her stability from her shape and not by carrying a lead mine underneath.

We suggest that an IWB should have a low freeboard, that is her deck edge should be as low as possible – consistent with the ability to heel over about 20° or more without the deck edge becoming immersed. The reason for the low deck-edge is personal safety. The high freeboard and over-hanging flare of modern motor cruisers is dangerous. In canals one needs easy access to bollards on shore and in locks, and for this reason many IWBs, and most *péniches*, have no guardrails. Falling overboard must be borne in mind as an ever-present danger. A low freeboard makes it easier to get someone back on board, or at least to proffer them a helping hand. More details of this will be given later on. As an alternative to guardrails, one should have grab-rails inboard.

Heating and cooling

For living aboard, you must think about both winter and summer, unless you are going to be a swallow (Europe) or snow-bird (USA), when you will only use the boat in the summer. For year-round use, you will need a sun-deck or shade-deck (or both). Think of the awnings you might need.

Think carefully about heating; even during winter in the Mediterranean, some heating is necessary, if only in the evening. There will be more about heating and refrigeration in later chapters on construction and domestic considerations.

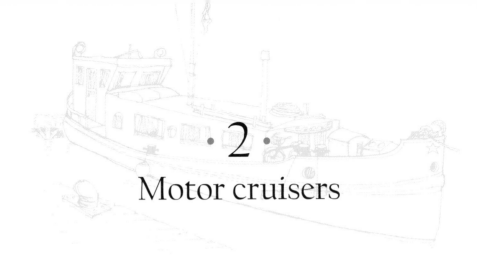

• 2 •

Motor cruisers

Most motor cruiser builders seem to build boats based (however loosely) on sea-going styles. This compromises their suitability for canal use.

❖ Dutch steel motor cruisers ❖

The classic Dutch cruiser of about 12 to 15m (39 to 49ft) length is similar, at first sight, to her seafaring sisters, with a high fo'c'sle, centre wheelhouse/saloon, and spacious stern cabin with sitting deck over it. These boats are pretty and popular. In spite of being from Holland, the land of inland waters, and being popular, they are not ideally suited for cruising, except temporarily as a summer holiday boat, which is their intended purpose.

What are the less good points?

We are lukewarm about wheelhouse/saloons for live-aboard boats. Fine for summer, but the year-round live-aboard will find them less cosy than a below-deck saloon, partly because their large window area is difficult to insulate. Condensation can be severe. A deck saloon/wheelhouse often means a galley below decks and it is inconvenient not to have galley and dining area on the same level. The cook should not be condemned to working in the basement.

These boats usually have flared, high bows, that makes it difficult to pick up moorings. We have seen people jumping a long way down onto a low pontoon; this is not good for the elderly. Many motor cruisers have to carry movable steps, similar to a caravan step, so that the crew can safely disembark onto a pontoon.

Some cruisers have a low platform astern, mainly because sea-going motor-cruisers berth stern-to in marinas or the Mediterranean. These platforms suggest that they are suitable for recovery of a man overboard. *They are not*, because they are too close to the propellers. (See Chapter 20 Coping with risks and dangers.) Small Dutch motor cruisers such as the Pedro make few concessions to sea-going. These boats use aluminium alloy upper-works which should present few problems on fresh water, and are popular with live-aboards.

Another type of motor cruiser which is good for inland waters only, is the class known sometimes as the Caribbean cruiser.

❖ 'Caribbean' cruisers ❖

This is an unusual type of glassfibre boat. (I have not yet seen one in steel.) Unusual, because the design had few concessions to older-style craft. Her chief features are a parallel-sided hull with low freeboard and a tram-car style long cabin on top. The wheelhouse is forward, and combined with the saloon, but the entire roof and sides can be slid back on top of the other accommodation. The boat is on one level, and the engine is placed athwartships, right aft and easy to get at without having to pull up cabin floors.

All in all, a sensible, original design which has been around for a long time and given good service. The boats need improved insulation for year-round living, but many are used for this. They are economical and their low air-draught enables them to navigate interesting waters inaccessible to larger craft.

A good source for second-hand boats of this type is the French magazine *Fluvial*. There is a large turnover, possibly because so many are used for summer cruising.

❖ Fast motor cruisers ❖

Speed is silly on canals and can cause damage to river banks. Even on open water, a boat's speed is limited to a figure based on the square root of her waterline length. If she is given more power than is needed, her bow will ride up and her stern drop and she will make a lot of waves. These waves use massive energy, increasing fuel bills and alarming the green lobby. The increase in speed, though dramatic in appearance, is small so cruisers built for fast inshore cruising are unsuitable for inland waterways.

❖ Broads cruisers ❖

The traditional type has now nearly disappeared from waterways as Norfolk boatbuilders have found semi-planing hulls to be more popular – and marketable. Well worth looking at are the boats used by the hire fleets, both at home and abroad, which are well built and simple to drive. Good, well-maintained examples of these can be bought second-hand but they are sought after.

❖ Decks: wood or plastic? ❖

Often motor cruisers are finished with 'wooden' decks. This is usually an expensive extra, looking well when new. Sometimes it is not real wood, but a plastic imitation. The problem with decks on small boats is that wood is mobile; it does not keep still. To have real wooden decks needs a good hard wood of 20mm ³/₄in) thickness that can be fastened down firmly on a bed of sealant. This would add too much weight to a small cruiser, so the habit has grown of gluing down thin planks with Sikoflex. The thinner the plank the more unstable the wood, and though Sikoflex is an excellent product, the finished job is only as good as the workman who did it and you will

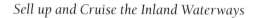

WOODWORK

Because motor cruisers are of modest size, one can survey the whole craft fairly easily, and because they have been built in professional yards the joinery is often of a high visual standard. Woodwork involves much plywood these days, the quality of which it is impossible to verify. The British Standards are a trap. We have known plywood to BS 1088 delaminate very quickly, while plywood from B & Q lasted on the upper deck for years. It is the unknown quality of plywood which makes it suspect. I prefer traditional panelling in beaded tongue-and-groove boarding, available in France at a fraction of the price in England.

never know until it is too late. There is also the question of wear which badly affects thin wooden decks. In the marina where we wintered last year were two boats that I would not class as old (approximately 15 years), from respectable yards, which were being stripped of their wooden decks because the wood (reputedly teak) had worn through in patches.

❖ Steel hulls ❖

For inland waters, a strong steel boat is far and away the best. Some cruisers are built like this, but not many, and they are often lightly built. Why are we so adamant about strength? The photograph (below) will say why better than any words. It takes a strong boat to cope with 200 tonnes of wayward barge.

This is a very good illustration of why your boat should be well fendered.

After all that hard thinking, let's have the first of a series of river and canal-side interludes to remind us of the pleasures of the waterways.

Waterway interludes:

Dining in Burgundy

St Jean de Losne is at the junction of the River Saône with the Rhine/Saône canal and the Canal de Bourgogne. There is a big basin here called the Gare d'eau, once an off-river parking place for commercial barges. With the decline of this business it has become a useful place for pleasure craft, with chandleries, hire-boat lettings, three *chantiers*, a dry dock, two marinas, and a supermarket, all within a short walking distance.

A favourite haunt of visitors here is the bar-restaurant L'Amiral, overlooking the bridge over the Saône. The small inside room can just about manage a party of 20 overwintering sailors wanting to celebrate (for instance) Guy Fawkes or Australia day. The proprietor Gilles is accommodating about Yorkshire Parkin, Wallaby stew and Peach Melba. In the summer, of course, we are all outside under the lime trees, competing with tourists for a table. The food is good but not fancy and certainly not expensive, so do not expect a *soignée* establishment. You can have Burgundian dishes like snails, parslied ham, and *boeuf bourguignon*, or good old steak and chips. This is Burgundy and the portions are huge. The friendly atmosphere makes up for the fact that at peak-and-panic times in high summer your order may go elsewhere, and you will need to swap plates with the next table, but nobody minds.

· 3 ·
Workboats

Workboats, no matter in which country, or on which river or canal they are found, have much in common. Perhaps the major differences are those of propulsion, and material of construction. Otherwise conventional barges found in the USA or China are not much different from those of the UK and Europe.

❖ English workboats ❖

In England, apart from narrowboats and wide barges, you have Humber keels, Norfolk wherries, Thames barges, assorted small tugs, de-classed passenger boats, lifeboats and so on. Several Humber keels are still navigating the canals of Europe. Many of them were originally owned by the same family. They are barges of conventional build, and having been originally designed with a big square sail, they slip through the water well. Sadly, the pool of unconverted Humber keels is exhausted, and most of the conversions I have seen have been by amateurs. Nothing wrong with that in the hands of a good amateur, but the range of quality is enormous. If you are considering buying a Humber keel, get it checked over.

Most wherries were clinker-built (lap-strake) of wood, and not many now survive. They were sailing boats of shallow draught and wide beam, and make good homes with or without sails. I believe that replicas could be simply and cheaply built of steel nowadays. They would do well in Western Europe, particularly on the rivers, being of a better shape than narrowboats. They are more sea-kindly, but though they used to go to sea on occasions, cannot be considered as completely suitable off-shore as, for example, the Thames barges are.

❖ European waters ❖

Leaving the English canal system one moves into a different world of inland waterways. Continental canals are widespread, so your choice of cruising ground is wide. The waterways cross continents, the distance you can travel (though not in one day) is almost unlimited. There is water uncluttered with pond-weed and water-lilies, and room to raise the engine speed enough to charge the batteries as one goes along. I am not knocking England's miniature waterways. They are charming, old and interesting, and for those interested in the history of canal engineering, there are wonderful things to see, and wonderful canal-side pubs with real ale. I, brought up among sea-faring folk and weaned into the ocean, need more space. That's just me; you may think differently.

❖ Buying foreign second-hand workboats ❖

In this world of inland waterways, one finds that the wild diversity of boat types that have developed through history is no longer so important.

There are many different types in the Netherlands and, because the barge population is large, there is a steady turnover in craft. About 25 years ago, the Dutch government wanted to rid the waterways of the clutter of uneconomic small barges and offered a subsidy for building a big new one to any owner of a small cargo barge that was sold out of the country. There were bargains to be had, and we bought *Hosanna*, length 27m (88ft) in reasonable condition for her age (built in 1931) for the price of a second-hand diesel engine. This extraordinary blip in the market is over, and you would now have to pay a fairly high price for a barge in good condition.

What are the best types? Answer: All of the hundreds of them. Which of these make the best boats for leisure use and/or living aboard is a question of personal preference. The type you would really like may not be available these days. *Hosanna* was often called a *luxe-motor*, and knowledgeable Dutch acquaintances suggested she might be a *Katwijker*, one said a miniature *Steilsteven*. Never mind what the boat type is called. *Do you like her?* If yes, then that is the boat for you.

Materials and methods of propulsion have changed and standardised to a great extent over the years. We saw barges in China on the River Li Jiang that closely resembled European barges, except that their motive power was

A barge on the Grand Canal in China. PHOTO: SHUMAN CRAWSHAW

PUSHER UNITS

There exist 'dumb' barges or *schleppers* which are towed or pushed by special tugs, and this format could be used for pleasure boating. This might be of interest to those people wishing to live in semi-permanently moored houseboats who move only for a shortish summer cruise. Houseboaters could live in the spacious dumb barge and hire the services of a pusher tug to provide power when needed. Commercial pusher units are too big for domestic pleasure purposes.

This might be economic in certain countries' tax systems. I imagine a dumb houseboat of squarish form, measuring say 24m by 4.5m (78ft by 15ft) giving a living floor area of about 95sq m (114 sq yds), which is a good size, and to use with it a pusher tug measuring 5m by 2.5m (16ft by 8ft) with a 120hp engine.

We have heard recently that a firm on the British canals have suggested just such a scheme for English wide canal barges. They propose hiring out the pushers.

provided by giant outboard diesel engines. Aids to navigation and navigation marks are being increasingly standardised (except in England, Ireland and the USA where the sensible standardised continental system of conventional signs has failed to penetrate). The authorities who administer the waterways are now more accountable, and at the same time, pleasure boating has become more commercially significant. The type of boat most suitable for living aboard, or for making long cruises, becomes a distillation of all the history of boatkind. Choose the features that matter to you most. If you are an historically-minded purist, have your papyrus raft by all means, most of us want something a little more enduring and containing more creature comforts. In much of the waterway world, there are seasons; and the discomfort endured by the working artisan of centuries ago would not be tolerable these days.

We are dismayed that the British Government is drastically cutting funding for the waterways. Even though the cash was previously promised, it seems that barging has to pay for administrative mismanagement of various farm schemes. The British boat industry is a major part of our national economy.

❖ A basic inland waters boat (IWB) ❖

Considering the waterways we have cruised, we think there is a basic style of boat that would be suitable for most of them. A few local variations of a minor character may be needed perhaps, but the basic shape we have devised would suit all waters from the Amazon to the Zambesi. We will look at this, together with the local variations that are still essential.

Climatic considerations

Mostly, the style variations are to do with climate. All inland waters in Europe have hard winters. Only the extreme south of France offers a reasonable chance of a frost-free existence, and moorings there are crowded and expensive as sea-goers flock inland to take advantage of lower winter mooring rates. Larger boats are experiencing increasing difficulty in finding a place in the coastal areas. If you move, you lose your place. Beaucaire, for example, which used to be a popular wintering basin for pleasure barges has changed policy and crams more smaller-sized boats into the available space, increasing their total financial take.

Even in the south of France, however, there is no guarantee of good weather. We once had 3in (76mm) of snow on our decks in Aigues-Mortes, and in Languedoc a boat hangar collapsed from the weight of snow on the roof. The mistral is a vicious cold wind that can reach force 12 and blow for days on end with a temperature barely above freezing point. On good days in winter, the sun is warm enough to eat lunch al fresco, but at sunset you'll need heating below decks. So, although the ability to make progress through the water is not much different anywhere, the accommodation and steering positions might have different requirements because of climatic considerations. (We described a serious mistral in our book *Watersteps Through France*. It's not a nice experience.)

Even Florida is not all semi-tropical. It can be icy up there in the region of Fernandina Beach, and freezing in Georgia and the Carolinas.

If you navigate only in the tropics, or in the Continental summer, then you should have the above-deck sides of the boat well open to the breeze or else close everything down and have air-conditioning, in which case you might just as well stay at home. The river passenger boats, such as the Old Flotilla and the Mississippi steamboats had galleries along the sides and cabin decks two or three storeys high with windows

A typical péniche-style boat (14.6m) designed for European cruising which can be bought or chartered. PHOTO: CLASSICBOAT LTD

giving light and air throughout. The Old Flotilla boats (which were built in Scotland in the early 19th century and shipped out to Burma in flat-pack (there is nothing new under the sun), were also three storeys high, but the captain steered from low down, standing exposed right in the bows of the ship so that the first class cabins' windows would not be obstructed ahead, where the cooling breeze came from. This was in the 1850s, they knew how to look after the gentry in those days.

The conning (steering) position

Traditionally, boats have been conned (steered and manoeuvred) from the stern. This was because the rudder had to be aft, and old-fashioned steering gear was heavy, and to have linkages or chains to enable the rudder to be worked from elsewhere would have been awkward, so the conning position was on top of the rudder. This suited sailing ships because the helmsman could see all the sails as well as steer, and it facilitated an uncluttered hold area. It is not the best solution under power, and soon steam ships started to have a conning position further forward connected to the after steering gear by a bridge which went over the hold. Soon the conning position came to be called 'the bridge', and eventually the hold was sub-divided, which increased safety. Conventional wisdom then was that the conning position should be one-third of the ship's length from the stem. This is actually the normal point of pivot of a ship when going ahead and turning.

Many ships now have moved the bridge right up into the bows. The first to do so were not the tugs, or the Great Lakes steamers, but the Old Flotilla in Burma, immortalised by Kipling in *The Road to Mandalay*. Now we have container ships and ferries so fitted. This has all been facilitated by hydraulic steering and engine controls which are now readily available to boats of a much smaller size.

The steering position is not a vital factor, being a matter of personal taste. Many canals have sharp corners and mooring basins with limited visibility when leaving. If you have some 35m (114ft) of steel sticking out in front as you approach a corner, it is necessary to send somebody up into the bows to be the first to spot impending doom. If you are steering from forward, this is unnecessary, and it increases comfort in the pouring rain.

I suggest that a forward steering position makes a lot of sense on a power-driven boat for inland waters. However, a word of caution applies to the inexperienced. The Broads hire fleet operators used to sell their holidays with the slogan 'if you can drive a car, you can handle our boats'. They neglected (or ignored) two facts. One was that most of the hire fleet are the length and weight of 40-tonne trucks, and the other was that when you put over the steering-wheel of a truck, it starts to turn with its forward wheels, and the back end follows inside where the front end goes. This means that most of the truck traverses inside the turning circle of the front wheels. With boats it is the other way round. The back end of the boat is deflected sideways and as the boat turns it covers more ground outside the axis of turn than inside it. Steering a boat is more akin to steering a car-plus-caravan while reversing and that really confuses some people.

If you steer from forward and the stern swings widely outside the rest of the boat, and if you concentrate on where you are going, you do not notice the interesting things your back-side is side-swiping. One has to cultivate a consciousness that the back is not going to follow the front as faithfully as you would like.

A benefit of forward steering positions is that sterns do not get cluttered up with boaty things. At the blunt end there is more deck space than in the pointed bows. Sterns make nicer places to sit and/or lounge, leaving the pointy bit at the front for anchors, winches, ropes and spare fenders. The middle of the boat, the widest bit, is where you need the saloon. Cat-swinging room is important when confined below by bad weather.

However, there are serious disadvantages to a forward steering position, especially for boats that are very nearly as wide as the locks. It requires more skill to line up the boat with the lock chamber while steering towards the entrance, especially as the water near the lock gates can be disturbed. This is important if your boat is not as directionally stable as you would like. In principle, long narrow boats hold their track much better than short fat ones. Also, the helmsman steering from aft has the whole boat in his field of vision but if he is right forward, dire things may be happening behind him.

SURVEYING A USED BOAT OR BARGE

Unless you have above-average knowledge of boat construction, maintenance, and self-confidence (and/or idiocy), you should have a professional survey on the boat or barge that you desire. The art of surveying is best left to professionals. Here are eight tips for commissioning a survey:

1 Make sure your surveyor is experienced with the type of vessel you have in mind. Many surveyors specialise. Use an appropriate specialist.

2 Make sure your surveyor carries professional indemnity insurance.

3 Agree the fee beforehand. Good men do not come cheap. You will have to pay his travelling expenses, too.

4 The vessel must be out of the water.

5 If the surveyor is good he will find the odd horror-story: ask for an estimate for correcting it. (All used boats contain at least one real problem, it should not necessarily put you off. Defects can be corrected, the price is the criterion.)

6 Your surveyor will almost certainly miss something, simply because there is so much to check. It may not be anything vital but it can be irritating. You cannot complain about missed minor defects. The surveyor undertakes to use his 'best endeavours', but cannot guarantee to discover all minor defects. Be understanding.

7 We repeat again: the surveyor *must* be a specialist. It is no use asking a yacht surveyor to survey an old barge, nor the other way round.

8 Ask for a valuation to give to the insurance underwriters.

· 4 ·
Narrowboats

Narrowboats differ from other types of boat quite fundamentally: in the main they cruise special waters and they should be considered separately.

There are two types of canal in England: broad and narrow. The locks of the latter are about 7ft (2.1m) wide and a maximum of 72ft (22m) long, which necessitate a special narrow class of boat to navigate them. Surprisingly, there are more miles of wide canal than narrow. The trouble is that the two main wide sections are separated by a short length of narrows at Foxton. Narrowboats which can cruise both broad and narrow, are very popular at the moment. They sell like hot cakes. Why?

- They are cheap. Possibly the cheapest way to get afloat in a boat that is strong, and forgiving (very important, that).
- They are surprisingly comfortable.
- They make good floating homes if your space requirements are modest.
- They look historic and picturesque with their traditional painted decoration.
- There is an enthusiastic cult whose members are helpful to anyone who wishes to learn (and listen).
- There are plenty of waterway miles to suit them, not just in the UK. When and if you tire of England, the Continental system is available and many narrowboats cross the Channel. This has its problems which we will discuss later.

None of the traditional work boats formerly used on the English narrow canal system are in commercial use any more so your chances of getting one for conversion is nil, but new ones are being built expressly for amateur cruising. They are ideally suited for the English canals, where the vast majority give great pleasure, and they are not bad on European canals.

Their 7ft (2m) breadth makes their accommodation long and narrow. One is unable, realistically, to have a corridor with cabins leading off; usually cabins open off each other in sequence, but in spite of the restrictions, a well-designed interior is attractive and comfortable, and enough people swear by them to convince me that they are excellent for canals generally, with a few caveats.

Narrowboats can be bought second-hand, new as a completed boat, as a bare hull for self-completion, and also in virtually any state in between.

❖ How to find a narrowboat, and what to look out for ❖

The expansion in the narrowboat population is remarkable A boat is not a caravan, and needs a different approach, though there would seem to be some similarities. In parts of the English canal system the overcrowding is getting serious.

For a time it seemed that anyone who could weld started making up bare hulls for home completion. Some hulls were badly designed and constructed, but there have always been good builders. Check your boat's provenance without relying absolutely on the inland waters magazines, some of which don't seem to conform to the objectivity of the mainstream yachting journals.

Many boats were built with holiday letting in mind, rather than to respectable safety standards. If you are planning to remain in the confines of the English canal system, this is unimportant, but be aware that the unusual configuration of a narrowboat means that certain safety measures must be taken for navigation in estuaries and/or foreign-going.

Originally, the motorised narrowboat had her engine at the after end of the hold, forward of the cabin. There was a small conning position at the stern and in bad weather, the driver stood inside the cabin doors and steered from there. There was little room for the crew to join him on deck, so for pleasure use, the engine was placed aft and even the stern shape itself was changed, giving rise to what is occasionally referred to as a 'cruiser stern'.

These variations have few safety implications on English canals, but some render the boat potentially unsafe for sea, estuary or even big river use. Check your boat with a knowledgeable surveyor before even contemplating the Continent.

The Last Farthing, *an excellent narrowboat, moored at Pont l'Eveque.*

Buying narrowboats

This is relatively easy, both in terms of finding your boat and financing it. Dozens of adverts exist for both new and second-hand boats in the inland boating and/or barging magazines. Both used and new, these boats are a bargain compared with traditional sea-capable boats. However, we are unimpressed with the practices of some inland yards without seamanlike experience of ship-building. If sea trips are envisaged, check for shipwright experience and Lloyds approved or diploma Mig welders who know one type of steel from another. The good modern welder is a craftsman.

When buying a completed new boat you must check the quality of the fitting out. The secret is the standard of insulation which is a vital part of a steel boat. Undoubtedly sprayed-on foam is best but is more expensive, and cheaper boats are liable to have their inside steel painted in Waxoyl before lining with 30–50mm (1–2in) sheets of polystyrene. This was normal in older, pre-foam boats, so there's nothing fundamentally wrong with that, but because the insulation is not fully bonded to the steel, you get condensation between insulation and hull. This must be checked and if some cheapjack builder has fixed the panelling with No-more-Nails glue, you have a hell of a job. Often cheap initial cost means extra work and cost later on.

There is no nationwide standard for narrowboats. Some regions have locks which take them a little longer than others. About 20m (65ft) LOA seems to be a rough maximum, but we believe that narrowboats from Lancashire are shorter. This 20-metre LOA measurement is important on the Continent and it may become the maximum size of amateur-driven pleasure craft in the UK if Brussels has its way.

❖ Build your own? ❖

You can buy a hull in flat-pack form like a wardrobe from Argos – the Argosy class, perhaps. It comes with the steel parts plasma cut, shot-blasted and primed ready for welding; every part is numbered. All you need is an angle grinder to clean off the weldable edges, a Mig welder (which can be bought for about £400), and a shed. Mig doesn't like strong winds.

❖ Narrowboats abroad ❖

On the Continent, narrowboats cope well in canals and are seen all over France, Belgium and the Netherlands. They are uncomfortable on the big rivers. The Rivers Moselle, Saône and Rhône are OK for narrowboat navigation unless the weather is bad. Even on the Rhône, the commercial barges are not that big or fast, and with a little prudence about gales and floods, one should not be in serious danger or discomfort. Narrowboats, being designed for the gentle British waterways, are not usually powerfully engined, so some have an inadequate speed to mount a river in spate. They might well get there in the end but moorings for the night are often some distance apart so there may be problems in conditions of fast flow.

The rivers Rhine and Danube are another story. Traffic on the Rhine is intense: fast, commercial, and impatient; the water is seldom calm for a moment. On these rivers the maximum permitted size for pleasure craft has been increased from 15m (49ft) to 20m (65ft)LOA.

❖ Clapotage ❖

There is a risk for narrowboats near big locks. Where the lock is approached down a long straight stretch, a special danger exists. A strong wind blowing over a few miles causes significant waves. On the approach to some locks there is nowhere for the wave energy to go – they come up against a vertical surface, are reflected back, and generate harmonics that can merge with the original waves to form a static wave pattern of steep, dangerous crests called *clapotage*. If a boat of any type finds herself beam-on to this wave pattern, (and it can happen if the lock is not yet ready to admit the approaching boat) she will be very uncomfortable and will experience heavy spray breaking over her. Much depends on the wave pattern, which can be so short that a narrowboat can find herself in a dangerous rhythmic rolling state. We know, with certainty, of one case where a narrowboat (in fact, a 'butty' – a towed dumb barge) capsized and sank, and we saw the yacht *Rainbow* considerably thrown about. We have heard of other cases which we cannot authenticate. How do you cope with these conditions? You stay made fast until the weather improves.

❖ Anchors ❖

In France, barges, including narrowboats, must carry an anchor while on rivers. This is not just bureaucracy; any mishap above one of the big weirs could be fatal if no anchor were available at short notice. For a 20m (65ft) narrowboat, one should have a patent anchor (such as a CQR, Danforth or Bruce) weighing 20kg (44lb) with 10m (33ft) of 8mm ($^1/_3$ in) chain cable on it. On big rivers, this bower anchor must be kept ready for letting go, however inconvenient. Do you think this is too big? Well the holding ground above a weir is often poor.

In *Hosanna*, where we navigated adventurously, we had a self-stowing stern anchor of 200kg (440lb) with an hydraulic capstan always ready for instant release. Laurel and I occasionally do some funny things, but we take precautions against unexpected mishaps.

❖ Wider boats in England ❖

What applies to narrowboats also applies to the English wide boat except that the wide boat is a more convenient shape for living aboard and Continental cruising.

· 5 ·

Construction materials

Before we start to go into boat design, we need to consider the construction materials, for this will impose on the layout. We lived aboard *Hosanna* for 22 years and cruised widely: 20 countries and 28,000 miles; and for our own life-style, we got it right. She was built of rivetted steel.

We once got into conversation with the managing director of a major boat-hire company and discovered that they sold off their boats after five years of use. 'Why?' We asked. 'Because they start to get shabby and need repair.' We commented: 'Build them of a longer-lasting material in the first place. Steel for instance. The hulls wouldn't get so knocked about in the locks, and a coat of paint tarts them up like new.' 'Holiday-makers don't worry about the hulls,' he said. 'They are put off by shabby interiors, and dirty ovens. It is no good having an everlasting hull if the interior is shabby. Hirers never look after things as they would at home. A fibreglass hull lasts about as long as the interior.' For his trade that makes commercial sense, but the important thing here is the question of use and care. A private owner uses his boat much less than a series of charterers or holiday-makers. The live-aboard owner takes care of the boat inside and out. Cleaning is properly done, damage will be quickly put right.

❖ Types of hull material ❖

The chief problems faced by IWBs arise when navigation gives way to parking, or when two boats want to be in the same place at the same time, or whilst locking. Domestic problems are less important but have relevance. The choice of hull materials includes steel, aluminium, glassfibre, ferro-cement and wood. We deal with steel later on as a special case. We prefer and recommend steel boats for canal use, and in Chapter 7 on Converting a workboat it will be apparent why.

Aluminium
This has its place, but is not ideal for IWB hulls because it is a comparatively soft material.

Glassfibre

It is comparatively easy at the construction stage; it needs less attention and small damage is easy to repair. It is prone to impact damage, and unless bruises and grazes are promptly repaired, the damage can rapidly become more serious than it should have been. A glassfibre boat for inland waters needs careful fendering. It does not require a big bash to cause serious constructural damage. They do not cope well with ice.

Wood

This material is forgiving, being elastic and strong. Cosmetic repairs are easy and it is the only material with some inherent insulation. The drawbacks: wood does not like fresh water, and boats rot faster on inland waters than they do in sea water. Select the right woods, but good boat-building timber is getting harder to find as the rain forests are depleted.

Ferro-cement

Ferro-cement is not suited to canal life. When well constructed it is fine at sea, but abrasion in canals is a problem. If built on a well-reinforced matrix, it can be repaired easily, but it is best not to sustain that damage in the first place.

We will discuss insulation later, and the chapter covering winter conditions and ice navigation (Chapter 13) is equally relevant to wood, cement and glassfibre.

For the average boat-owner, it is important to buy or build a boat that he (or she) can love. And when he does, he will not want to trade it in – he'll make it last. He should build to last.

❖ Hull shape ❖

How should the boat be shaped? The shape of sea-going boats is dictated by their ability to withstand waves. For the sea it is desirable that the hull should cut through the water as well as ride over it, and should not only do so below the waterline, but also above, as far as the foredeck. The foredeck should be strong and unpierced because that is where head seas will wash over. Her stern should be sea-tight because now and then she will have to run before a following sea that may break on board. Her transverse section should have a substantial reserve of hydrostatic stability because wave-forms can tip her over to a greater degree than is comfortable. This can be more readily achieved with some V-shaped cross-section.

Little of this applies to boats designed solely for inland waters. Some applies to boats capable of short coastal or estuary passages, but for the moment, consider the boat in its inland waters form.

Look at the traditional shape of inland waters boats. There are some passenger boats built with fine lines, mainly for cosmetic effect, but the vast majority of craft are blunt-ended, flat-bottomed, and straight-sided. There are reasons for this.

Inland waterway boats pay tolls, which are often calculated on the dimensions, L x B x D (Length, Breadth and Depth) for example, often only L x B. or even on length only. So it cuts running expenses (and mooring fees) to have as much boat in the length as possible. The limiting factor is breadth, and this is limited by lock width. We are led to a compact design, unless we wish to demonstrate our unconcern with financial matters.

The bows can be bluff (blunt) above the waterline because one seldom has to butt one's way through significant waves. Even below the waterline a degree of bluffness is acceptable because resistance to movement due to hull shape is comparatively light at slow speeds. That is to say, when speed in knots $< \sqrt{w}$, where w is the waterline length in feet, resistance will be reasonable. So, for a boat 15m (49ft) long, if you keep your speed below 7 knots, water resistance to forward motion will not be a major worry. It will concern fuel consumption though, which increases exponentially the faster you go. The slower you go, the less energy you waste. If you travel at over 7 knots, you burn up more fuel.

With a fair-sized boat in a canal, where there is usually a speed limit of about 6 kilometres per hour (slightly over 3 knots), the speed resistance due to hull form is virtually non-existent, the major parts of the resistance are skin friction and interaction with the bottom and sides of the canal. The best thing is to accept a bluff design and make it look elegant without those racy long-drawn-out ends that seagoing folk tend to equate with speed. Some of the Dutch commercial barges combine boxiness with a form of beauty. Even the constricted narrowboat gives opportunity: the traditional painting and decorating of them is eyestopping.

We must pause to consider the passage through locks, which has, or should have, an impact on boat design. This needs a chapter on its own because it is one of the major features of canals. However, the idea of locks brings us back to boat shape. Having a boat with parallel sides, rather than the elegant and graceful curves of the sea-going yacht, is an advantage in inland waters. It makes it possible to lie quietly in a lock, close to the wall. (Odd-shaped locks do exist, but are rare.) Elementary geometry confirms that one rope amidships will hold her tight, and one rope to adjust, as the water level changes, is easier than two – one at each end of the boat. It is also convenient when berthed alongside for two reasons:

One reason is that the main strain on your canal moorings are not those of wind or weather, but lateral movements in the water, caused by large craft going past. As we describe in the chapter on Canal effect and interaction (Chapter 19), these both pull you away from the quay, and also propel you sharply in one direction after another and it is the sudden changeover that causes the worst problems. With parallel sides you have a taut moor, and there is enough stretch in the ropes to accommodate small changes in water level.

The second reason relates to lock design. The archetypical parallel-sided boat is the narrowboat, which fits English locks exactly. On the Continent you can have a broader beam that fits the lock width of 5m (16ft). For example, our new boat is 12m (39ft) long and 4.5m (14ft 8in) broad. This combination of short length with broad

Our steel-hulled Faraway, *built to our own design, is afloat at last after many months of hard work.*

beam actually uses less steel for any given measure of capacity; the disadvantage being that she requires more concentration while steering.

❖ Choosing for cruising ❖

You will have to select your type of boat according to its cruising climate and whether or not she will be taking any short sea passages. For the boat that never goes to sea, you can take full advantage of open accommodation. Let the breezes blow through unless you are navigating the Arkangelski Canal; in which case you will have not only the icy blasts to contend with, you will have insects. In fact, you will have insects almost everywhere at some time or another. Boats on the American Intracoastal Waterway often have their on-deck sitting places (we call ours the verandah) completely isolated from the outside world by dense mosquito screens; this is necessary if cruising in the summer months.

When Bill commenced designing live-aboard yachts years ago, he analysed dozens of long-distance yachts, and considered their owners' opinions on the yachts they had designed/chosen. The lessons he draws from that experience are that a prospective owner of a new-build must:

- Firmly decide what is best for him (her).
- Consider successful solutions to similar needs.
- Be prepared to ignore 'expert' opinion when criticised (he inevitably will be).
- Go further and fight entrenched opinion for his point of view because, though he

is unlikely to be right in every respect, he will get what he wants, and if there are faults they are his own.

- Be prepared to oversee every detail of the building because no builder or designer ever understands what a live-aboard owner wants. With two uncomprehending experts in the frame, you need extraordinary persistence and determination.
- Know exactly what you want and darnwell get it. The best way of doing that is to build her yourself.

If you can't build your own (boat building is getting more and more complicated), then oversee everything. Be at the yard every day. There's no call to be unpleasant but do not allow anything to be done without your personal imprimatur. You will be a pain in the butt to the builder, but in the end you will do him a service, for contention and argument will be less likely.

The only day we did not go down to the yard when our current boat was being built, the engine beds were put in too far apart, making it less easy to access their outboard sides for maintenance. This fault was too expensive to put right.

Relais Fluvial at Pont l'Eveque.

· 6 ·
Building a new boat

This is the most exciting experience in boat ownership, but also the most fraught with hair-tearing frustration, empty bank accounts, arguments, misunderstandings, and interminable and unexplained delays. When you finally take delivery, it suddenly seems to be the most delightful pleasure you will ever have. Partners are apt to be a little less thrilled.

The first bit is all fun: choosing and making plans. Only people who know what they are doing should contemplate designing their own boat and/or building it from scratch. This can be satisfying if your passion is for long drawn out expressions of love. In our experience, naval architects are slow to the point of desperation, never produce what you had in mind (which you thought you had explained in great detail) and submit unexpectedly huge accounts. It is far better to go to a builder experienced in the type of craft you favour and look at stock designs. He will probably have several. Generally, IWBs (other than motor cruisers) have hulls built by one firm and then fitted out by another. This latter is convenient if you want to finish the boat yourself. Buying a hull with its engine fitted and stern gear operational is oddly referred to as buying a 'sailaway'. Given that the hull is a small part of the total cost, the process makes sense. The usual proportion of cost of hull to fitting out is between 1:4 and 1:6 depending on the luxury demanded. Beware! Often the 'finishers' are people with little knowledge of boats. Some started life as shop-fitters, used to short cuts. This is OK as far as appearance goes, but in boats one must have easy access to what is behind the furniture (which may have great nautical importance), and this adds to the difficulties and costs of construction.

Some people have their boats built on the Continent, and we come across examples where the experience has been spoiled by misunderstandings and arguments. Because you cannot visit frequently, if the build goes in the wrong direction it's hard to correct. Contract terms and language, both grammatical and technical, vary from country to country, as do building practices, and, though you may get quoted a lower price somewhere else, it pays in the long run to stay close to home. You can visit the yard and see your baby growing, but you cannot expect to interfere with the builder at the hull stage. With a reputable builder, you will get what you contracted for; so don't dither.

Remember, importing agents have a strong interest in remaining on good terms with the builder, and may have to decide which side (owner or builder) to support in the event of a dispute. They all deny this is a problem, but I know of examples where the owner has felt that it was. These disputes can be expensive, especially if lawyers get involved.

We are talking about barges here, not mass-produced plastic cruisers which are a different matter, though some motor cruisers are imported from the Far East and potential disputes multiply for these. Many of these boats seem to be quickly resold.

Helpful publications are the *Barge Buyer's Handbook*, published by the DBA, (see Chapter 7 on Converting a workboat). There is another small publication that summarises factual information regarding building in England: *How to Buy a Boat for Canal or River*, published jointly by the Canal Boatbuilder's Association and the British Marine Federation. It is oriented towards the British waterways but refers to the Continent too. It lists types of boat, builders, engineers and fitting out yards, and gives estimates of cost of build and even of running such a boat, not in depth, but enough to point you in the right direction.

One word of caution, referring to having a boat built in England for use on the Continent. Either you must know Continental waters well and have experience in their navigation, or you must choose a builder who does. Navigating the Continent in a wide barge is different from cruising a narrowboat in England. Before going ahead, study the literature and the magazines – the latter are informative, though oriented essentially towards British canals.

There are some specialist inland waters boat shows in England that repay reconnaissance. See the magazines for details, which change yearly - Birmingham in February; Crick in May; Beale Park, near Henley, in June; Preston Brook (Bridgewater Canal) August Bank Holiday. There are of course the London and Southampton Boat Shows.

❖ Check out the boat builder ❖

Whether you are having her built or doing it yourself (or a combination of the two) it is essential to know exactly what you want and aim steadily towards it. People who do not know what they want end up with what they get, often something unexpected. One of the most important policies (and the hardest to follow) is never to change your plans during building.

If you are having the boat built by a professional builder, you will probably have negotiated a price and signed a contract (see below).

In theory, you should receive your boat built exactly according to the plans for the price specified. Boat-building being what it is, the builder may find his profit being pinched, due to material price increases, labour problems and weather (among other vicissitudes). The moment the owner/customer varies the contract, the builder can heave a sigh of relief, and can charge like a wounded buffalo citing the fact that his whole work programme and critical path analysis (critical what?) are up the spout. Try to stick to the contract, but if you must vary it, negotiate a fixed price for the variation.

Check that the builder has resources to finish the job efficiently. There are builders on the margins of the trade who finance the current job by taking a deposit on the next boat. They are always financially behind by about half the cost of a new boat. In effect, their working capital is provided by the next customer. The builder can continue this way if all goes well, but one major upset can spoil the sequence.

Boatbuilders are seldom deliberately dishonest, but watch out for yards run by optimistic enthusiasts working on a shoestring. They quote low prices, and run into liquidity difficulties, especially if the business climate changes and credit tightens. We have known a builder, now out of business, who underquoted, hoping the market would pick up before he had liquidity problems. It didn't, and when the receiver moved in, he had a string of uncompleted contracts for which prospective owners had paid in advance. They lost their money.

If you are contemplating a deal outside your normal area, reconnoitre. Pick up gossip from other traders or customers in the pub. Other owners appear at weekends, see how they are getting on. They will all be optimistic on the outside, but listen carefully, perhaps to what they are not saying.

❖ Payment and contracts ❖

Commissioning a new boat from a builder means signing a contract and making stage payments. This is a legal minefield. Disputes can arise and become a pay day for lawyers, surveyors and other 'expert' witnesses. It is not unknown for small building firms to go into receivership or administration and your boat as she stands, perhaps half-completed, could be held to remain the property of the administrator, even though you have paid for all the work done. The RYA publish good advice on building contracts. Read it.

Notwithstanding contract terms, make sure all the items you have bought separately and left in the yard ready for installation, are clearly identified as your property. This is not paranoia; some of the nicest and most trusting people get taken, not by the builder himself, but by members of old professions. On the other hand, you will learn that everyone building a boat is an inveterate skip-raider, and probably become one yourself.

We have never had a boat built to a fixed-price contract, preferring to get the work done on a current basis under our own supervision, and paying monthly bills for labour and materials. I have no way of telling whether our method (which may not suit all builders) is more expensive or cheaper, but I feel as if I am in control. Sometimes that feeling is an illusion and I often suspect that nobody is in control; the boat itself assumes a personality and runs away with you. Boats, like children, need discipline if they are to grow up satisfactorily.

This whole process is a nightmare if you let it become so. Builders are not rogues (as a rule) and it is necessary to work with them. If, like Shylock, you insist on having your pound of flesh, you can end up paying the medical bills.

You will have chosen the plans and with luck, you will get what you pay for. Make sure you know exactly what you are paying for.

❖ Self-building ❖

Completing a bare hull by yourself is quite a different matter. You are in charge, you can change the details easily. It is a huge job, and requires courage, as well as basic skill and knowledge, more than you might find in the local library, though that can contribute practical advice and help.

We have completed or built four boats by ourselves. We know the problems; by God, we do. Are we:

- Over-optimistic nut-cases?
- Masochists?
- Workaholics?
- Too stupid to learn sense?

Take your pick, but we hope we are none of these; we are certainly not brilliant craftsmen.

The first boat was *Chanticlere*, a wooden 22ft (6.7m) 'family' weekend sailing cruiser – too fast for comfort. We were giving up yacht racing, but there were no anti-addiction patches for that. We gloss over that period, but she taught us a lot. Perhaps spending ages and a year's income on an unsuitable boat is part of the learning process – an apprenticeship in imprudence.

Fare Well

My (Bill's) hobby was designing the ideal boat. So when life in the City went sour in spite of the generous income, we decided to sell up and sail. It was the best decision we ever made, and the Ideal Boat for 1968 became more than a hobby. Alas, I did not know enough about detailed boatbuilding techniques. I fell in with an ambitious builder. I should have known better. Together, we made construction plans for *Fare Well*, a 55ft (16.7m) steel, deep-sea ketch. I signed a contract – the usual 33 per cent deposit – I was an investment analyst, for heaven's sake, not a boat designer.

The contract was for a painted steel hull, foam-insulated with engine and stern gear installed, and launched ready to moor at the bottom of our garden on the River Madway. (A typing error, but it stays because it is telling).

All went well. The builder's business expanded. He needed bigger premises. He went to a merchant bank in the City that was looking for a 'stake in the leisure industry' and borrowed hugely to buy a freehold riverside plot. *Fare Well* was nearing completion when I became aware of trouble. I was alarmed at the number of new contracts the builder was taking on, more than his work-force could handle, and spotted that he was neglecting our build in order to work on the next boat coming up for a stage payment. When he got the money, he switched to the next in line for a payment. I checked *Fare Well*'s progress; she was almost ready to launch.

I lunched with a worried director of the Merchant Bank. (Very valuable, City lunches!) They had got themselves into a fine tangle. As an investment analyst, I had agents to check on companies my clients were invested in. I set them off on my own behalf. On a Thursday afternoon I got warning that the receiver would move into the boatyard on the Monday.

Friday morning saw me at the yard. No boss. I got the foreman; call him Harry. He said:

'The boss has just flown to America.'

'To sell more boats?'

'That's right, sir.'

'He's had deposits on six boats that he hasn't yet started on?'

'That's right sir.'

'Launch my boat today, Harry.'

'Can't do that sir. The boss said nothing was to leave the yard. It's more than my job's worth.'

'On Monday, Harry, you won't have a job.'

'Like that, is it?'

'Yes. Put my boat in now and there's a case of whisky for you.'

Fare Well was launched without ceremony at 3pm on the Friday and with some relief, I motored her to a new mooring.

My job enabled me to be unusually well informed. Our advice is execute credit and professional checks on the builder before placing a boat-building contract, and watch him carefully. This is one reason to avoid building abroad at a time of uncertain economic conditions.

Hosanna

Our next build was a conversion. We bought the Dutch barge, that became *Hosanna*, the moment we saw her. This is normally unwise. She was an old boat (1931) and we knew only her recent history. Still, I have some experience of steel boats, from trawlers to battleships, and I saw signs of a well-maintained boat.

Owned by a prosperous company, she carried Indonesian peanuts from freighters in Amsterdam to a cattle food factory in Friesland. She regularly crossed the Ijsselmeer, which can be rough. All steel boats have minor defects that even the best surveyors miss. It was her first day on the market, a price had not yet been established. I made an offer that the agent thought might be accepted, and we dealt.

The cargo of peanuts was then discharged, and she was loaded with 25 tonnes of damp sand ballast. After sessions with a *notarius* in Balk, and an unhelpful British Consul in Amsterdam, we crossed the North Sea in February – running before a sea with 2m (6ft) waves caused by a rising north-east wind that had got to force 6 by the time we reached Lowestoft, with seawater frozen into ice on our decks. We don't recommend following our example, though it gave us confidence in our new boat, which had not let us down on a fairly hairy crossing.

We had no problems in converting her. We drew up our own plans, we found the evil spots that experience told us we would and put them right. We replated the turn of the starboard bilge although there was still enough steel there to pass a survey (4mm). We increased that to 8mm because we wanted to take her to sea. *Nothing ever breaks because it is too strong.*

Faraway

We have built our latest steel boat, *Faraway*, from scratch. I designed her, and discussed her hull with some experienced platers. They advised me to get the design redrawn using a naval architect's CAD which would save money in the end.

The CAD programme forms the hull in conic sections, easy to lay out and cut using computer-driven machines. It lessens the problems of three-dimensional curves and reduces the amount of heavy metal bashing that characterises steel boat-yards. (Reduces, but does not eliminate; the shed resounds with an anvil chorus played by over-enthusiastic tympanists.)

We avoided established boatyards and engaged a team. Lowestoft is not a yacht-building town, it builds small ships and is deeply into oil-rig engineering. The latter requires above average craftsmanship, and it is an industry in decline. The boys

Faraway *moored at Seraucourt, Canal de St Quentin.*

were all keen, obliging, good-natured fellows who often went voluntarily further than would have been expected. We had a good experience, if a little hair-raising from time to time. We wanted a hull only. There was no written contract. It was a question of:

'Can you weld that on so that water will run off?'

'Course I can.'

He did and I paid him what he asked for – always a reasonable sum.

Every day we were on board by 0700 as she took shape; holding tools, passing bits and getting in the way, as owners do. It is like being the midwife at the labour of your wife – the labourer at the berth of your boat.

The hull is only the beginning. It is spectacular; a special moment, that birth, but the up-bringing and finishing are equally important and not nearly so dramatic. Not a drama at all; more like a long-drawn-out expectation, hoping that the off-spring will grow to be a credit to her parent. Who wants a rebellious boat that will not steer?

The finishing is, for an owner, the vital part. This is where his or her personality must blend with that of the boat. You have to live this bit. It should be one of life's great pleasures. Buying a completed boat from one of the mass-producing manufacturers is like having your teenager thrust upon you fully formed at age 18, too late for any control or influence. The boat you dream about, think about, scheme about (and probably cry about from time to time) will be your creation. Even if it is ugly, it's yours. If it bites and you sit waiting at the Casualty department, you cannot be angry with it. It was an accident, wasn't it? And partly your fault. In the end it's all worthwhile.

❖ Builder beware ❖

Building from new will require rather more application, thought, effort, expense, and scheming, than converting, where you do at least have a hull to begin with. To build new involves expertise that must be paid for unless you have already acquired it the hard way through experience. Either way is expensive. Experience has to be paid for in the currency of error, and we all make some hum-dinging errors from time to time. You learn by error, the cost to your bank balance and self-esteem being compensated by this mystical quality called experience. Do not confuse experience with wisdom. *Nothing connected with boats has any relationship with wisdom.*

We are all mad, we boat people. I would today be rich (but not so happy) had I not made so many cock-ups connected with boats, bouts of over-confidence that I shudder to recall, lessons that can only be acquired through the chastening experience of failure. Sometimes, you do not realise what an idiot you have made of yourself until later. Experience is bought at a price. Laurel consoles me by saying that success is the penalty for aiming too low.

If you cannot face the possibility of being seen to have made an error of judgement, cannot tolerate a patronising condescension from know-alls, buy a ready-made boat from a mass-producer of aquatic Ford Mondeos. You can spend a fortune on a waterborne Maserati-like boat and still have a stumer instead of a stunner because it does not do what you want or expect. There are competent people who build boats suitable for inland waters and the Dutch do not have a monopoly. There is also a market for floating caravans with short masts for the TV, sold to sit in at weekends in the marinas, while you start the engine and have tea, but we hope our readers will want more than that.

Builders who produce sensible boats that are adaptable to individual tastes tend to charge a little more, but you get what you pay for. Boat design and construction is not yet out of the age of the nautical equivalent of the coach-built car. The owner may not aspire to having a unique, specially designed and built extension of his personality, but he wants to personalise his boat, and this involves far more than dangling a dolly from the rear-view mirror. Marketing is the enemy of contentment for the individual, for it tries to fit us all into pre-conceived moulds. People who aspire to boat-ownership will not fit into moulds, whether guru-inspired or not. I do not expect everybody to want what I want. To me, one of the joys of boating is the quayside chat in which two contented boat-owners say what they enjoy most about the boats they navigate, and are happy to discuss the differences without argument. You learn like that.

❖ Problems to be faced ❖

Building a boat, such as a barge, from the keel up is not to be attempted without expertise. We mean that. Even with over 60 years of sea experience, I would not attempt it from scratch. Perhaps *because* of 60 years etc might be a better way of putting it. A knowledge of ships and the sea, though essential, is not enough on its own. One must know the techniques of being a shipwright. The traditional shipwright's skill really matters.

Fortunately you can buy hulls in various stages, ready to fit out yourself. Once you go down this road you are in the same position as someone doing a conversion except that your vendor will provide some drawings that are approximately right and which help when cutting fittings etc. These help but *always measure on the boat*. (There is an old saying: 'measure twice and cut once'.) Never expect a finished boat to conform exactly to the drawings. A fitter works to the nearest thou, a joiner to the nearest sixteenth, and a shipwright works to the nearest ship.

I mentioned earlier the contemporary method of ship-building. These CAD programmes (Computer Assisted Design) cost serious money, but they unfold the lines drawing and reduce it to conic sections which can be rolled on special rollers. The programme feeds this data into a plasma cutter that cuts the plating and the rollers roll, all automatically. Some programmes even run the welding of certain sections, all untouched by hand. The job barely needs a human being and one company I know no longer employs any shipwright-platers. This method of ship-building is cheap (once all the gear and the programmes have been set up) and quick, and far from labour intensive. Even the paint job is done by robot.

❖ A kit of parts ❖

There are several firms offering hulls in kit form – all of it right down to the engine beds, rudder posts, bulkheads, and bilge keels, with each carefully cut piece numbered and primed with welding primer. One might be tempted to think that assembly is a doddle, similar to an aircraft model kit.

One such (a trawler) was being put together in the same shed as *Faraway*. We were out and afloat first, even though they had more men at work. Unfortunately, building from kits is not as simple as one is led to believe.

I observed various snags. The plate edges are primed in the same way as the plates themselves. Though the primer is called welding primer, it does not weld as well as clean, shiny steel because the weld burns off the primer and leaves the edges foul, as well as creating a bad atmosphere for the welder to breathe. (Remember he is a human being too, and you cannot ventilate the work because MIG welding does not like draughts.) Best to grind off the welding primer for half an inch at the edges, and all that grinding is a heavy and expensive chore.

No matter how the steel was cut, when the project is up on end and the weight starts to distort things, the parts do not fit together with the sort of precision you might have expected. A boat is designed so that the water will take her weight evenly. She does not rest comfortably on her keel when out of her element. The trawler resounded with hammering as wayward metal was forced into shape, like a scene from the darker parts of Wagner. Swearing echoed round the shed and upset the roosting seagulls.

Aboard *Faraway*, the steel plates were not rolled. Lugs were welded on and the cry was 'Do we put a "come-along" there, she'll soon do as she're told.' Then lugs were ground off unless they were useful as foot-holds as they often were. We developed a vast respect for the 'come-along', and often use one ourselves to work steel. (See photo on the next page.)

For advertisements offering part-ready hulls etc, the inland waterways magazines in England are best. This activity seems to be more developed here because demand is stronger, though some enterprising agents are arranging imports of part-completed barges from Eastern Europe. The quality I have seen is good, but transport is a limiting factor. Larger barge hulls need shipping as deck cargo and then trans-shipping for delivery over here. In the yard where we built *Faraway* there were both an English-type narrowboat and a wide boat, both being amateur completed from hulls.

Recently, I have come across a barge completed to a finish in Poland. It was OK but lacked the air of a boat that had received the touch of her owner throughout. I worry about what might have been done out of sight, and like to see a boat in its underwear before admiring the finished product.

Laurel using a 'come-along' to straighten a boat awning stanchion.

❖ Steel quality ❖

One problem, given a world shortage of steel, is to ensure that the steel is of best quality. Steelworks vary in quality control, and steel, being an alloy, depends on the mix and the method of calendaring. Some Eastern European steel I saw being used contained patches that powdered when being cut by oxy-propane.

We once came across a magnificent barge of 38m (125ft) LOA that had been built of the best materials, painted a shiny blue enamel, and fitted out by an eminent interior designer. She was reputed to have cost £2 million, and had a paid crew. Her owner did not keep her long. I do not know the reason why he disposed of such a handsome boat, but I suspect that her immaculate finish could not cope with the brutal bashing that a hull receives in working locks. In addition, she would be always in close proximity, and occasional contact with, some rough old boats with bent plating, and jetties with jagged edges. The lesson is that it is impossible to maintain an immaculate finish to the hull if you are using the boat to enjoy the inland waters. A certain amount of bashing is inevitable, no matter how careful you are. In this context, note that commercial barges are immaculately painted at bow and stern, but the hull sides are not. It's a waste of paint.

It is possible to buy a new barge, fully fitted and ready for use. Of course it is a replica, and usually made of much thinner plate than a working barge. Is this a disadvantage? It all depends on the use to which she will be put. A working barge is on the go 365 days a year, her hull being continuously abraded by the silt in the shallow water, especially the starboard bilge plates. A pleasure barge, even a live-aboard, is unlikely to do a third of that time under way. So the boat suffers only a third of the amount of plate erosion.

Typically, a working barge loses about 3mm of plate in 60 years, a little more round the starboard bilge. This is an average figure; in places she will have lost 7mm, and in others she will be as good as new. You never can tell. Re-plating is expensive, so working barges of 38m (125ft) or under were generally built with enough steel to last the 60 years without problems, but circumstances have changed. The last price I heard for new rolled steel was £690 per tonne, ten times what it was 25 years ago. Owners are more cost-conscious nowadays. Working barges, once built of 15mm plate, are now built of 12mm. Hulls being built by a firm in the English Midlands have 6mm plating. Others are cost-cutting even more, relying on owners not knowing the form. I have seen a smallish barge built of 4mm plate. In my opinion, this is much too thin (and any thinner would be illegal for a French registered vessel).

As we have said, an IWB is bound to get knocked about, far more than a sea-going yacht. The impact resistance of steel is high, but we are dealing with moving objects with substantial kinetic energy even when moving slowly.

PLATE THICKNESS

The minimum plating thickness for any inland waters boat is 6mm; if she is over 15m (49ft) long, raise that to 8mm, and 10mm for boats of 24m (79ft).

Our new boat, *Faraway*, 12m (39ft) LOA, has plating of either 10mm or 12mm depending on what part of the hull it is used. The upper works are of 5mm, and she has deck-edge rubbing strakes of 75 x 75 x 12mm angle and a waterline rubbing strake of 75 x 12mm flat bar at the chine.

Our barge *Hosanna* of 27m (88ft), was built in 1931 of 8mm plating with frame centres at 350mm. Frame spacing is important. The floors (frames across the bottom) were 8mm x 250mm deep with flanged tops. Most important, that. This is strong. If the skin thickness is to drop to a mere 6mm, frames should be closer spaced, perhaps 250mm, and of heavier gauge. Frames must be flanged; fin and bulb steel is not satisfactory.

You may notice that I mix up millimetres, centimetres and metres. In the boat-building world they use millimetres only. They would not talk of 35cm spacing, it would be 350mm. You come across enormous figures, but it avoids confusion, they say, and of course metrication was meant to dispense with confusion. Ho, ho! Also, although we give Imperial conversions for metric measurements and vice versa, we frequently leave millimetres to stand alone as it is sometimes difficult to give sensible conversions to inches.

· 7 ·
Converting a workboat

Of the various ways of obtaining an IWB, possibly the most satisfying method is to convert a commercial barge. It gives you credibility by association. You know that the boat is basically easy to handle. If your idea of boating fun is to have a clone of a thousand similar boats, left to look after itself in a marina when the weather is unkind, and get anxious when the loo needs fixing, then steer clear of any sort of conversion. If you want a boat that has been converted by somebody else (leading to switches that cannot be found and fuses in unknown locations), this chapter is not for you.

The first thing to do is to find a fundamentally sound ex-commercial boat suitable for the life, navigation and aims that you wish to pursue, whatever they are.

The Dutch Barge Association (which dropped the 'Dutch' and became, for no good reason, the 'Barge Association –DBA') has a first-class book available to members on buying a barge called *The Barge Buyer's Handbook*. (Whatever the Association calls itself, the DBA is excellent). To buy a barge for the first time, whether converted or unconverted, begs for problems, therefore it is a very good idea to join this helpful association and learn from the articles published in their journal *Blue Flag*, which reveal a fount of both anguish, achievement, and experience. The modest subscription is money well spent.

The *Blue Flag* is probably the best club journal (from a practical point of view) in the pleasure boat field. It usually contains several advertisements for barges in various stages of undress, as well as plenty of small businesses who will help you clothe your boat. It contains useful notices of moorings to let. One needs a secure mooring to carry out the basic conversion. Finishing details can be done anywhere on an as-and-when basis. That is normally the case.

❖ Where do you find unconverted barges? ❖

The Netherlands is a prolific source, but good barges are usually snapped up by canny Dutchmen. People buy up good quality unconverted barges and move them to places where they will get a better price. Nothing much you can do about this; they are where the action is and geared to do a quick deal, just what commercial sellers need. There are several specialist barge brokers but I believe the better ones are in France. The Dutch play a straight bat but drive very hard bargains and I think their system is loaded against the foreigner.

France, like the Netherlands, is a country where the number of smaller barges is gradually being reduced, though in late 2008 a good grain harvest created such a demand for barge transport that many old barges are being re-conditioned for work. Given the economic climate, this situation may not last long.

The buying process in France is loaded in favour of the buyer. The price is agreed and a contract exchanged and a survey is arranged. Usually the broker organises this, called an *expertise*. The rule is that what is visible and accessible is the buyer's look-out. The defects are there for him to see, and he should have seen them. But the condition of the boat underwater, and her stern-gear are assessed by the *expert* (surveyor). He lists the defects (such as a chipped propeller or a slack rudder bearing) and it is up to the seller to put them right before transfer. Much depends on the pernickityness of the *expert*. Alternatively, seller and buyer can come to an agreement adjusting the price according to what needs to be done. Another alternative if the seller thinks the *expert* has been over-picky, is for the seller to get a counter-survey at his own expense and let the *experts* fight it out. This can cost a lot, as French *experts* can be inflexible as well as possessing large doses of *amour propre*.

The French firm H_2O are busy barge brokers and usually have a good choice on their books, including some whose owners have lost enthusiasm. In my view, it is advisable to pay H_2O a visit after a quick check on the Internet. There are usually several barge-owners about their premises at St Jean-de-Losne (near Dijon) and you will get some atmosphere and hear some horror stories. If your enthusiasm survives then you are on your way. Even if you do not find what you want there, you will be able to view some interesting barges and gain the knowledge to be able to cross off or add features that you hadn't thought of before.

There are two other yards at St Jean-de-Losne of varying degrees of poshness. You will discover them with ease. All, in my experience, are straight dealers.

It is possible to find a part-converted barge that has fallen on hard times. Many people start converting but fall by the wayside. There are five main reasons for this, so watch and avoid them:

- *Insufficient funds* This can be due to an under-estimate of what it would cost. The only advice we can offer is that, like government projects, whatever the method or plan, it will always cost more than you think. Make a best realistic estimate and add 30 per cent for contingencies and set it aside deliberately and conscientiously. You'll need it.

- *Cash flow* Conversion takes up time when you might have been earning, but one has to go on living. The conversion cash must be available as and when it is needed. The converter may have to stop to earn money, while the part-converted boat eats its head off.

- *Condition* The barge is in worse condition than the converter had reason to believe. All second-hand goods are liable to this snag.
- *Lack of berth* Because the conversion takes time, the converter is forced to quit a convenient berth and cannot find an alternative.
- *Other problems* The converters may have family or health problems.

We cannot solve those problems for you, especially not in advance.

❖ Find a good site ❖

An important factor in conversion is a good berth to do it in. Immense amounts of time can be lost fiddling about on a difficult site. There are criteria that are essential and/or desirable. We will discuss these from the point of view of the impecunious. The better off probably won't do the work themselves anyway.

- Get the boat to the site without too much expense, trouble or danger. Danger, because Murphy's Law dictates that the boat you want to buy is awkward to access, it will be mid winter, and you are obliged to move the boat away from its original berth straight away.
- Include the cost of relocation and essential extra equipment you will need in your offer for the boat. It is a bargaining point, but do not expect any seller to yield much.
- Don't expect to live aboard even in primitive camping conditions in the early stages, you need accommodation close by. Don't waste time and energy in travelling.
- The site should have reasonable facilities for launching and/or hauling out, not necessarily very close because boat transport specialists can move even large boats easily and at reasonable cost over short distances. Avoid frequently dunking the boat like a doughnut; Launching boats of this size by crane is inadvisable – their length makes them difficult to sling without bending them in the middle. Craning is a specialist business.
- Your site should be under cover, if possible. Working in the open air in northern climates imposes limitations that add to the cost and time, and makes partners nervous. Erect a substantial and semi-permanent cover that won't blow away in the first gale.
- It is a plus if the site has a small crane for moving equipment and materials. Alternatively, investigate buying a second-hand fork-lift truck at a sell-up auction. Buy, rather than rent because the total work will always take longer than you think and there is always a market for second-hand equipment. If there is another user nearby, come to a friendly arrangement.
- A site near workshops is advisable. Get to know them. Convince them you are not rich. Affability and tolerance pays handsome dividends. Both British and Continental workmen are good friends to have on your side. Driving hard bargains seldom pays off in the long run. (Being generous at Christmas always pays off.) Our site on a business park gave us access to small engineering firms and the close-by 'greasy spoon' café was a boon in cold weather.

• Draw up serious plans. These cannot be done in advance of the purchase because you do not yet know what you are getting: the field is limited.

You've found a convenient berth, and bought your hull. Now, you have to get her on site. If she can be navigated, you should take her yourself, because you will learn a lot. If you cannot and hire a delivery crew, then try to go some of the way yourself, a weekend perhaps. This is your best chance to learn about your new baby.

Delivery crews can be contacted via the DBA or via H$_2$O. Warning: reliable ones don't come cheap, so take this into account when choosing your boat. Also bear in mind that crews work to time and are not always careful in the way they treat the boat.

The sooner you can bear to move on board, the better. It can be uncomfortable: camping with hazards; you move about dodging holes in the floor, and things are fixed temporarily with clamps, but the time and money saved will be significant. Check that the site allows you to do this. Ours didn't, officially. To keep the social services off our backs (*What? Two 78 year olds living on a chocked-up unfinished boat in a hangar with no sanitary block and only a 10 litre can of water? That can't be allowed!*), we made friends with the manager of the site, and got classed as working night-shift, in case anyone from the council came snooping. There are ways and means.

❖ Shortening a barge ❖

The boat you want may be too big for you. Don't worry; if she is straight-sided, she can be shortened as part of the first stage in conversion. Dutch boats do not lend themselves to shortening as most have an elegant, even beautiful sheerline (curved deck). Boats are best shortened by having a section cut out of the middle and then the two ends are joined together. It is not difficult, and the amputated portion is a source of steel that you will undoubtedly need, important with high steel prices. What remains unused, sell for scrap.

With a sheerline, the join would make a sharp interruption in the elegant deck curve. It would look wrong unless you spent a lot. On the other hand, the French *péniche* is built with a straight deck and is parallel all the way. Shortening is easy and many interesting examples exist. We think 38m (125ft) is too long for amateurs, and suspect that the bureaucrats will soon impose restrictions on such a size for private use, as they already have done at sea, 24m (79ft) has been discussed, it could even be 20m (65ft).

The living accommodation in a *péniche* is aft and surprisingly comfortable for a family. You could (we have seen an example) cut out the entire cargo hold and join the pointy bit directly to the blunt end containing the living accommodation, leaving the machinery intact. Minimum expenditure, minimum work and a usable live-aboard boat.

Boats that have undergone this treatment but have been left with three or four metres of the former hold, look better proportioned, finishing up just short of 20m

(65ft) long, a convenient length. There is more deck space. This is undoubtedly the best route to a low-cost conversion that looks business-like and is easy to handle. You can move her away and live aboard the old *roef* (cabin) while attending to the remaining part of the hold. Believe me, this is worth considering.

❖ Tools and equipment ❖

It is not worth buying expensive machine tools for a one-off job. It is best to hire them for short periods as and when needed. But you will need to plot the work carefully – how good are you at critical path analysis? Some expenses that can pay off are:

- *Scaffolding* This is always in demand and costs a fortune to hire. If you can get it at auction when a builder goes bust, do so. You will be able to sell it on completion. Make sure it is not stolen: it seems that scaffolding is regarded as anybody's in boatyards, so are ladders and buckets, and even industrial vacuum cleaners. Paint your name on every piece.
- *Cover* It depends where you do the work, but if there are other vessels nearby, an expendable cover is desirable for shot-blasting. Shot-blasting is never popular; the dust travels miles unless screened. The ideal site is in a large shed, but even then covering for painting and blasting is essential if other boats are near-by. The dust can hang in the air for ages.
- *30-amp power supply* This is the least you will need. If you can get 3-phase, so much the better.
- *Good, long ladders* These are essential. The deck of a boat when hauled out and chocked up, so as to leave room underneath for work and/or painting, is a long way from the ground. Carrying heavy items up ladders is neither easy nor safe: hence the convenience of a crane or fork-lift. We found a 12m (40ft) ship's gangway that had failed its test. For us, it made a good sloping access to deck level.
- *Bucket on a rope* You'll save a lot of time using this to move small items.
- *Security of tenure* Conversion is going to take longer than you think. Moving a half-completed project under duress can be a nightmare. Make sure you can cope with the rent. Putting the landlord's back up can cause difficulties. Boat-building involving steel-work is a noisy and unpopular activity.

There are many Health and Safety regulations about ladders and work habits that must, of course, be scrupulously obeyed, though if you respect all of them you will never finish the job.

With a steel boat, it is possible to cut a substantial hole in the bottom of the hull to obtain access in the early stages. This saves time and the original piece can be welded back before finishing the interior. We did this with *Hosanna*. Be careful with old steel hulls; cutting and/or welding close to rivets is fraught with difficulties (see page 50).

Put your name on your ladder and fasten it securely.

❖ Health and Safety ❖

Avoid commercialising the project by setting up as a business. There are gains, but you will invite bureaucratic interference – business rates and taxes, VAT etc and you will be more likely to fall foul of the Health and Safety man. Some of these officials are first class, even a positive help, but the profession contains too many know-alls to take chances. Boat-building is an activity that defies strict Health and Safety regulations. Rely on your own judgement and common sense.

If you are employing direct labour, other than engaging a professional firm to do work, it is advisable to get insurance cover. If employing freelance craftsmen, make sure they have their own insurance cover. (They usually do, but never make assumptions.)

❖ Registration ❖

The Recreational Craft Directive was introduced in 1994 to ensure a consistent level of safety in boat design and manufacture (see the British Marine Federation website (www.britishmarine.co.uk)). To avoid problems, it is important that the original registration of your craft be continued to exempt you from this piece of bureaucracy.

If you buy your boat abroad (and if it's a barge you probably would) it is necessary to get her registered. If you want her on the British register then you must find the nearest British Consulate. If, after a long wait, the fourth deputy-assistant clerk deigns to speak to you, an insignificant tax-payer, he may help you through the process. It isn't difficult. Best to get two sets of forms in advance. Take with you the Bill of Sale or notarised contract. Fill in the form for registration. If you want a Boat name different to the one on the Bill of Sale, now is the time to do the change – it is a nightmare afterwards. You need two sets of forms because the chances are you will have filled in one form incorrectly (comma in the wrong place?). Just when the consular clerk is congratulating himself on having won, you trump him with spare forms and while he is still recovering from the shock he agrees to help you complete the right part of the forms correctly, collect a fat fee and give you a temporary certificate. It is not as bad as that. You can always put the boat on the Small Ships Register more cheaply online.

❖ Converting abroad ❖

Where exactly is the work going to be done? The advantages of working in a country where you speak the language and know the conventions are important. On the other hand, unless you have a secure weatherproof site, there is much to be said for starting the work in the north of Europe, getting the boat into a movable state and moving south to finish in a warmer climate. It makes a difference.

Much depends on the extent to which you will need help in the earlier, more complex stages when the work is likely to be too heavy for an inexperienced amateur working on his own, even with specialist tools.

In our major conversions, we have contemplated having the work done in Eastern Europe. Countries such as Poland, Romania and the Balkan states have a tradition of ship-building, hard work, skill and low prices. Your problem is that unless you plan to live on site and sign an open contract that allows for *ad hoc* changes, you will need to get plans drawn up by a naval architect in a clear and unambiguous form that a professional ship-builder can use unsupervised. Fag-packet, or back-of-envelope designs are OK if you are there to resolve ambiguities. They will not do in the case of a firm contract between parties that have no common language. Even if you are quite good at everyday Romanian, say, do you know all the technical words and the legal and professional conventions? There is another snag: the builder will work to the plan and deliver the boat as on the plan. We have warned against changing your mind about this or that, on pain of rising cost. You get what you contracted for, and you collect the boat.

Because we are people who have strong ideas, we have always opted to keep complete control of the whole operation. If you want a boat to cruise in now and then, this is not so important, but living aboard a boat requires a degree of intimacy with your craft that you must enter into voluntarily, like a marriage. We do not relish living aboard somebody else's ideal boat, and do not grumble at our own errors of judgement. If you do much of the work yourself, or are at least on site with the work force, you know the boat from the start, and when snags eventually arise (and they will) you will be better able to cope.

Dutch boat builders have a reputation as first-class steel boat-builders. Based on experience, I am wary. Putting together a decent basic hull is not that difficult. One judges excellence by attention to detail. But here are some examples of bad practice that I have seen in Dutch builds. Watch out for them:

- Steel boats should have deck drains so that water does not lie in the scuppers. Many Dutch boats are built without them.

- Butt-straps should be riveted on the *inside* of the plating. This is more difficult to do because when inside they need notching into the frames. It is cheapjack to put the butt-strap outside the plating, and dangerous too, because the strap will be 10 or 12mm thick, the edges will not be ground down and the blunt edges can catch on piling or other obstructions. This can dislodge the strap, perhaps only by a millimetre, but it can shear the rivets and destroy the watertightness of the riveting.

- Look behind the panelling of the accommodation. Most people think the Dutch barge *roef* (or after cabin) is quaint and beautiful. *Hosanna* was built in 1931 by Boot Brothers of Leiden, one of the better builders in Holland. The wood panelling had not been treated or sealed either on the outside, or the hidden part. This is bad practice and led to severe insect attack, probably brought in by the insulation material (untreated wheat straw) that is a fire risk as well as being inefficient. It allows condensation to form on the steel skin that can cause corrosion (though in *Hosanna*'s case this latter had not happened).

- The overhead insulation was screwed-up newspapers wedged in place. *Hosanna* was typical. Economy is one thing, but this was another fire hazard.

This parsimony in detail did not affect the fact that *Hosanna*'s basic hull was sound and when converted gave us 22 years of pleasure. Be sure what you have is basically sound, and then improve it.

❖ Converting in Britain ❖

Within Britain, there are important differences in localities. Avoid the south coast or the London region because the labour and property costs (for worthwhile sites) are high. On the south coast you will find good yacht craftsmen but they command high rates of pay, and the less well-skilled demand the same rates. Skills on the south coast are for light construction types of boat. A canal boat conversion needs construction to concrete bunker standards. When learning about boat-building many years ago, my instructor asked me:

'What would you use to fasten these two steel angles together?'

'Half-inch bolts, Chief?' I offered.

He threw the angles down, their resounding clang reinforcing his gesture of disdain. Contempt spread over his face. 'Half-inch bolts is for watch-makers,' he said.

Boat-building is not an exact science like brain surgery. Everything should be twice the size you first thought of.

Ordinary motor cruisers can be fitted out almost anywhere, but barges are special, and there is no legacy of barge-building around much of the British coast. The best places to go for fair-priced expert help is to the East Anglian ports where there was once much work servicing oil and gas rigs whose specifications are unbelievably strict. The standards of skill in that industry have left dozens of small, skilled enterprises working informally and hungrily. They are more accessible if you have to bring your unconverted barge across the North Sea on her own bottom, which matters because this is a step that can be fraught with problems. The dangers of this unconverted delivery journey rise exponentially with distance. Recently we saw a barge bought with the intention of sailing her round to Ireland. After several disasters and a stranding she could not continue; she was condemned by the Coastguard, and broken up. Incidentally, that barge had spent her working life carrying gravel. Gravel is one of the most corrosive cargoes imaginable, after salt. Ascertain whether a barge that you contemplate buying has been used for gravel, and expect the worst.

Scotland is still busy with the oil industry, but south of the Tyne there are many small ports that relish barge work. Not the big, well-established yards with designated parking spaces for the managing director, the firms you need are based in sheds surrounded by remnants and off-cuts saved on a 'come-in-handy' policy from which you may benefit. Even the boss drives a 15-year-old pick-up, and the only union to which everyone belongs is the United Skip-raiders Union. We are founder members.

I would recommend consideration of Lowestoft as a base for conversion, At Lowestoft there is still an active oil or gas rig industry to maintain the production platforms, and skills are available. At the time of writing, the old shipyard of Brooke Marine, forced into closure by Harold Wilson, has huge building sheds to let, either in whole or part, equipped with 10-tonne overhead travelling cranes, and good security. Prices are modest because some government-appointed group has caused a planning blight by proposing to abandon Lowestoft's industries and build thousands of executive waterside homes. The Brooke Marine site will probably be available for some years yet. The regional authority will soon use up available funds paying exalted fees to consultants who know little about the area and nothing about the sea.

That's not surprising. The field of ocean expertise is so wide that nobody can know more than a fraction of the pool of knowledge. The fascination of boats is that you never stop learning. Whatever an expert tells you, there are always exceptions, and it is a penny to a pinch of fairy dust that your case is the exception. It's tough, but fun.

As well as Lowestoft, the same can be said about the Humber, the Orwell, and the Essex and North Kent coasts.

❖ **Bringing a barge to the UK** ❖

Now, what if you've bought your boat on the Continent but want to do the work in England? You'll need to get her to a channel port and then make the sea crossing. Do your research beforehand. Choose carefully the ports of departure and arrival. Almost certainly the barge will not be fully equipped for the inland voyage, let alone the sea crossing, though it is customary (even obligatory) for a vendor to leave some mooring ropes on handing over. There will be no book of instructions. This is the fun bit, finding out what this knob does (whoops!).

Inland passage

For the inland passage, you will need a personal qualification to drive a boat of this size. Make sure you have enough fuel for the journey; there are not many filling stations and you will no longer be eligible for red diesel. If the vessel is in commerce, get the vendor to fill her up before the sale and include the fact that she has fuel in the tanks stated on the Bill of Sale.

This voyage should present few difficulties once you have got the confidence to manage a large boat. It's not difficult. But make sure you know all the rules for the country concerned. This is not difficult in France or Belgium, where the authorities are more concerned generally that you are not a menace. It is different in the Netherlands. A nation almost pathologically tolerant of drugs, they are wary of 'dangerous' foreigners with boats. Their water regulations are draconian and vast numbers of grave-looking water police pounce on minute infringements with unbelievable enthusiasm. Dutch sailors see nothing wrong in all this. Perhaps they do not get harassed, only the poor b-----y foreigners. We ourselves have had no bother because we learned early on in Holland to take elaborate precautions of an intensity that should not be necessary. Having spent the last year or so in Lowestoft, we hear many stories from experienced cruising yachtsmen navigating properly-equipped cruising yachts who have had run-ins with the Dutch water police. One cannot expect the same standards of seamanship for amateurs as from professionals. The administration should allow for a small measure of flexibility when dealing with minor infractions that do not cause significant hazard or danger. After all, we British have never been subject to bureaucratic bullying in our boats and we use our freedom responsibly.

The sea crossing

In Chapter 21 we look at sea-crossings for inland waters boats, which you should study, even though it concentrates on a voyage to the Continent. The same gear should be on board. The authorities can prevent you from sailing if you don't have basic equipment.

❖ A preliminary conversion plan ❖

Assume your captured changeling is at a good site with a slipway available and you have shown the prize to your admiring and/or dubious friends. It is now time to plan carefully and commit yourself thoroughly to those plans. Here are three essential first steps:

1 Carry out a careful survey looking at her from your own point of view. Check carefully your draft plans and see whether it might be necessary to make alterations. Take time to *think* and *make lists*.
2 Empty the boat. *Hosanna* still had some of her peanut cargo aboard when we brought her back to England, and the local cats delighted in the exodus of rats from under the ceiling boards.
3 Now you can see it clearly, make good any faults in the steelwork.

❖ Preparation ❖

You must insulate the accommodation areas and this needs careful surface preparation. The best insulation for living quarters is sprayed-on foam, which insulates against heat, cold and sound, and nowadays it's also fire-resistant. In my view there is no alternative. The foam adheres to bare steel, prevents hidden corrosion and discourages pests. Spraying can be professionally done in one day, and though the bill will look heavy, the saving in time and effort, and the increase in comfort, will pay off handsomely.

Preparation takes time, do it yourself to save costs. To start, you must clean the steel, remove all dust, debris and bits of welding rod. As you will need to shot-blast the outside of the boat anyway, do the lot together. The interior can be blasted to a less stringent standard.

- Slip the boat and chock her up.
- Remove the ceiling boards. (Ceiling boards in a boat are under your feet – you might call them bottom boards.)
- Cut a 450mm (approx 18in) hole in the lowest central bit of the hull plating, taking care not to use oxy-propane close to any rivets. Save the piece you cut out and grind clean the edges of the hole and the cut-out ready for welding back later.
- It is likely that you will find a ton or two of small debris and rat-shit in the hold.
- Shovel it out through the hole. It's hard work but not nearly as hard as lofting it over the side.
- Wash the hull out with a power washer.

You will already have rigged up covers over the outside, and you are now ready for shot-blasting. This miserable business is best done by contractors. At best you can go away and come back when it is done. I cannot understand how anyone can be persuaded to do it for a living. The outside of the boat should be shot-blasted to S3 standard, and the inside to S2$\frac{1}{2}$.

The engine room is probably best left unblasted. Whether you shot-blast the accommodation depends on the clutter therein.

Usually the contractors will air-blow the steel clean afterwards and the price should include shovelling the used grit out through the hole in the bottom and carting it away. The cut-out piece must then be professionally welded back in place. Clean off the whole area with an industrial vacuum cleaner.

The contractor then sprays the surfaces, inside and outside, with a thin coat of epoxy holding primer which must be done straight away. You now have a beautifully clean inside to work on. (That won't last long!) The painters can come back the next day to put another coat of epoxy resin on the outside only.

If you cannot shot-blast the interior, clean off the steel and wash it down with N/10 ortho-phosphoric acid. Let it dry and go white. Clean off with meths.

❖ Ballast ❖

We prefer concrete which is anathema to the French and we think this is because they have never learned how to use it. Decide exactly how much you need and fit shuttering. Coat the blasted (or acided) steel with a liberal coat of Waxoyl and let it harden.

Now, instead of the conventional 5:3:1 mix, use a 10:2:1 mix which has little structural strength. Finish this off about 10mm below the desired level. When it is half dry, add a 10mm screed of smooth concrete.

The French fear that water will get under it and/or it would be impossible to move out. Our mix bonds well to the Waxoyl and we have never found water there, even after 22 years. And the screed is easily fractured and the weak concrete is easily broken out should you need to remove it.

❖ Roof ❖

Before shot-blasting the hull, construct the roof, overhead, deck-head, or whatever you like to call the top that keeps the rain out. Get the beams for it rolled beforehand because they will dictate the camber and they need to be even. Given a roof width of 4m (13ft), a camber with 15cm (6in) at the centre is about right. The rainwater must run off and boats are often not exactly upright.

The roof side-edges on self-conversions are generally made square. If you agree that a rounded edge looks better, have 1200mm (approx 4ft) lengths of steel rolled in a 20mm radius to form the edges.

Now make the roof upside down.

- Weld up the 5mm plating flat.
- Place the beams and stitch-weld them to the plate.

- Weld on the curved edges and the straight sides which you should make an inch or two higher than needed.
- Weld temporary cross-pieces near the foot of the sides to hold the whole thing rigid.

Don't be tempted to save a few pounds by using 4mm steel; 5mm steel stays flat better and helps to avoid the hollows and bumps that get left behind when steelwork cools down after cutting and welding.

It pays to make the cabin sides slope in a couple of inches at the top. Vertical sides look as if they are sloping outwards; an optical illusion that gives the conversion an amateur look. Shipwrights are aware of this.

The next stage is to get the roof turned over, using a crane, and lower it onto the boat without bending it. Then cut the sides to fit and weld down. Sounds easy, but it takes time and care. If you have got this done in time, you can put the roof in place for the shot-blasters to finish. You'll be lucky if it all works out to time-table, but with care it will go reasonably close. Having the roof on while shot-blasting the interior limits the mess.

Cut the window holes when the roof is welded up, but take care to tack on pieces of steel angle round the window holes to prevent the heat of the cutter distorting the steel. You can bash off the angle afterwards.

If you do not complete and/or fix the roof before the shot-blasters arrive, do not despair. The roof can be sent away to be shot-blasted in whole or part and they will clean and prime before it is returned. This is where critical path analysis comes in.

The next task is to fit lining guides or battens in the interior. The best material for these is tanalised tile-battens, usually cut in long lengths to about 35mm x 18mm section and obtainable from wood merchants who supply roofers. Order plenty;

WARNING ABOUT WELDING OVER RIVETS

When ships were riveted (a practice superseded by electro-welding in the 1930s and 1940s), holes were exactly drilled or punched, and then the two faying surfaces were coated with tallow. The surfaces were pressed together and riveting commenced.

The rivets were inserted when red hot. The head was backed up and the small end was hammered over, and so on many times. As the work cooled down the rivets contracted and the two faying surfaces were drawn tightly together and became ultra tight and waterproof.

If you now run a line of weld across a riveted butt strap, for example, or a lapped strake, the heat of the weld melts the tallow between the two plates and it runs out. Not only is the joint no longer watertight, but water can get into the joint and corrode away to its heart's content.

The job can be done, but requires elderly welders who were once riveters and who know exactly what they are doing. If you find one, look after him.

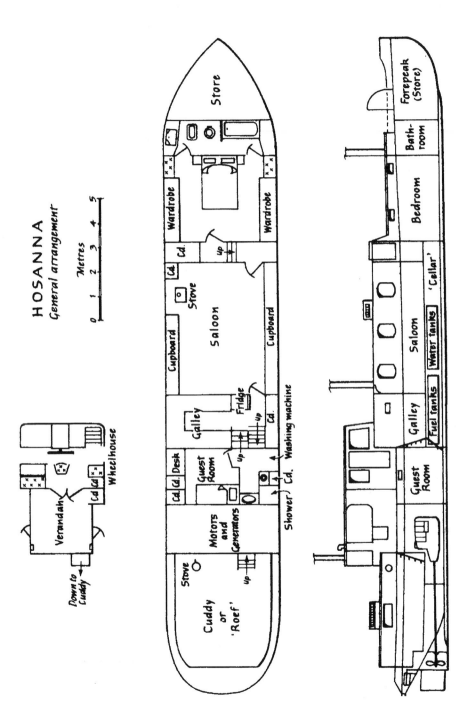

HOSANNA

General arrangement

Metres

0 1 2 3 4 5

Store

Wardrobe

Wardrobe

Cd.

up

Cupboard

Stove

Saloon

Cupboard

Fridge

up

Cd.

Galley

up

Cd. Cd. Desk

Guest
Room

up

Motors
and
Generators

Shower Cd. Washing machine

Stove

Cuddy
or
'Roef'

up

Wheelhouse

Verandah

Cd. Cd.

Down to
Cuddy

Forepeak
(Store)

Bath-
room

Bedroom

'Cellar'

Water tanks

Saloon

Fuel tanks

Galley

Guest
Room

Hosanna

it comes cheaper when bought in thousands of feet at a time, and is incredibly useful stuff everywhere.

The battens should be screwed to the frames with 5mm self-tapping screws. Nowadays one can get self-tappers with 'built-in' drill bits, you just hold the batten in place and with a strong power driver (ideally a pneumatic one if you have a compressor), drive the screw right home in one movement. Once the battens are fixed, you should then cover them with masking tape on the side that will take the linings.

❖ Spraying the foam insulation ❖

Before spraying, dust and sweep up. Tape up openings with sheets of hardboard. Carefully mask any fittings. Pipe-runs or channel plating for wiring must be shielded completely with newspaper and masking tape. Do this with care, as digging things out of the foam afterwards occupies an archaeological time scale and is intensely exasperating. When this is done you are ready for the foam sprayers.

How much foam? We specify one inch thick which usually means that we get 80 per cent of the plating at about 30mm, 10 per cent at about 20mm and 10 per cent at anything up to 150mm. Bear in mind that 15mm provides 85 per cent of the heat insulation that 30mm provides. Our yacht *Fare Well* was foamed to two inches (50mm) and was superbly well insulated. The problem is that the foam expands after it touches the steel so that it is a matter of judgement how much is sprayed. They give you a thicker coat than you ask for on the basis that it is easier to cut the surplus off than it is to set up the gear again to add more.

Then comes the real chore. Cutting the foam back to its desired thickness is simple, but beastly. It is important to cut the stuff off in chunks, rather than grinding or sawing it off and so making a dust which is deadly to breathe. (The foam sprayer is dressed in a protective space-type suit.) We used a bread-knife and it was exhausting, especially overhead. It's a chore that feels good to have behind you as you shovel out the over-spray. *A face mask is essential while removing foam.*

Now start on the fun bit, interior decoration and such, which depends on your taste. Advice on converting the *roef* or old cabin depends on its condition and what you want. In *Hosanna* we had to ditch the worm-eaten wood so we ended up starting from scratch.

❖ The engine room ❖

It is best not to shot-blast the engine room. Keep sand and grit out of it. The engine room on *Hosanna* looked scruffy, and we thought of painting it white. Even with methyl-ethyl-ketone, probably the most lethal grease solvent ever, we made no impact on a trial section. I consulted a metallurgist. Steel is porous, and over the years, the old steel had absorbed the blend of paraffin wax with old engine oil that the Dutch owners had coated it with. The steel was superbly preserved, but had a black surface resembling a waxy stucco that would not take paint. We found a product called Waxoyl which seemed similar to what the Dutch had used and was not expensive. It worked well. We even used it at the bottom of the chain locker in the fore-peak. The sides of the engine room when we sold her looked exactly as they had done 22 years before and they had had no attention in the meantime. However, they still looked like grotty black stucco.

❖ VAT ❖

The DBA have been fighting a court case to have work and/or fittings on residential barges free of VAT. They have had some success, but expect the Revenue to appeal as it is our money that they throw at the lawyers. This is a current subject and you should follow events reported in the *Blue Flag*. In our own case, and under different criteria, we had no difficulty getting VAT exemption with *Hosanna*, which we declared and registered as a 'barge'. Her size and tonnage qualified her, and once she had passed onto the files everything went through easily, over and over again.

Only certain items are VAT exempt, generally the sort of professional gear you would expect. It is important not to give to government bodies information that they do not strictly need or request. The less they know about us the better, not that all civil servants are obstructive. Some are, but one often finds a friendly and interested person to deal with.

Do not rely on concessions and interpretations of European law being the same in all European countries. You may argue convincingly in English but it is unlikely to wash overseas. If you think a small 'present' might act as an inducement to co-operation, be careful. In certain countries it might, but as foreigners, we do not know the form. At the petty level, most European countries are pretty straight nowadays and they do not take risks by underhand dealing with foreigners who may be secret '*agents provocateurs*' of Brussels.

Much that concerns the converter will also apply to those who build from scratch.

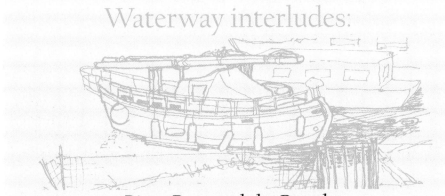

Waterway interludes:

River Bure and the Broads

The river Bure is one of the rivers that link up the enchanting waterway in the east of England known as the Norfolk Broads. These are man-made lakes, the result of mediaeval peat diggings later flooded by the encroaching sea, long used by watermen and sailors, for both commercial and recreational purposes. The country's earliest sailing regattas took place here, long before the Solent got into the act. These regattas were known as 'water frolics' and, apart from sailing races, there were all sorts of fun and games for the merrymakers.

The Broads are linked by about 120 miles of navigable rivers and dykes, forming an extensive and varied waterway. The clustered villages on the upper reaches of the Bure are busy in summer, in contrast to the wild and remote nature reserves further north.

Bureaucracy reigns now. Some years ago Broads navigation passed out of the hands of navigators and was given to the newly created Broads Authority that in accordance with the ethos of the time is dominated by the Green lobby. Soon, the bittern became more important than the boat.

The mouth of the River Bure empties into the Yare just past Yarmouth Yacht Station. This is the place to moor your boat if you want a look at Yarmouth, a town with plenty of history and museums to go with it; literary associations including Dickens, (*David Copperfield*) and Daniel Defoe who described its beautiful quayside in glowing terms. There is also the Golden Mile of seaside attractions, and a thriving marketplace.

You would be lucky to find Cromer crab or longshore herring on offer in the pubs of the Broads, where with a few exceptions, fish and chips and fast food carry the day. But in Yarmouth marketplace you will find the local food. Here in summer you can buy local fruit and vegetables, crabs and a wealth of seafood: kippers and bloaters, fresh longshore cod, and from the fish stall in July, emerald green samphire from the salt marshes. Buy a bundle of it, wash it, and discard the woody stems. Cook for 15 minutes in salted water, and eat it with your fingers and plenty of butter, pulling the green flesh off the stalk with your teeth. It tastes like asparagus, and it's wonderfully full of iodine.

The Yare joins the North Sea two miles further on from Buremouth. The Broads are also accessible from the sea through Lowestoft, Oulton Broad and the River Waveney. The limiting factor, apart from draught, is bridge clearance. The river Yare has no obstruction as far as Norwich but both the Bure and Waveney have low fixed bridges.

We moored for some time opposite the mouth of the Bure, where the boatyard was refitting *Hosanna*. We were in the short reach between Breydon bridge (leading to Breydon Water and the routes to Norwich and Lowestoft), and Yarmouth Haven Bridge, which takes the A12 across the river; this bridge lifts to allow craft to go to sea.

From this strategic position we were able to watch, sometimes with sympathy, sometimes with exasperation, the mistakes made by river craft, and the reasons for them. It was quite a lesson in boat handling.

If you come from Breydon Water under the bridge on an ebb tide, and do not notice the mouth of the Bure on your left, you can be swept past the notice saying NO HIRE CRAFT BEYOND THIS POINT under Haven Bridge. If you don't hit something under the bridge you will be quickly out to sea. If you see the notice and turn round, it will take a long time to claw back to Buremouth against the tide. The turn into Buremouth is an awkward one, more than 90°. The tide can be strong, and the posts at the turn indicating the channel are not just for mooring to while you lower your mast and sails. Many craft cut the corner and ran aground, and either awaited a tide, canted over, or were hauled off by the boatyard's workboat.

On a happier note, the water between the bridges is now so clean that the fish have returned, and we watched a little boat beam-trawling up and down the reach. He brought us a bucketful of beautiful sole, which he is not allowed to sell (EU regulations), so he gives his catch away to friends.

After the Yacht Station, there is no safe mooring upstream on River Bure for about nine miles till you reach Stracey Arms Mill. *Hamilton's Navigations*, an excellent guide to the Broads, often says 'no mooring, all reeds'. We used to moor a half-decker in the reeds or rond, with a rondhook. This may not be a good idea in these days of many motorboats passing – some of them going a bit too fast.

You will travel through flat, remote marshlands, where an occasional windmill recalls the time when all the dykes that drain these water meadows and reed beds were managed by windpower. Cattle still graze these levels, and the reeds are still cut for thatch. Over it all is the enormous sky, and the light that so entranced the water-colourists of the Norwich School.

The riverside villages are small and charming, clustering close together on the denser sections of the Broads. Most of them have a store for basic commodities, as well as a pub. If only the one-time glories of Suffolk and Norfolk cuisine were to be had more easily, the suet puddings (not just beef, but with chicken, fish, or fruit) the dumplings, the crabs, and kippers.

You can choose to take the wilder way, up the River Thurne to Potter Heigham, the last village before you reach the nature reserves of Hickling Broad and Horsey Mere, where birds have priority – there are wall-to-wall swans, and you might see a swallowtail butterfly.

You have another chance to see wildlife by cruising up the River Ant to Barton Broad, where bank holiday regattas give a different meaning to the wildlife aspect. If you opt to stay with the River Bure, you will come to delightful villages with everything you would need on holiday, including Roy's of Wroxham, the 'biggest village store in the world', still where it was when we went there for ice cream 70 years ago, but bigger now.

There is much to see, hear, and enjoy on the Broads, not least the absence of noisy motorways and traffic fumes, replaced by the chuckle of a coot or the cry of gulls wafted inland from the sea. There are ancient churches, Ranworth has a mediaeval painted rood screen with a wonderful St Michael, the ruins of St Benet's abbey where once a year the Bishop arrives by wherry in cope and mitre and conducts an open-air service for holiday makers. The immense skies never fail to catch at our hearts, and the ripple of water where we learned to sail; the memories will always be with us. Remembering how we would shoot the bridge at Acle, lowering both mast and sails together without stopping, carrying our way until we raised the mast and topsail and picked up way again on the other side. Just the thing to mull over when sitting on a sunny evening with a drink and a bowl of fresh caught shrimps, preferably the tiny brown ones that are a bother to peel (though the shells are tender enough to eat), and allow long conversations while you enjoy them.

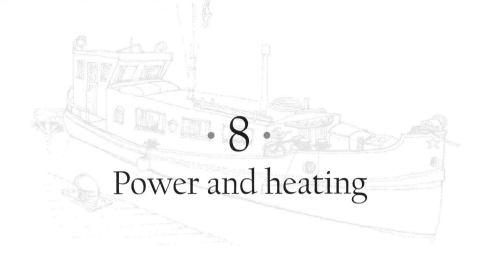

· 8 ·
Power and heating

❖ Engines ❖

Install the engine(s) as you build the hull. I designed *Faraway* with Perkins 4236 diesel engines. They are well-tried, all the snags have long ago been eliminated, and I have known them for years. I placed a provisional order for two while the design work was being refined. When construction started, to our horror, we were told that the 4236 had just been discontinued – it did not meet EU green standards. No replacement model existed in the same power range. We had to alter engine beds to fit different engines. Extra work, more delay. It is better to get important gear of a size that affects the design and build, in store before you spend money. They are unlikely to go down in price.

Make sure you have plenty of space in the engine room. Be able to stand up without fracturing your skull. Swing a cat. At one time *Hosanna* had a Cummins engine and tightening the cylinder-head nuts required a torque-wrench of 400 foot/pounds. Even if you could pull 100 pounds horizontally, the radius would be 4ft (1200mm). That engine ought to have been installed in a ball-room. And where, in God's name, do you find a torque wrench for 400 foot pounds? (The agents, as it happened.)

Hosanna was a rare barge in that she had three engines and three screws. It happened like this. We had a bare engine room. I found that three Perkins 4236 engines plus three sets of the appropriate small stern gear would cost less in total than a single Cummins or Volvo of equivalent horsepower and its single lot of stern gear. As I had once driven the old HMS *Illustrious* with three screws, I knew the immense manoeuvrability that this gave.

In practice, we had the centre engine keel-cooled so that it would never overheat by weed choking, and we used only the centre engine in canals: it gave us an economical speed of 3 knots. For manoeuvring and for the big rivers we used all three engines and got plenty of power. She was wonderful to manoeuvre, and it was all cheaper than a single larger engine.

TANKS AND FUEL SUPPLY

With the end of red diesel for pleasure craft, it no longer pays to have enormous tanks and return to Britain every couple of years to top up. Hosanna had bunkers for 5 tonnes of diesel and we have topped up cheaply in Romania, the Ukraine, and Tunisia. If you want to stay permanently on the Continent, install decent-sized bunkers - at least giving enough fuel to steam 1000 miles and still have 20 per cent left. This is because sources of white diesel are rare by the waterside (In France we have obtained it in St Jean-de-Losne, Lyon, St Mammes and Arles.) and will remain so because the trade is seasonal. It has always been an anomaly that pleasure boats could have diesel cheaper than lorries, but it was a question of availability. Our own politicians displayed a modicum of intelligence over this matter but were outvoted at Brussels. European politicians never listen to arguments from the public. Internally, the French, who are a pragmatic race, solve their problems by serious street protests which sometimes result in burning down government buildings. That makes the politicians think a bit.

Some boat-hire bases will sell white diesel to private owners, but they charge the Earth. They argue that the trade is seasonal and that the turnover is not enough to enable them to buy at fully commercial prices.

❖ Propellers ❖

You may be offered low-cost screw propellers that are called 'bronze'. They are almost certainly not, unless they are very expensive. Bronze is a word used with gay abandon to describe many differing non-ferrous alloys, some of which look like bronze. The proportions are critical, as is the inadvisability of incorporating cheaper metals in the mix. We have seen some poor quality cheap props imported from Italy that have been fitted to new construction boats from cheap-jack yards. Don't penny pinch on propellers.

It is acceptable to use cast iron props on inland waters, but they are not easy to find in small sizes.

❖ Electrics and voltage ❖

Decide on which voltages you are going to use. For a decent-sized boat, 12 volts is inadequate because of the voltage loss in long runs of wiring. 24-volt equipment is often unavailable as an option, and is more expensive. We have opted for 230-volt AC for most services in the boat, supplied via a Victron regulator through an inverter, though you will need 12- or 24-volt for nav equipment.

The Victron is a magnificent piece of equipment that bears consideration. I am suspicious of new gadgets that promise the Earth, but we have been living with this regulator for over a year now.

The principle is to have a large deep-cycle battery and supply the ship's AC through an inverter. Inverters and batteries are much more efficient and cheaper than they used to be. One has to keep the battery topped up, but one would do that anyway, and if you are under way the engine does it for you. If you are on shore power of 15 amps, say, it will feed into your circuits as much AC as you switch on, and rectify the rest into your battery. If you absent-mindedly switch on something powerful that takes you over the 15-amp load limit, you do not blow the pontoon fuse; the Victron makes up the deficiency from the battery via the inverter. When you have reduced the load, it will re-charge the battery. All AC switchings are sine-wave synchronised so that when the shore power at our mooring was cut in a thunderstorm, the Victron took over all the power supply with a milli-second delay that was not enough to affect our computer.

If you choose one, take time to get to know the Victron before you cruise. It has some funny little habits (Unusually for the Dutch the instruction manual is in mediocre English.) I have come to believe that it has artificial intelligence and occasionally has fits of sulks. Once it would not accept 230-volt AC from our generator. We consulted the agent and while waiting for a reply (he didn't know what to do either) the little devil solved its own problem and started working. On another occasion it stopped doing its stuff, flashed little lights at me but supplied no power. I went down to the engine room and switched it off. Teach it a lesson, I thought. After five minutes on the naughty step I switched it on again and it had repented, and decided to behave itself.

With *Hosanna*, I did the electrics myself and they coped well for over 20 years in spite of being described by one electrician as looking as if the cat had got at the knitting.

Now, over 20 years later, I opted to have the wiring done professionally. It looks better and it is probably safer but we are now fitting more complex gear than in 1986, not excluding the Victron. There are also many more types of lighting available now.

Experiments show that the coiled fluorescent mini-lights are the most economical at 230 volts. Halogen and LED are hopelessly wasteful, as are filament bulbs. These things matter in a boat much more than in a house for often you are dependent on battery as a resource. You learn to conserve energy in a way that should earn you a green medal. It is no good having halogen downlights everywhere if you are unable to light up the boat when you are dependent on battery power.

- Be careful when installing downlights in the deckhead lining. They need a reasonable space round them to dissipate the heat they engender.
- Be careful over earthing and isolation. Your steel hull can be eaten away before your eyes if you are careless.

We spent a winter fitting out at a local cruising club's pontoon. Our newly installed zinc sacrificial anodes disappeared within a few months, and our electrical installation had been tested before fitting the zincs. The reliability of the earthing

The pool at Berry-au-Bac.

bond on the pontoons on neighbouring boats is unknown, and we must have been sitting for some months in thick ampère soup. I took the question seriously, and have had an isolating transformer and galvanic isolator fitted, at uncomfortable expense. This was an experience that I do not wish to repeat: one cannot complain to a friendly club in which the members do all the work themselves.

We have fitted nickel-iron batteries of some 700 ampère hours as the main 24-volt battery. They came from Her Majesty, who had decided to test her submarines' equipment a different way. You can often pick up gear from magazines which trade old commercial shipping and barges but you should know what you are likely to find where. Small ports like Lowestoft, Hartlepool, and so on have people specialising in small ship breaking and/or conversions. Nickel-iron batteries have a long life, often 20 to 30 years, and have the capacity to take a lot of abuse, so I made the assumption that a considerable number of the cells (they come separately) would be in good order. I checked each one fully charged at 1.24 volts and none of the voltages had fallen more than a tenth of a volt in two months.

Be careful. When supplied, the Victron is not set up for NiFe batteries which have different characteristics to lead-acid. It can be adjusted for them by someone with the right programme. On the Victron stand at the Boat Show, I asked a man for advice on how to set up the Victron. He superciliously replied that they did not concern themselves with appliance batteries, even if re-chargeable. Perhaps he had mistaken the iron in a NiFe battery for the ion in a drill battery or perhaps he was ignorant. I returned a few minutes later when he was busy with someone else and found a man who was extremely helpful. It seems the Dutch don't do NiFe batteries, but their man in England does, very well.

❖ Heating ❖

You will need a snug saloon with a good stove. The big saloon which so many boats enjoy in the heady days of summer may cost a fortune to heat in winter. One owner of a converted 38m (125ft) barge we know says that his winter heating bill (for oil) was €3,000 in 2007.

From a planning viewpoint, three basic sources of heat are available (see also Chapter 9).

Using the engines for heating

When the main engines or diesel alternator are going, you can run pipes from the fresh-water closed-circuit part of the engine cooling and take the hot water through radiators and calorifiers. Doing this while under way uses free heat which would otherwise be pumped overboard in the engine exhaust. There are three cautions:

1 The engine cooling pump may not be powerful enough to service a number of radiators and/or a calorifier, and it may be necessary to put in line a central heating circulating pump as a back up. One can get these in 12 or 24-volt DC but they are expensive. A household 230- volt AC pump is cheap, but less efficient; you will surely have an inverter which can cope with it.
2 Engine cooling water is close to boiling temperature. Your radiators can get too hot to touch and the domestic hot water can scald. One can install a temperature-controlled by-pass to take care of this.
3 I think it is better to put the engine cooling water through a heat exchanger and have a separate circuit for the boat heating. We arranged the main central heating circuit to select its source of hot water with a change-over valve.

Note that these ways of heating are uneconomical if the boat is not under way, unless you are using a powerful generator and fit the piping to that. It is grossly uneconomic to run the generator solely for heating purposes except in case of emergency.

Electric heating

This is only an option when on shore power. Nevertheless, we have a small electric radiator and a fan-heater which could be used at a mooring with free electricity.

Oil-fired heating

There are three distinct types:

Hot-air ducted around the boat The heat source for this is from burning heating oil or gas. We have no experience except that we know of two boats that have caught fire due to a defect in this type of heater. One must check the oil burner regularly. It is a comfortable heat source, but makes a noise. Owners get used to it and guests are too polite to mention it.

A stove that burns oil The oil is drip-fed to it via an adjustable carburettor. A genuine flue-pipe is needed and an adequate supply of air to aid combustion. There are simple types such as the Danish Refleks, much used by fishermen, and the more elegant Dutch-made ones with fancy brass rails.

We have had both types and found them to be good heaters. Both sometimes flare up for no good reason but respond to a modicum of blasphemy and, like children, to a short rest and cool down before re-starting. There are times when the beastly things hoot like demented owls, but then for no apparent reason settle down and go properly. Both make soot if not looked after, and have almost useless handbooks.

The Old Dutch one is supplied with a water coil inside, and should not be run without either a circulating pump or a syphonic radiator to keep the water on the move. (The smaller version's piping is too small to cope with syphonic circulation.) We have found that at half-throttle, the Old Dutch gives off generous heat and will also supply domestic hot water and two small radiators. The Refleks is inelegant, but we had it aboard *Fare Well* for ten years, and after her new owners didn't like its looks and threw it out, we put it into *Hosanna* where it went on for another 22 years. It gave good, if occasionally temperamental, service throughout, without any expenditure on servicing.

House-type oil-fired central heating In larger boats such as *Hosanna*, our domestic radiators were supplied by a conventional domestic boiler. This required regular servicing. You would find such an installation a bit OTT in a Mediterranean climate, but good in a Continental winter.

Obtaining oil fuel at all is not easy in the sort of quantities needed by the live-aboard. In France, for instance, one is allowed to have a sort of 'red diesel' (on which one could, *illegally*, run the engines) which is intended for domestic heating and fuelling electricity generators only. This oil is called *fioul*, and to qualify for it one has to have a dedicated oil tank that is entirely separate from the bunkering tanks that fuel the motors. There must be no connection between the two systems. If building or converting, it is worthwhile seeing to this in such a way as to be obvious that there is no cross-connection. Such a tank should have a minimum of 500 litres capacity as *fioul* is delivered by truck and 500 litres is the normal minimum delivery (except at waterside filling stations). Make sure the filler pipe is more than 50mm (2in) internal diameter in order to take the standard nozzle, and that the breather pipe is 25mm (1in) to avoid blow-backs.

Solid fuel

Hosanna had, in her saloon, a cast iron wood burning stove bought from Norfolk Stoves Ltd, which was marvellous. In Laurel's studio there was an elegant enamelled Godin stove which took long thin logs. So powerful a heat did these give off that we had to put several firebricks in the furnaces so as to be able to get into the same room without scorching one's trousers off. We fed them on driftwood if in sea-going mode. We came across a whole dead eucalyptus tree floating in the Ionian

Sea and hauled it on board with our derrick where it overhung the width of the boat by several feet either side. An electric chainsaw is an obligatory service tool with a wood-burning stove, and it took Bill three working days to reduce the tree to stowable logs (he was younger then). We were rebuked by the Greek Coastguard for allowing the sawdust to pollute the sea (which was where the tree came from). So we used the sawdust: Bill soaked it in used engine oil, put the pasty mess in plastic bags for firelighters. Living aboard can be economical; that tree lasted two winters, though the branches looked a bit inelegant until reduced to logs (the two cats loved having a tree on board).

Otherwise we bought logs from merchants in the canals. Logs are sold in old-fashioned measures (pre-metric? called *stères* in France), a cubic metre of logs cut to one metre lengths. A metre is longer than modern stoves can take and presumably dates back to the sort of fireplaces in mediaeval castles; one reason for carrying a chain-saw. The price of *bois de chauffage* varies from region to region, it is lower in well-forested regions such as the Oise-Aisne-Ardennes area, and expensive in the Camargue to which it is transported by *péniche*. We paid €30 per *stère* in 2004 in Burgundy. In 2008, the price near Compiègne was €50 which puts the probable Burgundy price at about €60. If you wish the vendor to cut the logs shorter, you will pay more. An important point, when considering wood as a fuel, is room for wood stowage, and the stains and mess that wood leaves on the deck beneath. The ideal scenario for wood is to winter alongside a spacious quay. If you have to stow wood on deck, put it on a sheet of strong plastic.

We once saw a commercial barge pause in a wooded area while the *marinier* leapt ashore with a chain saw and felled a dead tree which he hoisted on board with his car crane, all without stopping.

Coal as such is unobtainable, but one can get sacks of treated coal that is similar to those obtainable from garages in England; this is easier to stow than wood. (This coal-like fuel costs twice as much in France as in England.) Burning solid fuel was a congenial method of heating but had two big snags, which made us opt for oil in *Faraway*. It requires much physical effort to feed the fire (chop your own logs – they warm you twice, is an old Suffolk saying) that Bill might find difficult in the future, and the amount of ash that resulted. The saloon required frequent dusting, and the ash cans had to be emptied daily, often surreptitiously. This is fun in windy weather.

One good thing about a solid-fuel stove is that one has a means of burning household waste (Greens, quiet please) which solves one of the boat-dwellers continual problems: how to dispose of household waste in this recycling age. No wheely bins on board, and no space for them, and few municipalities in England or the Continent (including Germany) offer the cruising boat-dweller any waterside facilities for triage or disposal. The lack of consideration for itinerants is an incentive to fly-tipping which nobody wants.

Make sure your bunker tanks are copious enough to give you long range without running short. You cannot reasonably fill up a barge's tanks with jerricans.

❖ Water supply ❖

Generally, one has better access to water inland than at sea, but taking on water can be a worry in unknown territory, or if caught in a freeze-up. *Hosanna* carried five tonnes of fresh water; we could last about three months without filling up. For *Faraway*, a much smaller boat, we settled on two tonnes. We have a 150cm bathtub, and even with frequent bathing the water lasts a month. The two tonnes is split between four specially made plastic tanks that are a better buy than stainless steel. Four tanks means that you can adjust their use to trim the boat level.

Lastly, there is the holding tank for the WC. For comfortable living, this should be of a goodly size. Not many places in Europe have pump-outs yet, but we bet that the European Commission will demand holding tank use long before anyone organises pump-outs. We opted for 500 litres. Again, its volume can be used to assist ballasting, but more important, if one has to stay in a marina for a lengthy period, one does not want to have to keep moving out to empty it, perhaps surreptitiously.

GREEN TIPS

Putting a small plastic bowl inside the stainless steel sink reminds me to use this for washing up when nothing larger is needed, and a pint jug by the tap regulates the kettle contents for tea or coffee.

Waterway interludes:

The River Shannon

The Shannon is 161 miles (256km) long, and runs southerly from the hills of County Cavan in Eire, close to the border with Northern Ireland, to the estuary at Limerick, where it reaches the Atlantic Ocean.

Commercial traffic on the river has long ceased with the coming of the railways, and out of season in a frosty early April when we cruised the Shannon, it was peaceful and beautiful.

At Banagher our day began with unfreezing the gas bottle so as to enjoy a large and sustaining breakfast: porridge, Irish bacon, white pudding, eggs and 'boxty' pancakes.

When the spectacular thunderstorm that greeted our departure from the dock rumbled away north-eastwards, the air was washed clean. The sky was a piercing blue; the light was sharp and intense, and the green land seemed lit from within, like an emerald.

Fishers, not just the few human ones, but myriads of birds, voles and other water creatures, frequent the river. Goats, cattle and horses graze the water meadows and marshes.

It was not yet Easter, freezing cold, and the Shannon is in spate against us. We were travelling north, I (Laurel) was wearing not one but two woolly hats in the outside steering position. The river had breached its banks, and the flooded fields either side present a vista of a long narrow lake with the tops of isolated trees; a marooned car had water up to its windows, and a seemingly legless cow waded through the floods. The water draining off the peat bog was black with an écru edging, like Victorian lace.

We stopped for the night at the village quay at Shannon Bridge (no charge for mooring), and went in search of a pub. Irish pubs in these riverside villages are dark, cosy, often timbered, and blessedly smoke-free. Reading the notice board gives a snapshot of local life:

'Midweek Taxi service, Mondays and Wednesdays.'

'Anyone interested in Ladies' boxing classes contact the Resource centre.'

In one bar, the TV shows the racing to a cluster of inveterate punters, cheering on their chosen horse. At weekends, there will likely be a folk group playing. The Irish love to chat, and their friendly curiosity is not intimidating.

We were intrigued to observe two hefty lads walloping into steak and chips –and glasses of milk. Well of course, they had given up Guinness for Lent.

Between Shannonbridge and Athlone is the site of Clonmacnoise, the monastery founded by St Ceiron in 545AD, on a rise over the Shannon. A mooring is provided here, at the Heritage Centre, and we went ashore to see the ancient stones and magnificent High Crosses. In the 9th century this was a place of learning unequalled in all Ireland, and here many wonderful manuscripts were inscribed. We lunched in the coffee shop. During the afternoon we negotiated the lock at Athlone (the first in 40 miles, not exactly taxing), moored at the Jolly Mariner and ate the home-made scones we bought at Clonmacnoise. The cold is making us hungry.

Athlone has nearly 9,000 inhabitants, a metropolis compared to other towns and villages we passed, and we ate out: steak and colcannon for Bill, mussels with garlic and cream for me, washed down with Guinness, Jamieson's, and white wine.

There was ice on deck the following morning. During the day we traversed Loch Ree, which is perhaps the hairiest part of the journey. It is a large lake, 'Dangerous in high winds' as the guide says, and we had a stiff North-easterly breeze. It is 10 kilometres long by 5 wide, enough to create choppy conditions, and though it was bright and sunny most of the time, one can lose sight of the next navigation buoy, let alone the shore.

We arrived at the pretty village of Lanesborough, deserted at this time of year, which provides moorings for passing craft. The Lifebelt Bar provided welcome food after a cold 32-mile day.

The next day was our 54th wedding anniversary, so after a protracted but satisfying breakfast (one gas ring at a time as we thawed the gas bottle) we did some shopping. (Take your shopping bags with you in Ireland, plastic bags are no longer handed out, and the countryside is infinitely cleaner for it, as in France.) At Mrs O'Brian's, who had charged our camera batteries overnight, we bought an orange blossom candle ring to celebrate. We stopped at Tarmonberry lock for a picnic lunch, graced by our candle ring, and continued the 28- mile stretch from Lanesborough, to Roosky, where we moored at the public quay.

Here we treated ourselves to an anniversary dinner at the Shannon Key Hotel, only a step away from the boat; and had a wonderful meal of saffron chowder and hake on crab claws. When they learnt what we were celebrating, our waitress brought us a lily in a glass jug, and our dessert plates were decorated in chocolate: 'Happy Anniversary'. I am still trying to reproduce the saffron chowder.

When after the usual long breakfast next day, we headed north again, wintry showers considerably reduced visibility.

We made one wrong turning in Lough Bofin, into an arm that led eastwards, rather than north, but managed to pick up the marks again before harm was done. Rain over Lough Tap made visibility very bad; in one storm we lost sight of the shore and needed our Boy Scout pocket compass to make progress. Despite the excellent chart provided by the company, we missed the next red marker, turned into the wrong arm of the lough and had to retrace our steps.

The sun broke through occasionally, and we were again able to enjoy the piercing blue of the skies, and clean clear light; country colours bright and fresh as the illuminations in a mediaeval Book of Hours. In our wake, the peaty waters of the River Shannon foamed like the head on our evening Guinness.

We passed the Albert Lock at midday – the last lock of our journey, in the Jamestown canal, and arrived at Carrick-on-Shannon where our 90-mile voyage ended.

It was an immensely enjoyable trip. We must not give the impression that it froze or rained all the time. The weather is best described as that of a cold early English spring, with plenty of sunny spells. As it was sometimes difficult to make out the marks in bad visibility, we tended to conn from the flying bridge as we

The River Shannon at Jamestown.

were snug enough in our foul-weather gear. When the sky began to hurl white grapeshot at us (it's called hail) we could have done with a riot shield or two, but that is not a normal item of chandlery. Still, we got quite slick at changing over from outdoor to indoor steering positions when the hail got too lethal.

Of some worry to us were the few bridges across the Shannon, where we could have done with the clearance gauges we are used to in Europe. Roosky was the only one that was too low, and that was lifted for us the following morning (payment €1.50).

The infrequent locks (same fee) were large and efficient, but much more impressive were the moorings. Every village or hamlet had either a free staithe or a mini-marina, and there was always a pub close by, where food from simple to excellent was available. Both the villages and the people were charming.

As well as motorboats, a Broads-type auxiliary sailing yacht would be at home on these big loughs, the sailing in summer would be all you could wish for. There is also scope for taking over a trailer-sailor, as there are plenty of places to launch.

The following day Laurel browsed for souvenirs, mostly small items for the grandchildren, but on passing the workshop of Leitrim Glass, a cut-glass bowl called to her loudly, so insistent that she entered the Crystal Cave and bought it, there among the pink-powdered cutting and polishing machines, from the hands of the man who had created the beautiful thing. It was packed lovingly by its maker to withstand airline baggage handling, and now reminds us of the light from those clear and sparkling Irish skies.

· 9 ·

Living aboard

❖ A waterways galley ❖

Designing galleys for waterways boats requires as much care as you are prepared to give it. This will depend on what style of cook you are. For a boat to be used for holidays, or a summer cruise, the minimum gear in a convenient space is likely to be the best answer. You won't be doing the Christmas turkey or a buffet for 20 people; you will want catering and clearing up after meals to be easy. You might not even want an oven, just a hob and a means of reheating takeaways, plus of course the barbecue.

If on the other hand you will be spending a great deal of time, even living, on board, then you will give the galley much thought, according to the kind of cooking you do. Nowadays, you could if you wished, especially in a barge, have the full chef's panoply: an Aga-style range powered by diesel (which heats the water), a domestic fridge and freezer, and a microwave oven. If you are a serious cook you have space for a full-size food processor, the kind I gave up 30 years ago in favour of a mini blender and a wand-style beater, which have accompanied me to sea and served me well even for quite adventurous cooking. You have space for your favourite kitchen tools and gadgets. You should think about storage for more sophisticated food supplies than a holiday requires, but rest assured, if one can cram the stores for an Atlantic crossing into the small and awkward spaces of a sailing yacht, you can get much more into a waterways cruiser or barge, especially if you plan it well.

Secure stowage
Unless you are going to spend part of the time at sea or in coastal waters you don't even have to worry about cooking and eating at an angle of 30°, because in inland waters this is a rare event. (Note that we never say never; extraordinary things do occur.) Unlike a seagoing craft, not all your crockery has to be well nigh unbreakable; though I must mention one drawback in inland waters that might not occur to you, and illustrate it with a story. You won't get waves and rolling and pitching, (except on the Scheldt, or the Danube, or crossing the Channel for which you take special precautions). But your boat will undoubtedly hit the side of a lock from time to

time. A friend kept her collection of crystal in a glass-fronted cabinet hung on the wall in her barge, as you would have at home. After a particularly severe bump entering a lock she found the cabinet and all her crystal shattered on the floor. So all furniture, fixtures and shelves in your waterways boat need stronger fastenings than household ones, as such a bump will otherwise dislodge them. By the same token, loose objects will be jerked off shelves and other flat surfaces, and it is as well to be aware of this when designing the interior of your boat. The decorative use that old Dutch bargees made of brass gallery rails round sideboards, shelves and mantels had a practical purpose as well.

Note also that water levels can change without warning and your boat may find herself aground through no fault of yours. If she settles on flat mud: no problem, but if she lies on a hump, she may settle down at an angle. Your discomfort will probably not last long, but could dislodge some loose objects, and/or empty a cupboard whose doors face across the boat. Shelves, drawers and cupboards are best mounted athwartships.

NON-SLIP MATS

You can also use high friction mats under precious items. Get this non-slip material by the metre rather than readymade into fancy and expensive mats, you can then cut it to size and shape.

❖ Built-in or slot-in furniture? ❖

In our new boat, to save time (we haven't much left) we adopted a principle of slotting in readymade furniture. This worked well with things like wardrobes and chests of drawers, but not in the galley. We put in a domestic fridge-freezer, but the so-called fitted kitchens of land-based manufacturers waste so much space that for galley storage we had a unit made to our design in pine by a local workman, and considered the expenditure well worth it. My experience with modern kitchens (living ashore while we built the boat) and the dozens of other kitchens that I have known over many years teaches me that happy kitchens should be made to measure, like shoes; not only to the space you have, but to the person using them. In my last kitchen ashore everything was too high for me, the average woman being half a head, or more, taller than I am. The shelves were too high, I needed a hop-up to reach them, which I couldn't always be bothered to use, leading to hopeful snatches that led to explosions on the kitchen floor of lentils, marmalade, or relentlessly unwinding rolls of paper towels. The bottom 9in (22cm) of the cupboard units were entirely wasted with a false floor, providing a kickstep. The gas hob over the oven was too high, leading to stir frying just under my chin, which would have horrified the Health and Safety people.

We designed a unit that was all drawers, except for a narrow cupboard for cleaning materials under the sink. The bottom row of drawers went right down to the floor, and was set in to form a kickstep; so there was not a cubic inch of wasted space. Above the sink is a plate rack, and above the worktop are shelves with a ³/₄in (20mm) fiddle rail to keep the contents in place. At the outboard end are a three-burner gas hob, and a 28-litre gas oven, under which is a big drawer for pans. Above the hob, tucked to the back, is the microwave, and above that a 600-watt mini-oven that was almost all I used in the building stage before we had any mod-cons. Everything above the work surface can be shut away with folding doors. The galley works extremely well, and we finished it as soon as we could; morale depends a lot on good food, in our experience.

We moved aboard long before the boat was completed, with only the mini-oven, a fridge-freezer (which was craned in through a hatch in the roof before the hatch cover was bolted down, so it had to come in; ready or not) a 10-litre water container, an electric kettle, a bed and a bucket. You get more work done living on board, partly because you are there to do it, and partly because the motivation is intense. You also learn fast what doesn't work. I cannot tell you how enormously satisfying it is to commission, at long last, something that you have been doing without: the loo (first on the list, obviously, with a 500-litre holding tank) a triumph that for us equalled an Olympic Gold medal, and far more useful. The sink and running cold water followed, pumped by hand at first, a luxury compared to the miserly provision of the 10-litre jerrycan, which, however, had the advantage of bringing home the necessity of water economy; living in a house for a year with hot water on tap had pampered me reckless.

Eventually we got an electric water pump working, the gas oven and hob installed, and I was back to enjoyable cooking. The 28-litre oven, though smaller than you would find ashore, *will* cook the turkey, and with good planning, the set-up can cope with anything.

❖ Cookers ❖

You can have pretty much what you would have in a kitchen ashore, powered by gas, electricity, diesel, or solid fuel, depending on space available and depth of purse. It needs careful planning to fit things in.

The smallest option

The equivalent to my old Primus is a single gas hob (£20), portable, takes butane cartridges which last 4 hours on simmer, and lasts 90 minutes on full power. The next size up are the mini (electric) oven-grills, about 7 litres capacity, is available with or without a hob: 620 watts (£25 to £50). There is an élite version, very compact with two hobs (£150), advertised as suitable for boats and caravans, but we think 2900 watts is too much power for the average boat, unless you have a huge generator (about 5 kilowatts would be required). In *Hosanna* we had electric

As the galley is the hub of the floating home we include as many useful appliances as possible and plenty of storage space.

cooking (domestic oven and hob), but she was a big boat and we had a 7 kilowatt generator. The hob was mixed: two gas and two electric. I found the gas more user friendly and hardly ever used the electric ones. Which meant we could cook quietly, without running the beastly generator.

Gas ovens

These don't come in miniature, except as the hob cited above. The smaller ovens advertised in chandleries and camping shops are about 28 litres and cost £250–£450 (smaller than a household oven which is usually 50 litres or more). They come with, or without, grills. You can go up in size (and price) until you have a 6-burner cooking range if you have the space, and enough room for a big gas tank.

Electric ovens

Apart from the tiny ones mentioned above, these are not considered ideal for boats, as they are usually 2000 watts, and not made especially for marine use. However, if you have a big enough generator you might consider a domestic electric oven, probably one of the smaller ones, such as I had on *Hosanna*. Double ovens usually have one oven of about 50 litres, while the smaller oven is 35 litres.

Diesel cooking

If you are reluctant to leave your Aga and have the space, you can have a similar stove, diesel-fired, which will heat the water and run central heating as well. They are large, heavy, and pricey. I had one in *Fare Well*, and I loved it; the warm stainless steel cover did the ironing beautifully, but though we had room in our barge *Hosanna* the price by then had soared beyond our means, and we settled for an electric oven, a big generator, a microwave oven, and a mixed gas and electric hob. The total cost of these four items was the same as the diesel cooker would have been, and in the 20-odd years which followed I did not regret the exchange. Diesel stoves nowadays cost upwards of £1500, or more than £2000 with a boiler.

Solid fuel stoves

These are an option, not for an Aga-style cooker, because there is no room for an extensive wood pile except on a very big barge, but certainly a small pot-belly stove will heat a kettle or a pan, so will the larger cottage-type stove you will find in the narrowboat catalogues. More on these under *Heating*.

Almost all boats, including sea-going ones, now have a barbecue. They come in every possible size and degree of sophistication, starting with the disposable ones (what a good idea that can be). You have only to choose what suits you and your space. Remember that many marinas forbid onboard barbecues, so far be it from us to suggest that an invisible spot with a discreet chimney could be a good idea. Bill has constructed various barbecues to hang outboard of the taffrail, his idea being that if the fire got too rampant, he could just let the whole lot slide into the water on the end of a wire, then haul it back. What actually happens is that at least one sausage leaps into the water, so we've learnt to separate the sausage links, so that the rest do not follow.

The microwave oven

The days are gone when my idea of installing such an item on a yacht was met with hoots of derision from the Primus brigade. My reasoning was (and still is) that 1300 watts, (for an 850 watts MW) normally for less than five minutes, is better than 2000 watts for half an hour (or more, as most electric ovens need 10 minutes pre-heating before you even begin cooking). In many ways, a microwave saves power from other sources, and is easily coped with by present day generators, and the larger inverters. I have used one afloat for 20 years, especially in hot weather, as it does not heat up the galley as other cookers do. It is handy to use as a meatsafe to keep flies or cats off fresh food, or frozen food that you are defrosting.

GREEN TIP

Even in very small boats a pressure cooker is worthwhile. The miniature ones take little space.

The speed with which a pressure cooker copes with otherwise long-cooking items, such as chicken carcases, beef bones, stews, oxtail, and such, is an enormous saving of energy. It is probably the greenest cooking there is, apart from frying your eggs on the slopes of Vesuvius, and brewing your tea at hot springs. Highly recommended, especially if it will simmer away on the stove you use for heating. I have even baked bread in a pressure cooker.

Compact and standard versions are now specially designed for boats, 12 or 24 volts, or with built-in inverters, which used to be expensive, but these might suit you, as inverters are now much cheaper and better. I have always had the ordinary high street store model, and the two or three I have had over the years have given no trouble.

The large inverters capable of providing all that a modest boat could need are now comparatively cheap and reliable, but they can rapidly drain your batteries unless you have at least a 700 AH battery-bank.

You can get a combined version of a microwave which has a grill built in. It is considerably heavier on power.

❖ Cooking ❖

Nowadays there is no need to treat cooking aboard as a Primus-in-the-cockpit-locker affair, as it was when I started cooking on a boat, more than 60 years ago. Lunch then was sandwiches, and hard-boiled eggs, lettuce and tomatoes if you could get them. Food was still rationed, don't forget; ham, bacon and butter were rare commodities and meat too precious to risk on a Primus. We ate a lot of bread in those days, and in the evenings sea stew: one tin of meat (any kind: corned beef, sausages, beef and gravy – no tinned curries then, or we'd have used them), one tin of potatoes, two tins of vegetables (again any kind), heated all in one pot on the Primus. The trick was to stir the mixture so that it became piping hot without burning the bottom of the pan. It was fast, variable, and wonderful food after a day on the water.

Now with foods of the world on supermarket shelves (or in our freezer), and sophisticated hobs and ovens available for boats, we can let ourselves go.

❖ Heating ❖

In northern waters you will need some form of warmth, even in summer, for those heady July days when the rain lashes down and the water churns under the lash of a chilly wind. In winter you will need more of it. Go south till the butter melts, as they say, and you will still need a little heat on winter evenings, and to survive the short spell of snow that we have experienced on the Riviera, in the Camargue, and even in Florida. In these days of mounting fuel costs it is wise to have different means of heating, and use the one that (temporarily we fear) costs less than the others.

All fuels have their drawbacks. Wood was cheap in France when we used it for our cottage-style stove, but the logs had to be chopped and carried, and the resulting ash cleaned out and disposed of. We could do that in our sixties. If you have the deck space for a pile of logs the solid fuel stove has a warmly welcoming glow, the larger ones will run a couple of

GREEN TIP

Boil your kettle and heat your stews on top of a wood-burning stove to use the fuel to the full. I kept a beanpot simmering on ours – haricot or Boston beans need long slow cooking.

radiators and heat the water. If it is one of the very small stoves you can (you hope) feed it with brushwood and canalside tree branches, and the odd bit of driftwood (found close to weirs – watch your footing!). See also Chapter 8.

Central heating

This can be run from a stove, whether solid fuel as above, or fired by diesel. You can have a separate boiler to run your heating, usually gas or diesel fired. The boat's engine can be used as well, giving hot water and heating as you travel. Diesel stoves for heating have drawbacks, they are sometimes tricky to light, and in a bad humour can emit gouts of black snow from the chimney that unfortunately don't melt when the weather warms up. Once coaxed into life, they are warm and comforting. Expect to pay £450 to £650 .

Electric heating

This type of heating is rare on board. An immersion heater in the hot water tank is fine for occasional use, also a low powered fan heater, but make sure you have the power to run them. In principle, space heating and water heating by electricity are only practicable when on shore power.

Gas heating

The warmth of gas is instant, and if you cook by gas and already have the bottles these still have their place, and are better designed than they used to be. The old-fashioned portable gas heater (the round reflective bowl with a mantle that screws into a dumpy gas bottle) stopped us freezing in the huge hangar where we built our current boat; turned up high it gives off a lot of heat. Like all gas installations these need good ventilation, which was never a problem on small boats or indeed in the hangar.

❖ Lighting ❖

Don't be tempted to use halogen spotlights throughout. We heard (our builder's workshop was a repository of scurrilous stories, that we and our boat have undoubtedly added to) of someone who furnished his new barge with these. When he lit them all the generator was unable to cope, even before he tried to use the washing machine or toaster. Halogen spots are neither cheap, economical, nor green. Get the right lamp, and most important of all, put it in the right place. If you want a working light in the galley or engine room, a strip fluorescent light, intelligently sited, is your best bet. I stress the siting, because I have suffered in many kitchens on shore where the lights have been carefully centred so that you cast a shadow on the washing up bowl or the frying pan. This is bad enough for young people, but for those of us struggling to maintain safety and hygiene with small amounts of washing up water when we've mislaid our specs, it can be a disaster.

Elsewhere, if you fancy cosy glows from old Navy cabin lamps, and why not, get one that takes compact fluorescent bulbs, which are the ones to use if you can, otherwise use a low wattage bulb.

You can unstep the mast of your yacht and cruise the waterways of Europe. Make sure it is as well secured as this one is – and the boat has plenty of fenders to protect her gelcoat.

Faraway's keel is taking shape – the bottom plates are tacked in place. We found a good boatyard in Lowestoft which had a large shed available for the build – good cover is essential.

Beginning to look like a boat now, *Faraway* is taking shape and her two main bulkheads are installed.

The superstructure is now being constructed; the windows are in place and the roof is being secured.

One of the pair of Nanni engines is installed in *Faraway*. Our experience has led us to always have two engines to ensure reliability – on our barge *Hosanna* we even had three.

◄ Laurel, the artist, gets all the paint jobs. Health and Safety wouldn't approve of the chair.

▼ This was a rather claustrophobic painting stint in the engine room.

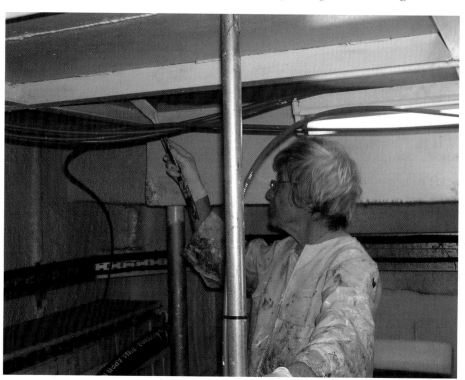

Bill is installing the cooker. We gave a lot of thought to designing the galley on *Faraway*, based on previous experience, and built in plenty of drawer storage units, a system which works well for us.

In the saloon we need plenty of space for our books, which were unpacked even before the panelling was up – and, again, here are lots of storage drawers. As you can see from these photos, *Faraway* is a real floating home.

Here *Faraway* has reached the painting stage...

... and now she is being towed to the launch site; notice the stack of timber on the wheelhouse roof.

PHOTO: DICK DALLASTON

This was an exciting time as *Faraway* waited on the slip for the rising tide to launch her.

Afloat at last – the First Mate is happy!

Even River l'Oise will sometimes freeze. Here thick ice is breaking up as the thaw comes at Sempigny, northern France.

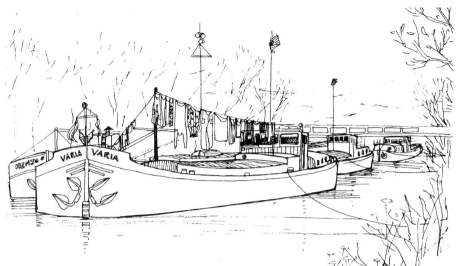

Arrête de navigation, Canal de la Marne à la Saône.

Oil lamps

Some of these charming old lamps still work on paraffin. Paraffin is not the stand-by it was in our young days, when freezing winters were aromatised with the waft of paraffin oil from the stove in the bathroom. ('It's only November and you want heat in the *bathroom*?') You will have to hunt for paraffin these days; country districts are best. Otherwise lamp-oil comes from a fancy chandler in a teeny bottle, deodorised and expensive.

Torches and inspection lamps

Be sure you have several torches, spare batteries for all of them, and that everybody knows where they are kept. Be fierce about putting them back in their place. No need for the high-tech floating stuff; avoid those flimsy ones that break when dropped, because dropping torches is one of those on-board things.

A larger lamp that can double as a spotlight is good for emergencies. Under this category come inspection lamps with a long lead, to plug in where needed. The bulbs get broken quickly, probably because they are used in dire straits and get dropped, knocked over, or even, if we've reached tantrum time, thrown at the bulkhead. The new low-energy bulbs are more robust than filament ones. We always have two of these lamps, and half a dozen bulbs for them.

❖ Electrical gadgets ❖

Unlike halogen lamps, it is surprising how many small electrical gadgets you can use on board without the ampère needle going berserk. (The big users are undoubtedly the washing machine and immersion heater, closely followed by the tumble dryer, 'fridge and freezer.) The Victron (see page 58) takes care of everything; we can toodle along economically, running the 'fridge-freezer (a domestic model) the water pump, computer and printer, chargers for telephones, power drill, and digital camera, radio, short spells of microwave cooking and toasting, the vacuum cleaner, the navigation instruments, and of course AC power tools as we are still completing the interior.

To give you an idea, we are running these things for 28 hours on a *jeton* (token) put into a box ashore. A *jeton* costs €2 and gives 5kw/hr. The minute you start heating water or doing the washing, the *jetons* expire at an alarming rate.

Before we left Lowestoft in July 2008, we were paying £360 a month for mooring with electricity included. Here, in a winter mooring in France, the berth is free but the electricity is dear. Win some - lose some.

❖ Baths, showers and laundry ❖

Set against marina charges in England this is not too bad, tokens for a wash and dry at an east coast marina cost £4, and we have heard of a Channel marina where washing and drying two drumloads cost £13.

You might consider baths a luxury. We find that showers do not do it for us; the long hot soak is a comfort to old bones, and gets you clean without too much effort. Drying is exhausting though, if we could find a gadget a bit like a shower that blew hot air all over us we'd be interested. (Yes, I'm sure there is one.)

Bath or shower, you need fresh water for it. See Chapter 4 on building from new for discussion of tankage.

There are washing machines for small boats, made of plastics: light and compact. They don't do quite the job of a full-sized one, but you would not expect it for the price of about £50. I would have been glad of one in the days of our ketch *Fare Well* when I did the washing by hand, or sought somebody ashore to do it – not easy in the Mediterranean of pre-laundrette days. A couple we met recently had a small mangle, such as used to fit on top of the twin-tub washing machines, to expel excess water before hanging the laundry out to dry. Note that some up-nosed marinas forbid hanging laundry on board

Just available is a mini twin-tub, 160 watts (wash), and 90 watts (spin-dry) which takes 3$\frac{1}{2}$lb (1.5kg) of dry washing (that's roughly two pairs of trousers and a sweatshirt). It needs no plumbing, is filled and emptied with hoses, spin dries in the second tub and costs just under £100.

You can install a normal domestic machine if you have the space. The only difference between plumbing into a house and into a boat is that:

- You must fix the machine securely in place remembering to hold it down to the deck as well as sideways.
- A tray underneath to catch drips is a good idea, especially in a steel boat, where hidden rust pockets can form in such places.

A mini dryer is also available at just under £100; it uses 400 watts and takes 2lb (1kg) load. Domestic dryers are fine if you have the space, but they do run away

Nita mangles her washing on Aeola.

with the power. A venting kit to the exterior prevents the condensation that is a pain on boats.

Having to purchase water as if it were petrol for the car is an excellent discipline, and concentrates the mind on how precious the stuff is.

As lifelong sailors, and having lived and cruised aboard a boat for more than 30 years, it struck us when we heard a victim of the Gloucester floods in England saying that she was rationed to 9 litres of water a day. That amount for a fortnight is the pretty exact equivalent of an Atlantic crossing.

We have much experience of using a little water to best advantage, and when we moved on board *Faraway* with no plumbing, the two of us managed for 2 months on 5 litres every 3 days. (Washing and baths were taken ashore, of course.)

Water saving

The best plan is to top up your tanks at every opportunity but here are a few temporary water-saving tips if your tanks are running low:

Washing up

- Wipe over plates with paper towels straight after use.
- Cover grills, racks, and oven pans with foil before use.
- For cutlery, fill a clean soup tin with hot water and a drop of washing up liquid and upend your knives and forks in this.
- Use paper towels to dry your utensils, to save on washing linen cloths.
- A spray of antibacterial surface cleaner deals with surfaces like worktops and cutting boards, and other things you would normally use a wet cloth for.

Cooking

- Tinned vegetables bring their own water with them.
- Use the microwave to cook fruit and vegetables, as you will use only a tablespoon or two of water as opposed to a saucepanful.
- Steam your food; the water under the steamer can then be used again.
- If you do cook anything in a saucepan of water, lift the food out with a perforated spoon and use the hot water remaining either to clean the pan, or make soup, depending on the food cooked.

Consider installing a rain barrel. A little ingenuity is necessary, but you will soon learn where the rain water collects on your boat. We used to collect three bucketfuls or more in a thunderstorm on *Hosanna*. We used the contents for washing.

WATER TANKS

Float a red plastic bead in the sight glass to make the water level easier to see.

❖ Refrigeration and freezers ❖

There are so many fridges and fridge-freezers made especially for the marine market nowadays, that you should have no difficulty finding one that exactly suits your space and pocket. They come in all sizes and prices and can be 12 or 24 volts or even multi-voltage. Small ones (60 litres) start at about £400, and if you want holdover capacity, just double the price. Gas-driven fridges are no longer available for health and safety reasons. For once I agree with H & S – the boom of the exploding gas fridge used to be heard on the Norfolk Broads oftener than the boom of the bittern.

Don't be too niggly with freezer space if you are living aboard. There are sometimes long gaps between shopping opportunities, and to have some frozen meals and ingredients available will help the cook. But the bigger the freezer, the more amps you use.

❖ Toilets ❖

These are the greatest comfort and the greatest pain on a boat. Whether you get the electric flush or the hand pump version, be sure of one thing: no matter what they tell you about reliability at the Boat Show, it will eventually go wrong. The pipes scale up. The loo blocks. It spits back. At worst you can get overflow. Understand your loo. Familiarise yourself with its workings *before* it gives trouble. Install the working parts (all pipe connections, valves, pumps or sea-cocks) in a place where access is, if not easy, at least not cripplingly uncomfortable. In *Fare Well* we were able to detach the pump and take it up on deck in a bucket, which made it easier to descale.

- Anticipate and prevent trouble.
- If leaving the boat for several days, put a cupful of vinegar in the pan.

- Use as little paper as possible. You can even install a bin for tissue.
- Seawater scales up the pipes much quicker than fresh. The sight of a sailor beating a length of piping on the quay to dislodge the scale is familiar to all sea-going yachties. It works. But wear a cap!
- Never put anything down the pan that has not first been eaten.
- Encourage the blokes to sit down to pee.

GREEN TIP

All our bath water is recycled to flush the loo. We had hoped that this great idea could be built into the piping, but it proved too complicated. We use a bucket – simple is best.

❖ Shopping and food supplies ❖

Those who embark on a canal trip in Europe, or on the Intracoastal Waterway with no experience, or only that of British waterways, may be in for a surprise as far as shopping is concerned. The density of England, particularly, is such that a town or village where supplies may be obtained is never far away, and nor is a pub offering 'good food' (so it says outside).

Whilst in Europe, keeping a stock of supplies is a good idea. European towns and villages are often well spread out, and you cannot count on finding a central mooring near shops in small towns. Even in France and the Netherlands, where water tourism is established, supermarkets built right on the canalside are slow to realise that a pontoon on the canal and a footpath to the entrance would be immensely helpful to

Place St Louis, Aigues Mortes.

BREAD STRATEGY

Wherever you voyage, have some way of making bread; sooner or later, you will run out. So where there are no villages we need other strategies:

- If you stop for the night close to a lock, ask the lock-keeper if there is a baker nearby, and if not, is he or his wife going for the bread in the morning? If so, ask if they will buy some for you too. (Resident lock-keepers are becoming more rare.)

- Often, a baker's van brings bread to villages these days. Watch out for a cluster of housewives responding to a few hoots on the horn.

- When you buy bread be aware that baguettes, rolls and croissants and similar breads are meant to be eaten the same day. Look out for robust-looking country loaves, some of which keep for a week.

- If all else fails, a packet of part-baked baguettes or a bread mix will come in handy.

passing vessels in need of supplies. It is exasperating to see SuperU or Carrefour close by, blocked off by an impenetrable fence. Reaching the supermarket on foot is likely to involve a two kilometre walk crossing a busy motorway.

In the USA, distances can also be great, and the surroundings very rural, especially in anchorages. The useful thing about American marinas in the sticks is that there is always a courtesy car you can borrow to visit a shopping centre. Not so in Europe, Though the Champion supermarket at St Jean-de-Losne will deliver.

It makes sense therefore to stock up when you can with supplies that will keep for a while, and stock your cupboard with emergency supplies of non-perishable foods that will keep the wolf from the door if necessary.

EMERGENCY SUPPLIES

Dried pasta, noodles and rice

Sauces for pasta, (can, bottle or packet)

Bread mixes

Packet soup

Part-baked bread

Long life milk

Cans: fish, meat, vegetables, fruit, beans

Tea and coffee

Sugar

Flour

❖ Other supplies ❖

Bread is not the only thing to arrive in small villages by van in Europe: meat, vegetables, charcuterie, fish and groceries may come this way too. Villages without a minimarket often receive a visit from these vans once or twice a week, and sometimes there is a market day. Ask, and you will find out.

Lock-keepers used to be a good source of garden produce and eggs, but times have changed, and fewer families live in the lock cottage and tend their goats and chickens, and vegetable plots. So it is worth looking out for canalside farmsteads, who may supply you with milk, eggs and so on, but these, too, are getting rarer. An elderly lady butcher of whom I asked directions to such a farmstead recently looked at me in disbelief. 'Those days are gone,' she said. 'They are all factories now.' Not quite, I'm glad to say, only a week after that melancholy rejoinder we found a quayside bar with hens scratching in the backyard, and new-laid eggs for sale in season. So travel hopefully and take your own containers.

Carrier bags

In many European countries, Ireland, and some states in the US, shops and supermarkets have ceased to hand out plastic bags, so it's back to the old days. Take plenty of strong canvas bags, string bags, and anything foldable, including a folding shopping trolley. If you shop by dinghy, waterproof bags are a good idea.

The downside of the plastic bag disappearance, of course, is that you have to buy bags to line your rubbish bins, instead of recycling the ones you bring your shopping home in. Which brings us to:

❖ Rubbish disposal ❖

Some countries in Europe are less fussy about rubbish, and some are considerably more so, than authorities in the UK. In some countries, four or five different coloured bins stand like soldiers, and woe betide anyone who puts the wrong item in the wrong bin. Fat chance, as they are quite often locked. In Germany they are very strict about rubbish, all tins must be washed and crushed (you can get a gadget that does this) and all glass and bottles washed and separated from their metal or plastic lids. This can be difficult when water is short, but you can always use canal water. We don't think that glass for recycling needs to be totally germ-free.

This leads to some ingenuity being necessary, and a certain amount of discipline:

- Burn rubbish if you can. Our wood-burning stove in winter took care of a lot of our rubbish.
- Locks almost always have a rubbish bin for vessels travelling through. Use it when you can.
- Always take advantage of any recycling facility, either in locks or close to the bank.
- Return to nature anything that fish or birds can safely eat but in the canals, where no tide runs, don't spoil the scenery with large fruit skins and cabbage stalks, which fetch up at the next weir with all the plastic bottles, coke tins and polyfoam MacDonald's boxes which other people (surely not you?) throw in the water.

❖ Storage ❖

Stowage or storage on a boat is an art. Ashore, things go in a cupboard or on shelves. Cupboards are rare on boats, and often your storage space is awkwardly shaped and sited, under the side decks, under bunks, and sometimes involves trap-doors to the space under the deck. These spaces are sometimes triangular in section. Ingenuity is required if you are not to lose some items completely, as we often do.

If you can build in drawers, do so. It is much easier to find things in a drawer than at the back of a deep cupboard or locker. In addition, unlike a house, you have to be aware of the weight of your cargo, and heavy things must be distributed and kept low down, in the bilges if possible.

> Label clearly and with care,
> Keep a list of what is where;
> Inventory all you stow,
> To stop you hunting high and low.

It follows that a bilge (or 'cellar' as we call it), that is dry, is where you put tins and bottles, and bulk supplies. The Belgians, bless them, often have a special ventilated locker in their cockpit for potatoes, which in their case are in constant use. By the same token, we keep our fruit and vegetables under the ladder down to the saloon, in wire baskets or ventilated drawers.

The 'cellar' must be kept in order with some form of container system. In barges, the bilge space can be quite extensive, and some sort of division or shifting boards may be necessary, to prevent objects migrating when the boat is subject to the bumps and bangs of a lively lock. Cardboard boxes are not recommended aboard, the wet is likely get to them at some point, and they harbour insects. Plastic storage boxes, such as can be found everywhere these days, are useful, but make sure they are sturdy, and are secured in place somehow; flimsy ones are not suitable for heavy stuff like tins and bottles as they can chafe through or crack if the engine vibration gets to them. Beer crates and flower troughs are stronger, as are the heavy-duty industrial bins sold in the tool section of DIY shops. Square buckets and wire baskets have their place. We have some cylindrical drums (many sizes) with a rubber seal round the lid, used for storing olives in the Mediterranean. They make good dry stowage for flour and pulses, anything in packets that could suffer from damp or insects. Not only can water and beetles not get in, but they have also proved to be rat proof. Label everything clearly; it's dark down there.

Drinking glasses deserve purpose-built stowage, on shelves with clips or holders, or a wooden base with rings cut for the stems. Failing that, cosset them with squares of bubble-wrap to stop them chipping and keep them in a drawer. We find it unnecessary to use plastic glasses, the everyday French glasses are sturdy, and tend to bounce, rather than shatter, if dropped.

❖ Healthcare ❖

It is to be hoped that your health is good, or at any rate that small medical problems (we all have them) are understood and under control. If you get sick or have an accident, what happens?

If you have health insurance, you are usually home and dry. We have survived

As you can see from this spacious saloon on Hosanna, *life afloat can be comfortable.*

without it for more than 30 years, relying on the NHS or local resources in times of trouble. Our experience of these things, both our own and that of other voyagers we have known in foreign countries, has been pretty good.

In Europe, we find that in case of accidents or illness that neighbouring craft, lock keepers, and local people can be extraordinarily kind and helpful, the former with practical help, the latter with knowledge of how to access local resources.

Keep your NHS European Health Insurance card in a safe place, so that you can produce it. You may still have to pay up front for treatment, but you should get repayment in due course.

The situation is completely different in the USA. We took out temporary health insurance here, as there is no social medicine in the USA. We needed it only once, for a tooth filling. Hardly worth it in retrospect, but if worse had occurred we might have been glad of it.

❖ Entertainment ❖

In winter, one needs some indoor entertainment. In a waterside community, there will be social activities. Then there is radio and TV. We have a small multi-standard TV, nearly ten years old now, which receives Continental domestic channels through an 'all-round' antenna. Not brilliant, but adequate. For long lay-ups, we set up a 1m (3ft) satellite dish on a short pole. Some people install a sophisticated gyro-stabilised thingy that lines itself up wherever you go. There is also a dish which can be adjusted from down below in the warm. Lacking that, Bill persuades himself that he needs the exercise if there is Rugby in the offing. Climbing out to adjust it gives him an opportunity to swear without guilt. Adjustment of the dish involves a shouting match from below: 'No signal – Red-yellow, red again, BLUE! You've got it!' which some might think was an argument if they did not know us better. For more specialist advice try www.maxview.co.uk.

You can tune your dish to Astra 2 for free-to-air stations over a large part of Europe. These include some radio stations such as BBC Radios 2, 3, and 4, as well as RTE, the Irish FM station – best for classical music. Apart from this, an ordinary small radio receives Continental FM stations. France Info (a continual 24 hours news service) broadcasts a weather forecast at roughly 8 minutes past the half-hour in rapid but clear French. It is also useful for picking up news of *grèves* (strikes), *manifs* (demonstrations or protests) and other items which can affect us all. France Musique caters for classical music and jazz fans.

Other stations broadcasting occasional news in English are:

- Radio France Internationale
- Radio Riviera
- Deutsche Welle Radio (Germany)
- Radio Netherlands Worldwide

❖ Internet and cell phones ❖

Getting online is not always that easy. Many Continental countries are way behind the UK in provision of Wi Fi, and marinas are slow to provide hotspots. Try MacDonald's!

Mobile broadband is expensive and not omni-present, but the owner of a boat called *The Last Farthing* has had good service from SFR mobile broadband – more expensive than a similar contract in England.

We use a Blackberry to communicate, but phone calls have largely given place to SMS and e-mail on this marvellous machine. In theory, it will access the internet but that would be expensive and slow. Short e-mails cost a penny or two, though enclosures, especially pictures, can run up a big bill as use is timed by the megabyte. The cost of SMS is negligible.

Roaming costs on your cell phone are usually high, but deals are occasionally becoming available.

· 10 ·

Essential equipment

In discussing items of equipment, essential or desirable to IWBs, we will not comment here on a kit for sea crossings (see later) but concentrate on items specifically of use for inland cruising. Navigationally, there is less than one would need at sea.

❖ Compasses ❖

I like to have a compass on board – it is essential in wide estuaries and channels for hopping from buoy to buoy, and calculating the aim-off when buoy-hopping. It is vital in bad visibility in estuaries or big rivers such as the Danube, where the channel divides repeatedly. In featureless terrain you can lose track of where you are, especially if your charts/guides are not up to date. When we last navigated the Danube delta, the latest charts were based on a false geographical datum and GPS was more than a mile out compared with the chart. The classic case was when the GPS placed our barge in a Ukrainian railway station. I think this experience is not likely to be repeated, though there may still be pockets of antiquity. Our car compass is useful even on English roads.

Not everybody goes off into wild rivers, and if you plan to stick to the domesticated canals (and why not, if that pleases you?) a sophisticated marine compass can be dispensed with.

❖ GPS ❖

A GPS can be useful. It gives you an accurate speed over the ground – a good way of estimating the current (but one cannot rely on the height data given by GPS). Some navigable rivers have kilometre posts so that you can check progress, but they are not always visible in flood conditions, and few canals have them. Mostly, then, GPS for inland waters is an interesting toy, except that combined instruments exist for maritime and land navigation: the sort of thing that gets 40 tonne lorries onto vicarage lawns. You are unlikely to get lost on a canal, but it could be useful in checking progress on a featureless stretch. It might help you find a convenient pub.

❖ Navigation lights ❖

You must carry the normal navigation lights, even if you do not intend to navigate at night, because you must use proper lights in poor visibility and you never know when you might run into unexpected fog. The white 'steaming' light cannot conform to the position demanded in the Col-Regs (International Regulations for the Prevention of Collisions at Sea, which apply in certain inland waters ie the Thames, the Seine, the Scheldt; that are accessible to the open sea) because of height considerations. Most barges have a steaming light on a short counter-balanced mast that one person can easily raise or lower at bridges. If you can design the installation so that the light rotates on an athwartships pin as it is raised or lowered, thus enabling it to be seen ahead from whatever position it is in, so much the better. The navigation lights (the red and green side lights) are supposed to be always below the steaming light. You will need the side navigation lights when in tunnels, many of which are manned, you will incur wrath if you do not conform.

You will need a searchlight in tunnels. Opinions differ on whether this searchlight should be a narrow beam or one with an horizontally spread beam. I find that the narrow beam does not illuminate both sides of the tunnel, important because there are often bits of junk either side to watch out for. I prefer a slightly less powerful (to avoid back-dazzle) searchlight wide enough to illuminate both sides. This is also more useful in the canals at night. You may not plan to navigate at night but occasionally one has no choice. You will also need a horn for sound signals.

❖ Binoculars ❖

Good binoculars are essential. One must see well to identify marks that are not always easy to discern, especially in late summer when the greenery acts as a screen. I recommend the usual nautical type with 7 x 50 lenses. If you can find them, get a pair with built in sun-filters, the sort you can flip in or out with a finger. An excellent buy would be the ex-naval type 1800A; finding a pair in good condition is unlikely, but you can refurbish them at modest expense and they are better than most others. The filters are important, looking towards the sun in the early morning or at sunset is difficult.

❖ Poles ❖

A long stout spar, known in England as a *quant*, is not often mentioned as boat gear, but is desirable, its thickness depending on the weight of the boat. This is useful for bearing the boat off when leaving the bank, or helping dislodge her if she takes the ground. A boat hook is not the same thing, a quant is heavier and stronger. Ideally, the lower end of a quant should have a short wooden fork which helps to prevent it sinking into the mud when you push. By giving a twist, it relieves the suction so you can withdraw the quant. We cherish pictures of poles left sticking up out of the water as the boat moves inexorably on leaving the hapless quanter clinging onto it until his grip loosens and he slides slowly down into the water.

Another shorter, lighter pole for depth-sounding should be 3m (10ft) long and marked in decimetres if you are metric. I prefer it to be marked in foot-wide bands, red, white, blue and yellow, alternately from the bottom. My reason is that a foot is a convenient length for estimating depths whereas a decimetre is too short and a metre is too long. We use a bamboo pole (called Cleopatra because it came inside a roll of carpet) for this. Bind it tightly with twine at the depth marks. This helps to stop the bamboo from splitting.

You *will* need a boat-hook. If you have a barge over 25m (82ft), keep one at each end; it takes too long running from end to end to grab one – you always need a boat-hook in a hurry if you need one at all. Avoid boat-hooks with a hook and a point; these betray amateur status. Never shove off with the hook end; it can be lethal. In fact, like rifles, never point the business end at another person or boat. The best hooks are the double ones shaped like a rounded letter M. At the fore end of the ship, I like a strong one with a 10ft stave of about 1½in diameter (3m by 38mm), and at the after end a short stave of about 7ft with a 1in (25mm) diameter. Avoid fancy teak or decorated varnished hardwood from trendy chandlers; get a commercial one with an ash stave and do your own varnishing if you want to. Our long one is marked as a sounding pole.

RETRIEVING ITEMS OUT OF THE WATER

Tools you will need for this are:

- **A medium sized anglers' landing net** About half a metre across is adequate, and its stave must easily reach the waterline. This is a vital tool for recovering objects that have been dropped overboard, or if you have pets on board, especially cats which frequently seem to 'take a voluntary' (sailors' slang for going overboard).

- **A magnet** This is similarly a vital tool. Strong magnets on a length of cod-line are invaluable in the recovery of lost objects, and are available at most chandleries. The heaviest object we have fished up was a bicycle, but ours has also recovered screwdrivers, bunches of keys and spectacles. (Attach a small steel tag to your glasses if they are plastic, and to your wallet if it has no keyring attached.) We grumble a bit at the price of the magnet, and cannot understand why they are so expensive. However, they last for years. Ours is over 30 years old. Keep it well-greased with lanolin.

❖ Brows, gangways and planks ❖

Another essential item is a long plank (which we call a brow – the naval term) to enable you to get ashore when the side of the canal is too shallow for your boat to get close enough. Commercial barges, which can be deep-laden, have planks of some 5m (16ft) and in order to be light enough to handle, it has to be as thin as is safe and

Hosanna *in her winter berth at Abbeville on the River Somme.*

as narrow as you can bear to walk on. This means it bends as one walks across and with no hand-rail (considered sissy but who cares at our age), one feels like a slack-wire circus artiste. The trick is to adjust your step to avoid the plank picking up a natural harmonic, in which event you will bounce up and down as if on a trampoline until, inevitably, you fall off. Hilarious for nearby crews.

In *Hosanna*, we had two brows, one consisting of two 200mm by 20mm (8in by ³/₄in) deal planks, side by side, just under 3m (10ft) in length, bolted together by short steel straps. This was satisfactory, but a bit heavy to get out on occasions, so for lesser distances we had a short plank of 4ft by 1ft (1.2m by 0.3m) that was easier to manage. In any event, have a couple of 12mm (¹/₂in) holes drilled either side at the inboard end so as to lash the plank or brow securely to the ship. (Read later in Chapter 19 what we write about interaction: the way a moored boat moves about when another boat goes past.) Note that officially *Hosanna* did not have the legally required brow. The latest regulation (we suspect they change annually to keep us awake) says that for barges over 24m (79ft), there should be a passerelle measuring at least 400mm by 4m (16in by 13ft) in length, fitted with a handrail, and the sides should be marked with a white band.

❖ Temporary mooring equipment ❖

If you see a good mooring at three o' clock on an autumn day, you may settle for it; but you may want to continue and hope for a better one further on. You can bet that there won't be, and you have to press on regardless till the locks close. There are no street lights on canals and you will need light. A short while after lock-closing time you can be reasonably sure that no commercial barge will be pressing on and you can just stop.

If you do 'just stop' in these conditions, try to find somewhere to nose into the bank, and a tree or something to make fast to. Making fast to trees is illegal, but needs must if the devil is driving. If there are no trees, then let go your anchor with about 5m (16ft) of chain cable. This could be uncomfortable if the wind gets up, but you need special equipment to do otherwise.

Hosanna was fitted with a 'spud-pile'. This is a long 15cm (6in) diameter pencil-shaped cylindrical pile mounted as an easy-fit in a vertical tube through the fore-peak. When let go, the point sinks into the mud and fixes the ship exactly. The only problem is raising it again. We had a strong multi-part tackle to do this, but the best way would be a simple hydraulic ram. This is a useful stand-by on occasions, though we did not use it all that often. It is only useful in shallow water.

❖ Fenders and other dent preventers ❖

On motor boats of the conventional type, the inflatable plastic ones are the best. Unfortunately they do not last long because of the bashing they get (that is their *raison d'etre*, after all). Because of their intense use on inland waters against rough surfaces they soon get scratched. A yacht's best solution is three or four of these (cylindrical) with a horizontal plank fixed outside them. Watch the contraption does not catch over the edge of a lock when descending. For marina mooring, fender-sox are a good idea, but they last in locks only the blink of an eye, as they also get torn and bashed in service; they do not protect the basic fender much and the whole business costs more than ever. We do not recommend woven or plaited rope fenders for yachts; these attract oily shingle and scratch it into your paintwork.

For steel barges, motor tyres are undoubtedly the best fenders, but they are not allowed in locks. They last much longer (indefinitely even) than anything else, but upset the owners of smart motor boats against whom you may lie. We always have a

Here a 'pudding' fender takes the rub.

few small ones painted with white chlorinated rubber for politeness' sake. Or when necessary, put the tyre in a plastic bag. Again, woven or plaited coir fenders are scratchy, though they have a traditional feel. They weigh a ton when wet.

If your boat is very broad, then you may not have much room to fender yourself in locks. Aquafax market what they call 'narrowboat' fenders of black plastic at a modest price. These look like old fashioned policemen's truncheons. We bought four but haven't used them yet.

Have at least one large 'pudding' fender, a sphere of at least half a metre in diameter. It has to be plastic, and one should save it for those occasions when only such a fender will do, springing off, for instance.

❖ Life jackets ❖

You should carry a life jacket for each member of the crew on board. We expect visitors to provide their own. On inland waters, one does not need the hyper-buoyant expensive thingies offered to the sea-going sailor. You need a comparatively convenient buoyancy aid. You are obliged to wear one when locking and it must therefore be comfortable to bend down and work in. A cumbersome life jacket can itself be dangerous. We have only one set of oilskins and they are Laurel's size, which means that she is the one who goes out and gets wet. She has realised this, so I expect to get a set of oilskins next birthday.

❖ Other useful clothing ❖

Have a couple of pairs of heavy-duty leather working gloves. You may keep your mooring ropes in good condition, but you will moor alongside others who do not. There is much angling in canals, so you can find even your pristine white nylon moorings infested with fish-hooks. Mud, clay and fish-hooks can play havoc with your hands.

Avoid the temptation to walk about on board barefoot. You're bound to hurt yourself somehow. We favour old-fashioned boat shoes of the gym-shoe type; you will often be walking over slippery surfaces, and the treads on the modern leather shoes do not seem to grip like the older ones. Having said that, Laurel swears by her generic Docksiders.

❖ Marine VHF radio ❖

This is also now a requirement. A small boat can manage without VHF on the canals, but in the estuaries and big rivers it is essential. The EU is laying down draconian requirements for VHF/DSC together with AIS under a scheme called RAINWAT. We Brits had no say whatsoever in anything our EU legislators do for us, and Britain did not even take part in the discussions!

These rules are intended to govern coastal and inland waters, and are of particular significance for IWBs who have to navigate in estuaries where there are big ships

This marinier *carries a small car aboard his double barge.*

on passage, controlled by expert pilots who will not have time for amateurs who do not understand or obey the rules. I foresee trouble ahead unless procedures are simplified. Both the DBA and the EBA (the European Boating Association) are trying hard to get some common sense in these regulations. The latter, EBA, is a vague body representing pan-European amateur boating, but it is either reticent about its activities (more than likely) or does not have very much effect, equally likely. The British representative on the EBA when I last encountered this body was a most able man, but even he cannot move mountains.

❖ Land transport ❖

Personal transport is usually carried on board. The bicycle is common. A small motor-bike is a live-aboard sign, but big bikes need the same disembarkation gear that small cars require. Barges often carry cars on board. *Hosanna* carried both a Mini and a FIAT 600 at times (though not together), the Fiat was the better proposition. Though old, it was well built. Its metal work was scratched and rubbed but it remained rust-free. We drove it all over Europe from southern Italy to Britain (twice) and it never let us down though we had occasionally to perform emergency maintenance (it never needed routine maintenance – at least it never got any. The only tools needed were a hammer, a screwdriver and a little mole wrench.) Finally, the car was pushed into the Rhône at Arles by vandals. France has its youth problems too.

KEEPING A CAR ABROAD

If you do not carry a car on board, you might consider keeping one on the Continent for use while laid up for the winter. The question is, foreign or British registration? For the former, you must be personally registered in the country concerned – a bureaucratic difficulty. Some people have had trouble with the registration of their boat that way. We keep our car registered in England and we usually repatriate it twice a year or more. Watch for the MOT date, there are no days of grace for that. While we carried our car on board we made an Off-the-Road declaration, saying that it was on board a ship outside British waters. This worked while we cruised from country to country at sea, but might run into difficulties for a boat always on inland waters. Try it and let me know!

The Mini came with us down the Danube and was useful. We landed it several times, and after a winter in Greece sailed to France with it, where it dissolved into a heap of brown powder. One cannot legally scrap a car in France unless it has been properly registered there. Re-registering a British car in France is worse than any complicated parlour game.

On a practical note, how did we embark and land the car? We had an old-fashioned cargo derrick, but this needs some expertise in its use. The modern merchant navy is not experienced in derricks. Once many riverside towns had quays at just the right height for rolling your car ashore on planks, we have done that at several places. More recently the commercial barges have taken to having their own hydraulic cranes and the special quays have gone. Observe the French barges. Most have a substantial car and handle it with a long-arm hydraulic crane. But you need a 38m (125ft) barge to have the room and weight to do this (remember that when the car is suspended over the side of the barge, it will make her heel over significantly.) If you can afford to buy a folding hydraulic crane (called a HiAb), go ahead. Second-hand ones are much in demand.

An alternative form of transport is available to older bargees. The electric mobility scooters for the elderly (we call them methuselagondas) can easily be carried and more readily landed. These vehicles offer many advantages to boat dwellers. One day, all towns in Europe will be over-run by them, but so far, they are not common on the Continent.

A wheeled trolley for moving heavy items is worth its space – you can get folding ones.

❖ Flags ❖

It is obligatory to wear the ensign of the country in which the craft is registered. In Belgium, a craft under way has to show at the stem-head a red square flag with a white rectangular centre. No other country requires this. Most Belgian barges keep the flag showing at all times.

Members of the DBA have Admiralty approval to fly a British flag called the Pilot Jack at the stemhead. This is not for decoration. When one approaches a lock, the lock-keeper cannot see the ensign at the stern and has no idea of the nationality of the crew of the boat. The Pilot Jack consists of a Union Flag surrounded by a white border and clearly signals to the lockkeeper that this is a British boat.

Q flags (Quarantine flags) are no longer obligatory in Europe.

❖ A blue flag ❖

This is required for navigation. We do not mean the journal of the DBA, but the object after which it is named.

Let me explain the purpose of the blue flag. When two boats or barges approach each other head on, the Colregs lay down that they should keep to the right and pass each other port-side to port-side, or red to red as professionals say. This is sometimes inconvenient in rivers, especially those that meander. Rivers flow strongest on the outside of bends, and convention allows the barge going up-stream to ask for the privilege of taking the inside of the bend to avoid having to plug against the stronger current. It is the up-stream going barge (the *montant* or *bergfahrer*) who has this right. If he wants to exercise it, the traditional way of doing so is to wave a blue flag from the starboard (right-hand) side of his wheel-house. The on-coming barge, the *avalant*, or *talfahrer*, acknowledges with a similar blue flag. Because of the inconvenience of standing there waving a flag, or because the flag is sometimes inconspicuous, most barges have a blue board, about one metre square, mounted on a hinge so that it can be displayed and seen by an on-coming vessel. On big rivers with large barge tows, this cannot always be seen in time, particularly at dusk, so a quick-flashing white light is added near the centre of the board.

You will not be expected to be so elaborately equipped in a small cruiser but should be aware when blue-flagging is occurring, and it does no harm to have a simple blue flag rolled up ready for use. The chances are you'll never need it, but for private barges, the square blue board is more or less essential. A barge is a barge, and some concessions to professional practice are required. It is axiomatic that most collisions between ships are caused because one captain does not understand what the other captain is trying to do. We must understand the practices of professionals of long habit and experience.

❖ Life rafts ❖

These are not required except for sea passages and forays across wide estuaries. If you have a serviceable dinghy that can be easily launched, you have what you need. The dinghies in big barges are often of steel, which makes them heavy, but it enables them to take a lot of punishment. You'll recognise those that have been well-used by the dents – to the point of a hammered finish. Most pleasure boats settle on a glass-fibre or inflatable boat and have an outboard to go with it. It is possible that you cannot find a mooring convenient for the shops for a bigger boat, but we have never found a dinghy necessary on inland waters, except in the USA.

· 11 ·

Boat maintenance

Maintaining boats is more important than many light-hearted boat-owners believe. Boats are meant to be pleasurable, but *rien sans peine*: the French say: 'no pain, no gain'. Boats, and perhaps some owners as well, need as much looking after as a house, and like a house, you hope that having a new one (boat, or owner) will obviate some of the work. It doesn't.

It need not be a desperate chore unless you are imprudently going to buy a virtual wreck. (We know, we've done it.) Fortunately for us, inland waters maintenance is not nearly such hard work as for sea-going craft, where conscientiousness is often a matter of life or death.

A full, detailed treatise on boat maintenance would make a largish book by itself and we have no space for it. There are too many types and sizes of boats, engines, deck gear, navigational equipment and so on. All we can do here is give some idea of what the newcomer to boat-owning is letting himself in for. We don't want people to buy their first boat ignorant of the responsibilities that go with ownership. She may be *your* boat, but your lack of maintenance can result in damage to others, persons and/or boats.

❖ Maintenance schedule and log ❖

The subject can be divided in several ways. There are the smaller chores which, when cruising, need attention almost daily, and there are the long term projects which can be done at intervals, possibly years. They all need thinking about, and if you keep a ship's log (and you should for many reasons) have a maintenance schedule written out as a reminder (a memory-jog log).

We use an A5 day-to-a-page diary, and preferably one with a sound sewn binding. The so-called 'perfect' binding, named not for its characteristic lack of perfection but because it was invented by a Mr Perfect, will not last for months of more or less continuous daily use, frequent back reference, being dropped to the deck a few times a day, and tromped on by the ship's dog. There is a space in the back for notes about next year. This is our maintenance log. Without some form of discipline like this, I procrastinate.

❖ Engines and generators ❖

You are unlikely to need a major routine overhaul of your engine because, as an amateur, you will not drive it as hard or as long as the manufacturers, who write the manuals, fear you will. We had backing for this (to our great relief) when our first live-aboard boat *Fare Well* had passed 2000 hours of engine use. The book said it should be now given over to an agent to reduce to a kit of parts, etc.

We were in Gibraltar at the time and got talking engines with our neighbour, who turned out to be a technical manager for Perkins, who made our engine. I consulted him (always pick a free brain if you can) and he asked:

'No black smoke? Starts and runs well?'

'Yes.'

'Use much oil?'

'Very little.'

'Then change the oil and filters regularly, and leave it alone.'

This is applicable to an engine that is used *regularly*. Those that are walked away from and left to brood all winter, need more attention. Details of what the manufacturer requires to maintain your engine are in the handbook. Advice on laying up engines for winter appears in every autumnal edition of the practical yachting magazines.

What is necessary for main engines is also necessary for diesel generators, which often get overlooked. Because their moving parts are smaller, there is less margin for faults in manufacture and/or fitting and, in our experience, generators give far more trouble overall than their bigger cousins that drive the boat. The problem is not helped by insistence that the generator be housed in an acoustic barrel, making it all but inaccessible, and requiring long fingers with four double joints in them. The Volvo 2002 was the worst, but all are bad.

I stress the desirability of having a generator that runs at 1500rpm instead of 3000rpm. These figures are convenient for making alternating current at 50Hz. In the USA, generators turn at either 1800 or 3600rpm to make juice at 60Hz. The slower revving engine is under much less strain and runs more quietly with less vibration. You pay more for the luxury, but it's worth it.

The most important maintenance for engines is that mentioned informally above by our Perkins friend.

REGULAR MAINTENANCE TASKS

- Look after the oil levels, oil changes, and fuel and oil filters.
- Remember that the fuel filters and the water inlet filters also need changing regularly – these clog up frequently on inland waters. When we bought *Hosanna* in Friesland, we planned to cross the North Sea in winter and to cut down on time, we asked the agent to get her ballasted and fuelled, and to replace the filters. We should have done the filters ourselves. We crossed the

North Sea in quite rough weather (a north-easterly force 6) without serious incident and it was only when I checked the fuel filters after arrival, that I discovered that the filter element (the part that mattered), had been replaced by a pair of old woollen socks. We were not impressed.

- Install an engine hours meter and do the jobs by the book, except that the advice to check some things every day is a bit OTT for amateur use. You don't grovel around inside your car engine every day.
- Check oil levels in the gear box from time to time.
- Keep the stern tube greased by giving the greaser gizmo a turn each time you go into the engine room.
- Once a year, go over the engine with spanner and screwdriver and adjust loose hose clips or bolts.
- Once a month, check drive-belt tension on pump drives and alternators. You soon get the feel of this; I reckon the belt should give about one centimetre when pressed down between the pulleys.
- Look at electrical terminals and check crimp terminals for metal fatigue. I don't like them, but electricians find them easy to fit. Most of the electrical failures I have experienced while under way have been due to crimp terminals coming adrift.
- Tighten up now and then on the stern gland, and with every other slipping have the stern gland examined and the packing renewed. This latter depends on the age of the installation; old shafts in old bearings get worn and slack.
- Do not forget that rudder bearings need the occasional helping of grease, and that at intervals they might need re-packing. If you are buying a barge and having a survey, make sure the rudder bearing is properly examined; it is possible that, if maintenance on this has been neglected (it often is), the rudder stock itself may have worn down dangerously.
- Check the steering action annually if it is mechanical, but grease it more often. (You should use a lot of grease on a barge.)
- If you have hydraulic steering, check the level of hydraulic oil in the system at least once a month, or at the start of any significant voyage.
- If your deck drains over the side through gaps in the toe-rail, these need no attention, but if water runs off down internal piping, put a powerful hose down them once a year, or in autumn if laid up under the trees. Try to avoid a build-up of leaves in corners.
- It is important to regularly check the airhole in the base of the gas locker, and check the flexible gas hose. Is it in date? The gas locker should be marked PROPANE or BUTANE in 30mm letters. Important because this is where the stop-cock is and a fireman has to know that.
- Navigation lights: you probably go years without using them, but check them at the beginning of each season.
- Check the horn/siren.
- At the end of each season see to all those items that need renewing or repairing. Now is the time to get them done.

❖ Anchors ❖

The anchor windlass gets little attention on inland waters. Anchors are seldom used except on big rivers such as the Danube, but they are important for ship safety in certain circumstances: getting a rope round the screw just above a weir for example.

It is no use having an anchor (and it is obligatory) unless it is kept ready for use. The basic crab winch with its curved spoke handle is the usual fitting, and it requires regular greasing. I suggest you examine, and use it, twice a year.

❖ Slipping ❖

With a motor cruiser, this is easy to do by travelift, but in fresh water you don't do it very often. Pulling any kind of boat around when it is out of its element puts unusual (and often unallowed for) strains on it.

Barges only need slipping every two or three years in fresh water, though in sea water it should be done more often. There is considerably less galvanic action in fresh water and the anodes last longer. Note that the makers recommend magnesium anodes for fresh water as an alternative to sea-going zinc. Strictly speaking, the anodes could be of any metal in roughly the same part of the periodic table, but some metals form a coating of chemical salt which inhibits the anode from working properly. Anodes are expensive. Until recently, we never had any serious problem with galvanic activity affecting the hull of any of our steel boats over 35 years. On the other hand, a builder who installed a propeller shaft made from the wrong type of stainless steel, left us with a bad problem when the shaft corroded in little deep pits or holes about 5mm across. Check your metals carefully.

Finding places to slip or dock on the canals is difficult. The Netherlands are better served than France or Belgium. France is normally cheaper but currently has seen a dramatic boom in barge traffic and the *chantiers* (boatyards) are full of old barges being tarted up for trade; so there are no cheap offers around at the moment. In any event, most *chantiers* do not welcome pleasure barges because the owners are not considered to be serious.

If they are not busy, they become accommodating. We have slipped *Hosanna* twice at the big bargeworks at Arles and had a good experience. We were once in the dry dock at St Jean-de-Losne, which is also good. We have had work done at the barge yard at Arques, again good. None of these were as expensive as yards in England. Smaller barges must watch out when slipping because barges are slipped sideways (laterally). The chocks are designed for bigger barges and are about 10m (33ft) apart. This leaves a lot of boat to sag between the chocks. If you have a delicate boat, watch out. I was very glad I had fitted *Hosanna* with a long, strong, centre-line keel and two bilge keels.

This method of slipping with widely-spaced chocks is the reason why France does not normally permit poured-in concrete as permanent ballast (whereas for the Royal Navy, it is the material and method of choice.) French *péniches* are built with lighter scantlings than Dutch or English, their hulls under water are not maintained and they corrode, and so the weight of concrete in the interior can cause the widely-supported hull to collapse. It has happened – I have seen the pictures. Why do they not space the chocks more closely? The reason is that the chocks are pulled up the slope together with a mechanism for equalising the strain. The more chocks, the more elaborate and expensive this mechanism has to be. The slipway at Arques is lateral.

❖ Be in tune with your boat ❖

Learn your boat's language. It is talking to you all the time, not only in sounds, but gives off signals to almost all the senses. Not taste perhaps. Though come to think of it, whether the water in your bilge is salt or fresh tells you something. Bill often dips in a finger and gingerly tastes it.

Sounds
We don't think it's appreciated enough that a small noise, paid attention to, can alert you to trouble that could cause a lot of grief if neglected.

- We know when our water tanks are full, not so much by the sight gauge as by a popping noise in the breather pipe. A gurgling noise in the fresh water pump indicates the tanks need re-filling, as does an odd noise in the hot water cylinder if you have one.
- A DC motor slowing down suggests a failing battery.
- Rough running or a change of note in an engine, should be investigated.
- The sound of dripping needs looking into.
- An intermittent rasping sound behind the linings can be your first indication of a rat.
- Something not very heavy falling over on deck in the early hours on a calm night: strong possibility of a stray cat, rat or fox, which will almost certainly leave traces, never leave edible rubbish on deck.

Touch and feel
In a sailing boat, a change of wind sets the sails flapping and gets everyone up on deck to see to it. One is less aware in a canal boat, but if you are moored you can often feel that a big barge is coming by the movement of your boat. Bumps and lurches tell you that the barge has arrived, and in close quarters is feeling her way past. Usually commercial barges are good at this, though they can come terrifyingly close. Barges passing on the move are completely different (see Chapter 19 on Canal effect).

If your fingers feel something is damp, it could mean a leak, but if it is also cold then condensation is the likely cause. Many live-aboards in winter create themselves a form of double glazing. We have seen clingfilm used to good effect on small windows, you can shrink wrap it on with the gentle use of a hair dryer. Bubble wrap can be neatly taped to the window. The aluminium frames of windows are the

A 38m péniche *lifted by the stern for maintenance at Arques.*

usual suspects, a double layer of masking tape laid over them cuts it down, but is hard to remove come spring-time. Damp holes and gaps behind linings can be filled with polyurethane foam (the DIY version in spray-cans) – wonderful stuff.

Sight
This is the normal way of noticing anything out of kilter. Rust stains, flaking paint, oil drips, mould, wood powder under a plywood panel are all saying 'Pay me some attention'.

Smell
The loo is the obvious offender, and its associated holding tank. There are eco-friendly products to cope with this.

A smell of mould alerts you to a ventilation problem.

All motor boats smell slightly of diesel, one gets used to it and only the visitors notice. However an unaccustomed strong smell of diesel, and any smell of gas in the accommodation needs an urgent check.

Unexpected smells in the forepeak store when it is opened up suggests that something has spilt. Plastic containers of chemicals will chafe through owing to engine vibration, and the contents can be dangerous. (Always decant any flammable material from the plastic can or bottle that it is sold in if you are going to stow it away out of sight for a period.)

· 12 ·
Using solvents, paints and glues

This advice is mostly for treating steel and wood. I (Laurel) know very little about painting GRP, cement, or aluminium hulls.

Painting is something all boatowners must learn about. Manuals and CDs obtained from the manufacturers are helpful, especially if you actually follow the instructions, but there are things they don't tell you about. One of them is solvents.

❖ Solvents ❖

Few manufacturers come clean about their solvents. They call them by mysterious names such as T49, and warn you that all warranties are void unless you use them. Having painted an 87ft (27m) barge for more than 20 years, and a steel ketch for ten years before that, (and I'm still at it) I am aware it is industrial quantities of the stuff you need, not expensive little tins and bottles from the chandlery. So here goes, we'll attempt to solve the solvent problem as far as I can. This section comes with a health warning. If you have not got the manufacturer's dedicated solvent or paint thinners, try:

- Cleaning the brush with a different solvent.
- If it cleans the brush you are half way there, but before you thin the paint make sure that it is compatible. Mix the solvent with a spoonful of the paint in a plastic or cardboard cup. If it gels, separates, smokes, curdles, or disintegrates into little particles, it is not the right solvent, find another.

Some solvents dissolve certain types of plastic, not to mention skin. Cardboard coffee cups or jam jars are the best mixing containers.

❖ What solvent do you choose? ❖

Water
Many of today's paints and varnishes, emulsions, acrylics etc (even some outdoor ones), are water-based, and brushes can be rinsed under the tap. For interiors these paints save you a lot of grief, and are usually quick drying.

An old fashioned tack rag can be made by dipping a lint free cloth in water and wringing it out well. On to this damp cloth, sprinkle white spirit and a spoonful of ordinary varnish and rub and squeeze till well mixed. Keep in an airtight container, and use it to wipe dust off paint and varnish between coats.

Methylated spirit

This is good for knotting, and shellac-based paints. Will also clean off Biro ink, and neutralise phosphoric acid, see below.

White spirit

Used for most conventional oil-based paints and varnishes, it is the poor relation of turpentine, which is much oilier. Look on the tin of your chosen paint manufacturer's standard yacht paint or varnish, and whatever they suggest as a thinner under a fancy name is almost certainly white spirit, which is a lot cheaper by the gallon than in little tins. Wear vinyl gloves when using it; it eats through rubber ones quicker than a rottweiler. Do not use for two-part paints or epoxy.

Acetone

This is a powerful brush cleaner which is also useful as a general degreaser. It is harmful to skin.

Xylene

This eats through anything, so handle with extra care; it is used for chlorinated rubber paints such as Hammerite, and suchlike. It is a strong degreasant for wiping over the engine. It is harmful to skin.

TIP

We have had good experience with Witham Oil & Paint Ltd, sources for generic stuff like acetone and phosphoric acid as well as being paint manufacturers. They have outlets in Oulton Broad, Cambridge and in Lincoln.

❖ Specialist thinners ❖

Where we are in difficulty is with two-part polyurethane paints and varnishes, resinous mixtures, and epoxy paints and tars. Here you are pretty much bound to buy the appropriate thinners, as these modern paints are complex chemical mixtures, and so are the thinners that go with them. Xylene can sometimes help.

❖ Ortho-phosphoric acid ❖

If you have a steel boat, you will need this. It removes rust stains, and prepares steel for painting. Provided you have removed loose rust and scale, the acid in a 30 per cent solution turns any remaining surface rust into a paintable substance. Leave on for 15 minutes, wash off with plenty of water and dry before painting (or you can use methylated spirit which will dry quickly). It is available from chandlers in small amounts under proprietory names at enormous expense, and from the factory in bigger quantities. It also brings back the colour to teak and similar woods. An alternative is oxalic acid. Both acids and their associated salts are seriously poisonous, but the acids are good for removing those unsightly ginger stains that run down the paintwork. They are merely a cosmetic touch-up for this: it is the underlying bad spot that needs attention. You will see gallons of these acids being used by professional yacht crews in the few days before the owner's party arrives.

❖ Paint ❖

Let us hope that your initial paint job was done by a good contractor. Even so you are going to have some work to do, touching up here and there, and antifouling must be done from time to time. If you are self-building, you will save yourself a lot of grief if you ask your contractor to leave you at least 5 litres of the paint he used for the underwater hull, and another 5 litres of the above-the-waterline paint – with the appropriate thinners and data sheets.

Antifouling

Choose according to the hull material and the waters you will be cruising in. Antifouling should not be thinned; zap on plenty with a roller, and use a throw-away brush for the awkward bits and for any pin-holes left by the roller. Remember *not* to paint over zinc anodes or sensing devices. I have bitten the bullet in recent years

This amount of paint is needed for the exterior of a 12m boat. It's expensive!

and no longer clean trays and brushes when antifouling; it's a tough enough job without that. Though it goes against my parsimonious grain, I chuck them away in the appropriate bin as everyone else seems to do nowadays.

Paint designed to look good and be long lasting

These are the two-part paints and varnishes, the polyurethanes and epoxys that cure chemically rather than air-drying like conventional paints. In the short term they are more expensive, and certainly more troublesome to put on, but they save money and work in the end. I find it helps to write the proportions (base to cure agent) on the lid of the tin, as well as a splash of the colour, as my memory and eyesight are not what they were. Use cardboard coffee cups or glass jars for mixing small quantities, as these paints dissolve some plastics.

Laurel antifouling; afterwards she needed a stiff whisky.

TIP

Always close the lid of the curing agent properly and keep in a dry place. It is even more expensive than the base, and you don't want to waste it.

Treat these paints and varnishes with respect and follow instructions, and they will serve you well.

Quick-drying paint

I swear by chlorinated rubber paints for a quick improvement job, or things that want frequent attention like guardrails, chimneys, and decks. The formula (and the name) has changed in the last few years to be more eco-friendly, but the new versions seem to do the same job – namely a quick-drying coating where three coats can be put on in a day in summer temperatures. It has the advantage of being more flexible than other paints. If used for decks, non-slip areas can be created by sprinkling with fine sand (not from the beach –the salt in it would attract moisture) before the final coat. Wait a week before putting heavy chairs on the painted surface, as it will dent like cheap carpet until it is properly cured.

❖ Painting tools ❖

Brushes

Have plenty of throw-away brushes for touching up. Use better quality ones for painting and varnishing.

Electric paint stripper

We never use ours for paint stripping! Used on low heat, this is invaluable for drying out those nasty little rust pits so you can see what needs chipping off before repainting. Another use is for softening plastic pipe before sliding it on hose fittings.

TIP

While you are in painting mode and have several coats to put on, swipe the brushes through its cleaner after use and put the bristle end in a sandwich bag with the air squeezed out, then they will be usable the next day.

When the job is finished, clean brushes thoroughly.

Other vital tools

- Chipping hammer, for removing chunks of rust. Preferably the blade type rather than the welder's pointed tool.
- Wire brush, for removing loose rust.
- Masking tape. Some is straight, others are a bit stretchy for bends and curves.
- Take knotting (shellac-based knot sealer) with you. I have not found it on the Continent.
- A palette knife,
- A short-bladed scraper, well sharpened.

Laurel painting the drawers for the galley – and there were a great many.

- A set of small 'toothbrushes' (one steel, one brass, one stiff nylon), an invaluable aid for all kinds of jobs –buy at a £1 discount store.
- Plastic dessertspoons for measuring paint.
- Plastic and cardboard cups for mixing small amounts.
- Old kitchen cutting board for mixing filler.
- Rolls of kitchen paper for mopping up inevitable spills.
- Old screwdriver for prising off lids. (Never use the Captain's!)
- A sturdy tray, an old washing up bowl, or even a strong cardboard fruit box, make good , safe containers to stand tins and bottles while mixing, to limit the damage of spills. Most paint and thinners will eat through your furniture and clothing if given a chance.

❖ Glues ❖

Woodworkers among you will have your favourite glue in a big squeezy bottle.

- Keep strong two-part glue in the locker – the little tubes are big enough for most small jobs.
- Buy contact adhesive for large panels as you need it, as it will go off before you need it again.
- A small tube of Superglue is useful but don't let it freeze.
- We have had little luck with No Nails sticky strips. On the other hand small pictures, photos, thermometers, digital clocks, mirrors, anything not too heavy, are easily hung on a bulkhead with two-sided sticky fixers, using two at each corner.

GENERAL RULES FOR PAINT, THINNERS AND GLUES

Read the health and safety advice on the tin or packet carefully, all these substances threaten different hazards.

- Work in the open air if you can, don't breathe the fumes in.
- Wear gloves: rubber, latex or vinyl.
- Keep these substances away from naked flames, and do not smoke or eat whilst using.
- Do not store liquids in plastic containers and stow and forget. Such containers can chafe through in your bilge or forepeak, posing a fire risk.
- Anything decanted from its original container must be clearly and permanently labelled.
- Paint it proper, paint it right, use good stuff and you'll sleep at night.

· 13 ·

Overwintering in icy conditions

W herever you cruise on the Continent, you are likely to find cold weather, though that is a comparative term. We have had snow in the south of France, and ice in the Camargue, but it is not usually serious thereabouts.

Even those dedicated to a life in the sun need to transit through the central regions of the Continent – bad news for brass monkeys.

You will voyage down in summer, of course. But are you sure you can make it before winter? Accounts of boats that have had mechanical problems, crew problems, injuries, any of the myriad ills that boats and their crews are prone to, are numerous. It is not only mariners at sea who must be prepared for the worst. We inlanders also must watch our water-steps. We know of a boat that had mechanical problems close to the Langres watershed in central France and was frozen-in there for three months.

The channel areas of Normandie, Picardie, and the Pas de Calais are warmed (comparatively speaking) by the sea. It is the centre of France, with a continental climate, which freezes but this part of France contains some of the prettiest places.

In St Jean-de-Losne in Burgundy, one of the most popular pleasure boat and barge moorings, boats in the basin were frozen in over much of the winter, though the River Saône remained navigable.

Great store is placed on *le tourisme* by the French government and this has been passed on to the canal authority, the VNF. This latter body has nobly encouraged moorings and associated facilities on many canals and rivers, but they seem to have followed the central government attitude that, apart from the Alps, tourism is confined to the summer months. If you wish to cruise in autumn, spring, or winter, you will find that these facilities have been withdrawn from 30 September until 1 May. On some, you may find a mooring, but neither water nor electricity, and often the gate will be padlocked as well. If you are completely self-sufficient for all weathers, you may survive, but if you need some supporting services you must find a berth in one of the few private marinas, which in winter are full of local boats renting their berths by the year and virtually never leaving them.

For most owners, a bit of shore-powered electricity is highly desirable because it is almost the only way one can prevent freezing up while you are away. Most people want a trip back to see the folks for Christmas.

❖ Ice ❖

Our experience is that canals can freeze over anywhere on the Continent north of the 46th parallel, though, generally, main rivers will remain free except in their upper, less used parts. Often the ice is not all that thick and a well built barge can plough through it (*Hosanna* coped with ice that was three inches thick) but locks become impassable owing to solid ice jamming the gates. If that happens, there you must stay.

- Do not try to break ice by reversing into it; you are likely to divert lumps of broken ice into the propeller and ruin it.
- On no account let a glassfibre or wooden boat freeze in where there is no reliable electricity supply to ensure an ice-free area round your boat. The ice can cut and/or crush the hull. Steel boats should be fine, but aluminium boats might be vulnerable.
- If you have to leave your boat for more than a couple of days in winter, then you must winterise her.

❖ Winterising engines ❖

Most modern engines contain anti-freeze coolant all the time. *That* is no problem, but the primary cooling circuit is itself cooled by canal water. Again, no problem in salt water, but the canals are fresh. Here are some important points to note:

A Close the cooling water intakes and loosen the hose clips, allowing the water above the filter to drain out. Turn the engine over for a second or two to allow the canal water in the heat exchanger to be pushed out into the flexible exhaust. Make sure the Jabsco pump is empty. Then lag round the inlet seacock with insulating rockwool or similar.

A stern view of Hosanna *covered in snow at Aigues Mortes in the south of France.*

B It is important to clear out the Jabsco because if that freezes, the pressure can push the pump shaft seal out of place and thus allow water to enter the sump when the engine is next commissioned. This might cause serious difficulties.

C The inlet seacock is almost certainly metal. If it is a ball valve, it may suffer by having the water in the hole in the ball freeze and fracture the ball. It is also possible that no matter what type of valve, the water in the base of it may freeze and expand, thus fracturing the valve casting (hence the lagging).

For this latter reason, it is better to have the inlet seacock down as low as reasonably possible because the canal water will have a temperature gradient and be slightly warmer the deeper you go. It only freezes on the surface. On the other hand a low seacock will scoop up all the mud and small debris. Fun, isn't it? There is nothing like mucking out the muck from a blocked seacock filter when you have guests on board.

After the winter

- When the thaw starts, the first sign of trouble could be a leak due to **C**.
- On re-commissioning, undo **A** first;
- then restore **B**.
- Check the level of coolant in the engine. This is to see if there is any possibility of water having been left in the heat exchanger and freezing. This is not likely.
- Now turn the engine over and run for a minute or two. Stop it and check that the lubricating oil does not have a milky texture that would indicate water in the lube-oil. If there is, get help unless you really know what you are doing with diesels, and you wouldn't be reading this if you did.

I am not a diesel expert. I am a die-hard diesel user, and have picked the brains of the experts I know to write the above. If you have no access to a diesel engineer, then this might help you, but get expert help if you can.

For the rest of the boat, where burst pipes can occur, the only seriously vulnerable parts are the fresh water system and the central heating circuit (if any).

❖ Winterising the water system ❖

It is best to leave the fresh water tanks almost but not quite empty. They should be strong enough to absorb the expansion of a small amount of freezing water with room to change level. It is as well to have a bit of fresh water in the system because, when you return, the stand-pipes may be frozen solid (or cut off to prevent them freezing) and you would have no fresh water at all. If driving out to your boat during a cold snap, take a jerrycan of fresh water with you.

In a typical fresh water installation, the water passes from the tank via an isolating valve to a manifold and then to a pump. In most modern boats, the piping will be Hep2O or similar push-fit plastic which should not burst when frozen because plastic is flexible. That is the claim of the manufacturers, and it is partially true. Recently, our return to the boat was delayed by *force majeure* after a vicious freeze with temperatures down to −11°C. We had ill-prepared for this back in the autumn.

The pipes did not burst, but several of the elbows and tap fittings cracked and I had to replace them. (It is always those in the most awkward places that suffer. My knees also suffered.)

It is apparent that the ice in the pipes expands and, because the pipes do *not* burst, it expands longitudinally and pushes the fittings off the ends of the pipes. You do not find this out until you think the problems are solved, turn on the water, and notice the jet from a pipe end. What fun boats are!

Other vulnerable points are the manifold (usually metal) and the fresh water pump and expansion chamber. After the pump, the problem eases because the water is under pressure (Boyle's Law says it will not freeze so readily), but it is the pump that requires care. Cleghorn Waring advises that one should open the inlet and outlet snap-on fittings (easily done on their latest pumps). Then cover the pump or pack with rockwool. Best install it low down in the boat.

- *Give the pump plenty of time to thaw completely before switching it on.* We have a plastic pipe rising from a tank to a plastic hand-pump at the sink – an emergency stand-by which should be permanently lagged. We recommend this for a variety of reasons.
- *Do not switch any machinery on until the system is fully thawed.*

❖ Winterising central heating ❖

This is where the hot air brigade score, their system can be switched on immediately. Those with a diesel oil heater such as a Refleks can light it straight away provided it is not fitted with interior water-heating coils. If like Kabola heaters, it has such coils, you must make sure the central heating system is thawed so that water can flow round the whole system pumped by the circulating pump.

- *The whole system must be thawed before the stove may be lit.* This takes time. Do not rush it.

❖ Winterising seacocks ❖

The seacocks under the WC and bath etc also need attention. What we said about the engine coolant seacocks also applies here. Before leaving the boat, flush the loos with an anti-freeze mixture to avoid the pump freezing solid. Beware, some makes of loo have valves which do not like anti-freeze. Check with the manufacturer.

For all seacocks you should have wooden plugs of the right diameter available for an emergency (these should be part of your boat's normal kit anyway.) These may be difficult to drive in when underwater in freezing temperatures, but that is one of the pleasures of boating. As they say in the Royal Navy: 'If you haven't a sense of humour, you shouldn't have joined.'

❖ The thaw ❖

This is the danger period. Where we were moored last winter, there was 3in (76mm) of ice in the basin. As canal traffic started again and began to break the ice on the main canal, water was pushed into the basin as traffic approached, and pulled out as they went on their way. This lifted the water level by several inches, which then dropped. This broke up the ice into large sheets with jagged edges, dangerous for lightly built boats, as these moving ice sheets have knife sharp edges.

Boats have sometimes been damaged by being squeezed in freezing ice, which is uncommon except in Polar regions. In severe conditions I would have little confidence in modern glassfibre boats with few frames.

We come to an important advantage of the steel-built hull. A hull of 8mm steel or thicker, will not suffer (except for the paintwork) from moving ice. Thinner steel will also do well enough if the frames and/or floors and stringers are spaced not more than 350mm (14in) apart. Aluminium in yacht-sized thicknesses is vulnerable to ice damage, but it is glassfibre and wood that will suffer most.

A tough old wooden workboat with planking over 50mm (2in) will get superficial damage only, but pansy-yacht plank thicknesses are vulnerable, as is glassfibre in any thickness likely to be used in pleasure boats. These boats are almost all built with minimum thickness and a dearth of framing. The hulls are elastic and will pop out again to normal size when all is done, but the sharp edges of breaking ice cut into the gel-coat and will even start work on the internal rovings, and that is a danger. If you are leaving a glassfibre boat in cold inland waters, best get it hauled out on hard standing. Frost won't harm it but sheet ice will.

COLD BATTERIES AND ENGINES

Sometimes in icy weather, batteries can become sluggish. This matters more with modern diesels. Engines with indirect injection require pre-heating before starting. With a suspect battery, the current involved in pre-heating a cold engine can result in insufficient battery power to turn the engine over fast enough.

The solution is to remove the air filter and fix up a hair-drier or electric paint stripper to blow hot air into the air intake for a minute or so. Then she'll start.

❖ Other preventive measures ❖

As an alternative to haul-out, marinas in Rhode Island (USA) ringed the boat with a submerged hose into which had been drilled little holes (about 2mm diameter) every 300mm or so. One end of the hose is blocked and the other connected to a low pressure air pump on the pontoon. The rising bubbles prevent the water freezing

Ice in the bassin at Pont L'Eveque as the thaw begins.

round the boat. Another method we saw was to get a length of fireman's hose and fill it with closed cell foam, and then ring the boat's waterline with it. It took the pressure and movement of the ice.

I'd like to quote from *Hamilton's Broads Navigation* (edited by Jamie Campbell) ... 'Pushing a boat through ice, particularly one with a glassfibre hull, is a remarkably quick way to sink a boat. During winter and surrounded by ice, it may take a long while for anyone to find you.' That's good advice.

When we first bought *Hosanna* at Starum (Stavoren) in Friesland in January, we had to leave her for a fortnight to arrange our voyage to England. We bought a gas bottle and a small gas heater that screwed into the top, and we left this alight in the engine room, at very low setting, while away. When we returned we found the boat iced in with eight centimetres of sheet ice all round, except for a three-metre semi-circle abreast the engine room. In that semi-circle, about a dozen ducks were gratefully swimming. It took us a full day to break out of the ice and get under way. Though the canal at Starum was frozen, the Ijsselmeer was not. (It was rough, though.)

This has been a gloomy section but these things can be coped with, and they have not spoiled our pleasure to any significant degree. By recognising danger, you are half way to coping with it. It is an infrequent problem for the pleasure navigator. Just be aware of it.

Waterway interludes:

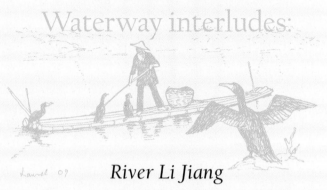

Lauvel 09

River Li Jiang

When we were given the chance in Guelin, China, of a boat trip on the River Li Jiang, we seized our opportunity. We rattled round our hotel, six of us in a building meant for hundreds. There were three Japanese, whom we bonded with better than the one lonely Swiss, and us two Brits.

Towels appeared with suspicious rapidity after Laurel had called from the bathroom 'No towels!' Was the room bugged?

Guelin is a karst (limestone) landscape of caves and fantastic rocks, narrow mountain peaks, three times as tall as they are wide, scribbled with scarps and clothed with twisted pine that Chinese artists have made famous in countless beautiful drawings. As the Guide leaflet told us, 'the picturesque landscape is exceedingly gorgeous'.

The tourist boat was closed in with windows – just as well as it was winter. We could see on shore the Chinese sitting in their blue padded jackets outside their cottages in the cold, round a brazier fed with the cowpats we could see drying against the whitewashed walls.

At the back of the boat a large area open to the weather was also occupied with braziers, but these were covered with steaming cauldrons and cooking pots, tended by hearty women, red-faced and smiling with huge stirring spoons like oars.

As we watched the scenery, we were given rice wine, and bowls of nuts. Fishermen with wide straw hats poled close to us on flat punts, each with one or two tame cormorants perched beside them, their necks ringed so that they could swallow only the tiniest of the fish they caught for their masters.

Lunch came with a mouth-watering waft of fish and spices, prawns and rice and deliciously unfamiliar vegetables, as we watched the rocks and hills slide by, and were told their names: Piled Silk Hill, Elephant Rock, Nine Horse Fresco Hill, Solitary Beauty, and Reed Flute Cave, which we visited in the afternoon. This was a wonderland of stalactites and stalagmites, with clever lighting to highlight the vast magnificence of it.

'Where rivers wind like ribbons of blue silk
And hills stand up like hairpins of green jade'

· 14 ·

Rivers

Having discussed boat types, we must consider the waters that they will navigate. These consist of lakes, rivers and canals. We set aside lakes because the smaller ones are like bits of river while big lakes are, in effect, inland seas, and outside our remit.

Most of your serious waterway cruising will be on canals but here we cover some specific points relating to rivers.

In *Rivers of the World* by Eberhard Czaya, his list of major European rivers is headed by the Volga, followed by the Danube. The Rhône comes more than halfway down the list. The Thames and Severn, Britain's longest rivers, are mere brooks; there are ten Thames's to one Danube, and two Danubes equal one Amazon.

Some rivers are canalised, but their significant characteristics are more river than canal. On true river navigations there are no locks at all, but these are rare. Most rivers used for inland navigation have a lock or two, otherwise the navigation can become too hairy.

The chief noticeable difference between rivers and canals is the current flow. If fully canalised, this is small, but big rivers used by larger craft have few locks and strong currents. In this category come the Rhine and Danube. In both of these we have experienced severe flood currents of about 20 kilometres per hour or 11 knots. This flow rate is hazardous and the river commissioners forbid pleasure navigation (even all navigation) in such circumstances. We experienced suspensions often on the Rhine and the Danube, also on the Rhône and the Meuse, and one can only wait until it becomes safe to navigate. In Europe, these floods occur mainly in spring when the ice and snow of the Alps and other mountain ranges are melting, but there can be violent thunderstorms in summer, causing flash floods and chaos because the lowlands that were once flood plains acting as a safety valve, have now been drained or concreted; the rivers have been straightened, trees cut down and there are no obstructions to inhibit the spread of floodwater.

Navigation on these rivers is controlled by Commissions with awesome powers. They expect rules to be kept, and the amateur is advised to check carefully and make sure he does not unwittingly contravene them.

It follows that rivers are more hazardous than canals, and boats should be well equipped to deal with the problems that arise.

❖ Mooring on rivers ❖

Finding a mooring, given that most facilities are reserved for commerce or for the huge hotel-boats, can be tricky. These latter craft, comparative new-comers to the river, have usurped many of the quays once dedicated to amateurs. They have absolute priority, even over cargo boats, based on rules that date back to the days before good roads, when passenger boats carried the mails and were often the only means of transport. It is no use arguing with them; it's best to make friends. We have often been allowed to make fast alongside one of them while visiting local shops, but don't expect an overnight stay for they often navigate by night. It interests us that passengers travelling through regions with excellent cuisine seem to prefer to dine on board. No nasty surprises that way, we suppose; no tripe sausage or frog legs.

Where the big rivers pass developed regions and/or cities, you will often find marinas in a side cut. These are pricey because marina construction and administration is costly in places liable to flood.

❖ Weirs and hydroelectric stations ❖

There are some alarming weirs (the upper Meuse for instance) where one finds a gaping waterfall close alongside your boat just as you leave the upper gates of a lock and have not gathered steerage way. An unpleasant surprise, as the water flow runs sharply towards the weir, sucking your boat towards the danger, particularly during times of spate. There are not always warning signs, so watch out!

At Schweinfurt on the Rhine/Main/Donau Kanal, the boat moorings are adjacent to the entry to a hydro-electric plant. Make sure your moorings in urban areas are not merely nautically secure but padlock them too, as idle soldiers from the nearby US Army base thought it fun to cast our boat adrift. (See *Back Door to Byzantium*). We have experienced this juvenile prank three times (once in Savannah, close to the US Marines training base,) and also in Cambrai, for which latter it is unlikely that Uncle Sam's soldiers were responsible.

❖ Estuaries and traffic control ❖

Estuaries count as rivers. In the big estuaries, expect to find the sea-going rule of the road rigidly enforced, especially Rule 9B. Often there is traffic control and small craft must check in and keep to specified channels so as not to impede the big ships, usually driven by on-board pilots. Give a wide berth to ferries whose captains are licensed pilots, always in a hurry to maintain schedule. They need a wide berth because their hulls are designed for ease of manoeuvring at each turn-round, and not for smooth economical passage through the water. They make a lot of wash.

Maritime VHF is obligatory. A low powered, hand-held set is not adequate, though one of these, in addition to the ship's set, is useful. If you use it for shopping or chat, do not use a channel in frequent use by shipping as it is illegal.

Samois-sur-Seine. PHOTO: MAISON DÉPARTMENTAL DU TOURISM DE SEINE ET MARNE

Other highly regulated rivers that need a mention are the Scheldt in Holland and Belgium, and the Rhine; the Hudson and the canal connected to it in the USA. Check the rule book; it is draconian and needs to be. Rivers like the Savannah and Potomac pose no problems, just avoid any commercial traffic. Keep to waters too shallow for big ship use, you are safer there.

The Mississippi and Ohio rivers are something else. The barge tows there can be bigger than those on the Danube, big enough to cause problems.

The St Lawrence river is not that simple either, but it improves the further inland that you go. The estuarial region round Prince Edward Island is worth exploring for the abundance of lobsters and friendly people, but that is virtually sea cruising.

We mentioned earlier that together we have navigated many other rivers. Most of those are out of the scope of this book. They tend to come under the heading of 'Adventure', which is not our present subject.

· 15 ·
Canal systems

❖ The origins of canals ❖

Canals were built as a means of moving freight that could not be carried by horse or by river. They existed in the biblical countries now known as Iraq almost 3000 years ago, and they had some sort of lock, not thought to have been the modern double-gate type, but rather a single gate and haul-up-a-slope system, probably based on slave labour which was then plentiful. (Most civilisations have advanced by exploiting slave labour, an uncomfortable thought.)

The Romans used rivers and canals. Fine engineers as they were, they could not transport their armies' baggage trains by cart even over their superior roads. Mostly, they used rivers, and where there were no rivers, they often dug canals. There are traces of Roman canals as far apart as Lincolnshire and Romania. Their canals were all in flat land, usually through marshes; and for centuries, canal development was limited by the fact that most land levels changed arbitrarily.

It was not until the modern double-gated chamber lock was invented in the 15th century that canal building expanded outside the flatlands close to river systems. This seems to have originated in the region round Milan, in Italy; and we give more detail in the chapter on locks. Even then, canals existed mainly in flattish lands. By contrast, the French developed their rivers; and the Rhône and Saône rivers were busy, but the watershed was crossed by mules until the cargo could be re-loaded on the River Loire. At that time canals as we know them did not exist.

The main factor relevant to modern times is that canal freight is hugely eco-friendly compared with other mass transport systems.

The table below explains why. It is a comparison by European Union environmental consultants of the environmental costs of road, rail, and canal/river.

	Pollution	Accidents	Noise
Road	2.36	1.78	0.87
Rail	0.33	0.12	0.70
Barge	0.34	0.01	0.01

The figures assume that railways are electric-powered, of which 20 per cent is hydro-electricity. These are revealing figures, no surprise that eco-mad European legislators get excited about canal and river traffic. However, shifting loads of a mere 350 tonnes by canal would not be economic, they decided. So there would be no subsidy for the traditional *péniche*, though massive subsidies would continue for their rivals the railways, which have powerful trade unions. The road transport lobby in Europe is equally powerful and also receives huge hidden subsidies.

❖ The English canal system ❖

This is very well covered in the English language by existing books and periodicals written by those better qualified in this respect than ourselves. See our bibliography in the Appendix.

❖ France ❖

Out of the 38,000 kilometres of canals and canalised rivers in Europe, 8,500 are in France – more than any other country.

The subject of canals in general is impossibly diverse and leads us to start with an overview of the French system. It is typical, being old, with occasional up-dates, and so includes most features of European canal life. It is also moderately well-organised without the heavy handedness of the efficient Dutch and German systems. The French are pragmatic and bend their rules here and there, which is easier for foreigners. As the French canal system is so extended and relatively novice-friendly, we will cover this country in some detail and discuss other European systems in general terms.

A brief history of French canals

Water transport has existed in France since Roman times, generally confined to the big rivers: Seine, Rhône, Loire, and Garonne. (The Rhine was not then part of France.)

After the invention of the gated lock, canals were dug, not primarily for freight traffic, but for political reasons. The early canal between Bordeaux and Sète had only a modest incentive from trade – largely the transport of English wool to Italy. It was more involved with the war between France and Spain, and Colbert thought his galleys could thus take the Catalans in Barcelona by surprise. Later, Napoleon thought of taking ships through, thus evading the Royal Navy at Gibraltar, but Napoleon did not understand shipping. The idea would never have flown.

France had huge expanses of interior and not much coastline so they needed routes for heavy transit both north/south and east/west.

After Germany defeated France in the war of 1870 and annexed Alsace and Lorraine, France was in a mess. Lorraine is rich in coal and iron, and France had to look for imports of these materials from elsewhere. Far-sighted men like Simon and Freycinet had long advocated massive canal and rail development, now this became urgent.

They turned towards Flanders and its coalfields. New steelworks were built round Dunkerque. The railways were insufficient to carry the quantities of raw material needed.

Belgium had developed a standard barge of about 350 tonnes capacity which they called a *péniche*. (The Dutch called it a *katz*.) They were built of wood. Freycinet decided to make this size the new standard and started to build canals to suit this measurement. This appears to be the first time the word *péniche* was used on the French canals. Today, the barges are mostly referred to as *bateaux* and those that man them are *batelliers*, though the word mariniers is used further south. France had traditionally localised names for their barges, such as *besognes, chalandes, coches, berrichons*, just as the Dutch use a multitude of names to this day. In France, the old names have largely disappeared. You may hear a *péniche* referred to as a '38', its nominal length.

A whole network of new canals was constructed serving the north-east and extending down the rivers Oise and Marne to reach Paris. The Belgian *péniche* was the standard, though the French started to build them of iron instead of wood. The River Seine was dredged and navigation improved.

France was in despair after their defeat by Germany and there is no doubt that Charles de Saulce, Baron de Freycinet, known by his nick-name as *la souris blanche* (white mouse) ranks as one of the heroes of his country alongside Gambetta, because in this, as in so many matters of infrastructure, he transformed the north of the country and made its industry possible. He ignored the south, which he felt could be dealt with later.

Modern French canals

The 350 tonne Freycinet standard served the nation well up to, and including, the First World War, but after that it needed updating. The system was badly damaged in the fighting, especially round Péronne and St Quentin, and on the Meuse. By now, larger canals were needed, and Dunkerque was connected to Lille and also to the river Oise, and thus to Paris.

Today even larger canals are needed. At one point France looked like getting them, but the recent (2008/9) economic turmoil will inevitably delay progress and perhaps threaten the whole concept. It does not take much to delay new canal ventures.

The French government, for example, planned a large-scale new Rhine-Rhône canal and even went so far as to vote the money for it some 20 years ago. It never happened. The French government changed and the new party supported the powerful logic of the rail and road transport unions. The French *routiers* (lorry drivers) have an industrial habit when upset, of loading their 40 tonne trucks with objectionable freight and parking them on important railway level crossings and letting their tyres down, thus effectively blocking two major transport systems. For reasons not unconnected with the French constitution and probably dating back to the Revolution, the Gendarmerie cannot, will not, or dare not interfere. France comes to a halt.

The *mariniers* (or *bargees*), have not the clout to carry out this sort of industrial action. The consequence is that the privately owned *péniche* is ignored and is gradually going to the wall while the European Union spends fortunes on overcrowded roads and railways. (See our pollution table above!)

In our opinion, what France needs in 2009/10 is to connect:

- The Rhine and the Rhône,
- The Sensée with Paris, and then
- Paris with the Saône/Rhône.

The remaining (*gabarit Freycinet*) canals would serve local interests and tourism (which cannot be overlooked). It must be realised that canals are international, like motorways, and need to be built to a common standard. Then we could get freight off the roads where it kills people and pollutes the air. The Paris/Sensée link will probably go ahead because (so my French country-dwelling friends tell me) Paris usually gets what it wants. These proposed developments would leave the uneconomic minor canal system generally uncluttered.

What is actually happening, now, on French inland waters? Commercial cargo-carrying has changed little for some years, but the government has gone flat-out for mass water-borne tourism, which has blossomed. Not satisfied with having turned their coastline into one long marina interspersed with short stretches of beach, they are doing something similar to their canals.

Canals cost money to maintain and as commercial revenue on smaller canals fell, France, in common with the rest of Europe, faced a re-think. In England we long ago abandoned our canals as serious freight-carriers because a narrowboat held only as much as a lorry and a half. In Europe, a Freycinet *péniche* carries about 350 tonnes, almost 10 lorry loads, and even that is uneconomic, except that some canny shippers of grain reasoned that if the barge took a month to get from the wheat-fields of Picardie to Sète on the Mediterranean coast they were both shifting and storing the product at the same time.

For the waterway cruiser, reduction in commercial traffic on the minor canals is good news albeit unecological. Traders in a hurry, which we *plaisanciers* generally are not, could traverse much of Europe swiftly on large waterways. Usually we are more relaxed and we can luxuriate in little backwater canals among the foliage. The trouble is that in France, the main canal authority (Voies Navigables de France, or VNF) is hiving off the smaller, uneconomic canals to regional governments or even to *départements*, who do not have the funds to maintain them well unless they can get hold of Brussels' millions, which, fortunately for us in this context, the French seem able to do with comparative ease. Thus the charming Canal de la Somme is being run (some say run down) by Picardie.

Heavy transport travels on the *grand gabarit*, or major canals, and tourism finds itself among the picturesque.

Tourism on French canals is mainly in charter boats hired out by large companies, as on the Norfolk Broads. Boat hire in France was developed as an off-shoot by a Broads company and, for a time, used ex-Broads cruisers that failed to meet the raised safety standards in Norfolk. Now, the French have their own excellent companies offering well-designed boats. If you like your holiday boat to look good, watch out for the *péniche*ttes, deservedly popular.

Alas, the success of the hire-boat business and its profitability leads to several contradictions in the way navigators are treated by the state, for instance in the case of qualifications.

Certificate of Competence

If you *own* a boat, you are required to have a certificate of competence. Getting this is a chore. On the other hand if you *charter* a boat of say 15m (49ft) length, and have never been afloat before, you may drive it away from the boatyard *sans permis et sans souci*, without a certificate and without a care in the world. So influenced by the enormous economic gains from water-tourism, authorities allow you to hire something large and lethal with no permit whatsoever, a privilege undreamed of if you were merely the owner of a small boat out for your weekend spin. There are draconian rules for owner-drivers who are generally much more experienced and competent than an insouciant holidaymaker who sees no danger and may have had a liquid lunch.

The boat charter business is big money nationally and the operators have clout. Individual boat-owners have no clout unless organised into an association and then it depends on the energy of the association. The RYA, for example, does not bother much about British yachtsmen on Continental inland waterways. The French equivalent of the RYA is sleepy. The DBA has some influence because its representatives on Continental committees are knowledgeable, but it still lacks the clout of being a big constituency. At least VNF consult it. The European Boating Association is poorly supported by the rest of Europe.

During the holiday season, the nicer parts of the French canal system will be crowded by charter boats full of holiday-makers who neither know nor care about the niceties of canal life. There is an etiquette, but they do not know it. On board is a rule-book of sorts because we are all driving large, expensive and potentially dangerous machines. Sadly, although there are written navigational rules which establish a mechanism which is the oil that makes the machine run smoothly, the etiquette is not written down. Private owners learn it, sometimes at the wrong end of a shouting match with an irate professional. We in our turn don't relish a fight with the idiot who has just cut in to the lock ahead of us.

Haltes Nautiques

One of the benefits of the new French attitude to water tourism is that local authorities bordering the canals are encouraged to develop *haltes nautiques*. These nautical stopping places offer a short length of quay heading usually about 25m (82ft) long, but occasionally longer, with cleats, bollards or rings, which have basic

Port du Somail, Canal du Midi. PHOTO: LE BOAT

facilities depending on its isolation. In some, one can find a simple 6-amp electricity socket of the domestic type, use of which is sometimes free. If there is a charge it may appear exorbitant, because the council uses the electricity charge to cover the general cost of the berth.

Some have fresh water laid on, and often there is a placard announcing what stores and services are available at what distance in the nearby village. This is magnificent service and the costs for the boat owner (if any) are reasonable. Barge owners take care, however. Often there is insufficient space for a barge, especially if there is already one boat moored there. Many of these *haltes* are not intended for barges, and the pontoons are sometimes lightweight and the bollards not strong. Barges beware.

If you are the driver of a modest-sized boat, please resist the temptation to moor in the centre of such a quay and thus leave no room for any largish boat at either end. Large barges might moor alongside you, overlapping you at either end, and using you as a fender.

At larger centres one may find a *base nautique*, a grander version of a *halte*, often having a man in charge, who will extract a fee. These have 15 amp sockets and fresh water. Usually, there are showers and lavatories. Occasionally there is some sort of boat service company operating.

Warning! Private boats like to cruise in the autumn and early spring, but many of these *haltes nautiques* close down for the winter and do so as early as 1st October in some places and do not open until May. One can see the logic at places such as Langres, on the main north/south watershed at an elevation of 1000m (3278ft), where it freezes in winter, and it is reasonable to cut off the water. It is also reasonable to cut off electricity at country *haltes*, because otherwise the non-tourist free-loaders move in, of whom there are many by the canals. Pontoons get vandalised during a winter without supervision, as happened at La Bassée, where a good mooring pontoon had been ripped to pieces and its wooden planking stolen. Unfortunate, as this is one of the rare locations where there is a supermarket close by. Still, VNF ought to reconsider whether as a general policy winter closure is desirable.

The last time we navigated the Rhône (2005) there were signs of similar facilities developing there, sorely needed as big barge moorings are not convenient. There were already '*plaisance*' pontoons outside the large locks for waiting pleasure boats. The rule in 2005 was that the locks on the Rhône, which cost a lot for each working, would not open for one lone pleasure boat. One had to form a convoy of 3, or wait for a commercial barge and lock through with him. After 30 minutes of fruitless wait, a benevolently inclined lock-keeper would take pity on you. Ideally one keeps station on a big barge and shares his locks, but not only do they leave the lock first, but they go at some speed when in the big rivers. The smaller Freycinet-sized barges might go at a speed you can manage, but there are not so many of these on the Rhône, which is dominated by huge petrol-carriers and even by sea-going ships adapted to go up-river. It seems that the facilities for pleasure boats waiting at locks on River Rhône are now (2009) much improved.

Stoppages

Stoppages (*arrêtes de navigation* in French; see drawing on page 75) are an unexpected halt to all navigation. You may be stuck in the midst of nowhere for days if there is an accident or breakdown in a lock, or on a stretch of water. This happens now and then, but is usually all over in a few hours. We experienced it at Chaumont when a strong gale brought several trees down across the canal. In 2008, we heard

of such an event on the Canal de la Marne a la Saône (in process of being renamed). A lock gate collapsed and trapped a number of boats, commercial and pleasure, on passage to the Med. This was an emergency, so it was arranged that a team of *éclusiers* would rig emergency gates and pass the barges manually. They passed three barges a day. The plan did not allow pleasure craft to pass. It was the professional *mariniers* who protested and demanded that the pleasure boats should be allowed their turn. This magnanimity should be recognised.

The longer, planned stoppages are called *chômages* in France. An annual *Liste de chômages* is published which announces, well in advance, long-term closures scheduled for essential maintenance. Get it from the VNF web-site, or from any VNF office. It usually comes out in the New Year.

Faraway starts her cruising life. Here she is moored (well fendered) at Peronne, Canal du Nord.

No, this is not an English canal scene, this narrowboat *Vector* is moored at Sereaucourt, Picardy on the river Aisne. Proof positive that narrowboats can cross the Channel safely.

▲ The Blue Flag rally,
La Villette, 2007; view of
the basin.

◄ There was an
impressive collection of
barges gathered together
at the Blue Flag rally.

▶ A *tjalk* is festively
dressed overall for the
occasion.

*PHOTOS: PAUL GOLDSACK
AND THE DBA*

▲ The tunnel at Riqueval over the Canal de St Quentin requires vessels to have a compulsory tow as it is 5670 metres long.

◀ Barge *Biggles* in a lock.

▼ *Cormorant* in Bastille Tunnel

▲ Tarmonbarry lock on the River Shannon.

▶ Pont du Coq.

▼ The St Nicholas lifting bridge opens to allow traffic on the River Aa.

French commercial *peniches* wait whilst the canal is closed at Creve-coeur, Canal de St Quentin.

The fortified town of Bergues, near Dunkerque, has its own tiny canal, measuring only 8 kilometres.

This 15-metre boat moored at Cambrai has a folding crane which is used for loading a car and a dinghy.

A typical pleasure cruiser, complete with bicycles for exploring the countryside, leaves the lock at Sempigny on l'Oise.

▶ Auberge Bon Humeur near Sancerre, France.

▼ A visit to Castelnaudary on the Canal du Midi, southern France, would not be complete without sampling their famous cassoulet, a dish of haricot beans, Toulouse sausages, pork and preserved duck or goose.

Hosanna *crosses the Pont-canal du Briare.*

We were once held up for days in the company of several loaded barges, far from shops and telephones, and with the canal bank inaccessible to crane ashore the cars that most of them carried. A meeting was held. A band of disaffected Frenchmen usually forecasts direct action, and VNF wished to avoid a riot. Fresh bread daily (or, even better, twice a day) is one of the rights of man as far as the French are concerned, so they organised bread deliveries. (We mentioned *rien sans peine* as a motto: there is also *rien sans pain*.) When French workers take 'action' the Gendarmerie usually do not interfere and government officials try to pacify the disaffected. Why French *fonctionnaires* (civil servants) have not learned to negotiate (as VNF did) after the protest but before the 'action' is beyond us. The worst example we came across was the unexpected closure of noted oyster beds for health reasons in the week before Christmas, when everyone in France eats oysters, and one-third of the annual oyster business is done. The ostrei-culturists barely hesitated. To make their point they burned down the government health laboratories.

If you wish to dig further into the history of French canals, read *Histoire des Canaux, Fleuves Et Rivières de France* by Professor Pierre Miquel, published by Edition°, ISBN 2-863-91620-3. Quite apart from its historical content, this book is written in beautiful language and will much improve your French grammar.

We next cover other canal systems and then outline the practical aspect of waterway dimensions.

❖ Germany ❖

There has been expenditure on some large canal systems in Europe. The Rhein–Main–Donau Kanal was completed, largely because it was part of the peace settlement and Germany was bound by treaty to do it. They did not exactly hurry: commitment made in 1946, job done 1992, not how we normally think of German efficiency. The second part of this project, the canalisation of the River Danube, was blocked by the Green Party, who did not want their beautiful river lined in concrete. It wasn't planned to be: there would be a lock every 20 miles, and then only in lengths with a steep gradient. The locks would generate hydro-electric power which would have been a 'green' benefit. It was voted out and now a new autobahn carries truck traffic with 40 times the air pollution of barge traffic. Such illogical hair-trigger opposition discredits more sensible Green supporters.

The German guide books are clear if you can cope with the word lengths. We treat them as word puzzles, working out how to divide the indigestible long words into meaningful bites.

River tourism in Germany is almost entirely by hotel boat, or short-stop passenger craft. It follows that a 12m (39ft) boat, or worse still a small barge, is not catered for. Having said that, there are wonderful places to visit alongside German rivers, so be insistent; find a mooring.

Provision of moorings

Germany has not got round to providing municipal moorings for pleasure craft, which in their experience are the size of a soap dish. Private marinas have few berths for larger boats. If you find a possible mooring, you will have to puzzle out for yourself whether or not you are allowed.

In Germany, they told us, everything is forbidden unless it is specifically allowed. Well, blow that for a game of marbles, if we followed that rule we would never have been able to moor anywhere. We became selectively blind to notices and if caught, blamed poor language skills. This is OK, provided you can work out which types of boat are *verboten*, for at every mooring there are always several types that are expressly not allowed.

The old town hall, Bamburg, Rhine-Main-Danube canal.

124

Moorings for pleasure barges are almost non-existent, and huge hotel boats have priority everywhere. We aroused a good deal of interest with our 27m (88ft) barge *Hosanna*, and with a little ingenuity usually found ourselves a place to stop, though sometimes with difficulty.

For the Rivers Main, Altmuhl and Danube (Donau in German) see elsewhere in this book. For more detailed, informative and reliable information on Germany in general, there are books written by those better informed than we are (see below and Bibliography).

Documents required

You will need your Certificates of Competence, insurance, and VAT. In addition for the Rhine, you will need a Rheinpatent if over 20m (65ft) length, otherwise you must take a pilot.

Maps and guides

Rhein Handbuch 1 published by DSV-Verlag ISBN 3-88412-156-1
Main, Main-Donau Kanal, Donau by Horn and Hoop ISBN 3-89225-254-8
Slow Boat through Germany by Hugh Mcknight, published by Adlard Coles Nautical

Types of boat

Pleasure boats in Germany are mostly very small. Commercial traffic, on the other hand, can be huge, fast, and frightening.

Types of lock

There is often a *sportbootsschleuse*, a small lock alongside the big one. In *Hosanna*, we were too big to use these and had to wait our turn for a place in the *grossschiffahrtsschleuse* or big lock, listening anxiously for the command on the VHF '*Englander, komm gleich*'. Sizes of small locks varied from 22m x 3.5m (72ft x approx 11^1/$_2$ft) down to 12m x 2.5m (39ft x approx 8ft).

❖ Belgium ❖

Belgium has an extensive and busy canal system, not as a rule as well-maintained as the French or German canals, and a lot worse than the Dutch. In Belgium, even on the main canals, you will find crumbling banks, unmarked dangers and a lack of tolerance towards amateurs.

There are beautiful and historic towns to visit in Belgium, and the welcome is there, but if you come by boat you are second-class tourists.

Provision of moorings

There are few provisions for pleasure boats that are not in marina-like surroundings and few stopping places on the canals themselves. Some of the older traditional temporary moorings are now forbidden, notably that by the windmills at Brugge.

Documents required

You will need your Certificates of Competence, insurance and VAT. This requirement is better than Germany, but not as good as France and Holland.

Maps and guides

Belgian Waterways (Geocart)
Michelin Green Guide (Belgium)

Types of lock

Sometimes these are ill-maintained, which can mean a long wait. The notorious lock at Evergem has been rebuilt at last.

❖ Netherlands ❖

The Dutch waterways are a delight, especially when away from the heavy hand of the state. We prefer the remoter parts in Friesland, which Hollanders treat as a backward region where time moves slowly. Dutch canals vary from small branch canals to busy and enormous main routes. The dimensions vary as do the services. Unlike the rest of Europe, one can get soil tanks emptied at many places, and at the main service stations, oil can be sucked from the engine room bilges if you have been unlucky enough to spill any. We have had generous assistance from Dutch barge families, usually without having to ask for it, for these people have an eye for boat problems.

Certain waterways in Holland are regulated by *Rijnvaartpolitiereglement*, meaning Rhine rules. These waters also cover the Waal, Lek and the Pannerdens Canal.

The Dutch people know how to welcome boats, they are a maritime nation, and a live-aboard barge is no surprise to them, as it was to the people of Hungary and Romania. Consequently you will find all that you need.

Provision of moorings

The facilities for boats of all sizes are excellent.

Documents

Take the usual documents: Certificates of Competence, insurance and VAT. Plus you must carry at all times (by law) the *ANWB Almanak of Watertoerisme*, (two volumes, in Dutch, with long pages of dense text and little punctuation.) The only pages we understood were the coloured ones with diagrams, until we discovered a few pages in English on page 27 of Vol 2. There is a valuable glossary.

Maps and guides

AWNB Almanak Volumes 1 and *2* (obligatory)
AWNB Vaarwaterkaart van Nederland

Havengids Nederland (Vetus) or similar
Dutch Inland Sailing Pilot or similar
(There are many alternatives to the above two.)
Green Guide Netherlands (Michelin)

Types of lock
These are modern, or at least well maintained, as at Terneuzen, which is operated with impressive efficiency and a short waiting time.

Types of boat
You will come across all types but generally in good seaworthy condition.

For further information and other waterways see Chapter 16 on waterway dimensions.

A CHECKLIST OF DOCUMENTS

- A permit to drive your boat, if appropriate (eg Certificate of Competence).
- A certificate of registration and/or ownership.
- A radio operator's licence.
- Evidence of payment of VAT, if appropriate.
- A certificate of third-party insurance, usually in the language of the country being visited (check).
- A crew list showing details of all on board.
- Passports for everybody on board.
- Visas if appropriate.

Take cash in local currency if you have not got a visa in advance and need to purchase one on entry. In less sophisticated countries, take a few hundred US dollars in small denominations.

· 16 ·
Waterway dimensions

At sea, your boat can be as big as you are qualified to manage. This affects many of us, especially those who envisage an occasional open-sea passage between inland systems in different countries.

For generations, Britain had no general limits on the size of pleasure boats. Nowadays, international rules (Europe) say that above 24m (79ft) the vessel *shall* be in the charge of a suitably qualified master mariner and (at sea) carry a certificated engineer. Smaller craft are exempt. There is a limit (< 20m/65ft) on the size of amateur-driven boats on the River Rhine.

This rule does not extend to the inland waters of all countries. The USA allows its inland waters to be used by foreigners without any documents other than a 3-month visa and a 6-month cruising permit. There is a commendable voluntary urge among responsible Americans to acquire some boat-handling instruction. In Europe, by the time this appears in print, the European Union may have settled on a sensible common cruising policy. See also Appendix, page 200.

❖ What physical parameters restrict your craft? ❖

The important waterways dimensions (after draught) are those which enable passage through locks. Most congenial waterways have the occasional lock, even the US Intracoastal at Great Bridge, (though that is big enough for any pleasure boat). The French, being a logical race, organised their water transport rather better than anybody else. The much-vaunted Dutch system has efficient locks and bridges, but with varying dimensions, and this means that they have dozens of different types of boats on their inland waters. The French could not tolerate so idiosyncratic an approach, and we have explained how Baron Freycinet rationalised the French canal system and introduced the *gabarit* (gauge or outline) named after him.

Here is a selection of the most significant waterway dimensions, country by country:

❖ Great Britain ❖

The main part of the 19th century narrow system has maximum dimensions of locks of 21m (70ft) and a beam of 2.1m (7ft). There are however shorter locks such as the Bridgewater and Taunton Canal that has locks of 15m (50ft) so check all lock dimensions when planning your cruise. Experts tell me that they have had no trouble with boats drawing less than 1m (3ft). Generally a height (air draught) of 2.7m (7ft) is considered a working maximum, but there are some lower bridges and tunnels. Some parts of the narrow system were subsequently widened to 4.2m (14ft). Some of the southern canals have a lower air draught. Canals available to wide boats are separated by some narrow locks near Leicester, which effectively, (and sadly) cut the British canal system in two. We have not found a publication giving all dimensions for all British canals but many can be found in *The Inland Waterways Manual* by Emrhys Barrell (Adlard Coles Nautical).

The Norfolk Broads have no formal length or beam limitation, but depth of water will limit draught to about 1.4m (5ft). Boats of more than 20m (65ft) length by 3.5m (11^1/$_2$ ft) beam will find the smaller rivers difficult and upper reaches impossible because of mediaeval bridges and bird protection. The River Yare is navigable by cargo coasters up to Cantley so poses no difficulties. Air draught is subject to large variations depending on tides. One should not try to go upstream into the Yare tributaries from Yarmouth without consulting tide tables and Hamilton's excellent *Broads Guide*.

Before navigating the Broads, one must register and obtain a licence for the boat and a certificate under the Boat Safety Scheme is obligatory. Temporary licences are available for visitors. I am not alone in saying that the tolls are unreasonably high, particularly for a visitor's licence. The Broads Authority is concerned with nature and conservation of wild life, and many boat-owners feel that they are unfairly milked for this objective.

The Thames

This river is tidal as far as Richmond. Above Richmond the river locks as far as Sunbury; the dimensions are great enough not to worry pleasure boats, except that max draught is only about 2m (6^1/$_2$ft).

From Sunbury to Staines, the official figures are greater than pleasure boats need worry about, though headroom is down to 5.5m (18ft).

The figures decrease as one mounts the river and one should get the *River Thames Handbook* (published by Imray) for varying details.

The Thames has some of the most draconian regulations we have ever come across, but it is a heavily used river and the authorities, rightly, are determined to keep it clean.

Licences to navigate are required. They are not cheap, and many good boats navigating safely on other waters will not qualify for a licence. See the websites www.visitthames.co.uk and the Port of London Authority www.pla.co.uk.

As well as physical dimensions which limit navigation in Britain, there are several schemes, bye-laws and regulations in force in different parts of Britain. All these are heavy in unnecessary verbiage, but they have some sensible things in common. In these regulations, however, is a plethora of detail taking (literally) hundreds of pages, that ought to be standardised. The powers of bureaucratic and safety-obsessed authorities and their expensive enforcement patrols cannot be ignored and are one reason why we prefer to navigate Continental waters.

❖ France ❖

The *Gabarit Freycinet*, which governs dimensions on French canals gives a lock length of 40m, from which subtract about 1m for the lock sill etc, leaving a length of 39m (NB we are not giving Imperial equivalents in this section.). You will find that the typical Freycinet *péniche* is often referred to as a *trente-huit*, or '38', even though many of them measure a full 39. This gives little room for error in making fast in locks with a disturbed fill-rate. Amateurs should not undertake boats of this size unless they have above-average experience. You would in any case need the PP licence, obtained by practical examination. Even then, we feel that such boats used for pleasure should be well ballasted to minimise their windage, which can cause significant problems when manoeuvring in strong winds. As we write, these qualifications are being revised.

THE FRENCH STANDARD FOR BARGES WHICH CAN LOAD
350 TONNES OF CARGO

39m long
5.05m broad
1.80m depth (draught)
3.40m height (air draught)

For amateurs, a strong bow-thruster is essential in longer craft. We note that commercial barges have always had some form of bow rudder, and nowadays more and more are having thrusters fitted. They know what they are doing and consider that €32,000 is money well spent for a 360° version. The non-rotating version is much cheaper. *Hosanna* had a 14hp hydraulic bowthruster (driven off the main engine) that cost less than £2000 installed. see also page 159.

Lock width is officially 5.1m, but can be slightly less as the lateral inward pressure on lock walls is considerable. We think 5m is an absolute maximum beam and it makes no allowance for fenders so that boats of this breadth rapidly lose their topsides paint in the locks. This minimal tolerance prevents damage caused by the boat being thrown about by turbulent lock-filling while inside the lock. Our new boat, *Faraway*, is 4.6m broad, and this allows for fendering in locks while minimising the way the boat can be thrown about from side to side. We have also a little more margin of error when entering the lock. Though long boats are more directionally stable than short ones, it requires nerves of steel and expertise to thrust 100 tons of steel into a stone-sided opening having only an inch to spare on each side.

Though locks take barges with a draught of 1.8m over their sills, this depth of water is not generally available owing to silting. Depth of water in the French canals has decreased over the years. One of the features of canal maintenance is that a canal well used by commercial traffic, does not need frequent dredging. The loaded barges dredge free of charge just by using it, their hulls pushing aside any accumulated silt while it is still soft. Canals that are now little used are silting up. Some have scarcely more depth than 1.4m, and it is dangerous to assume more than 1.6m. *Hosanna*, drawing 1.5m grounded frequently, especially in the Canal du Centre, which has virtually no deep commercial traffic nowadays. If you are going to cruise widely in Europe, I would consider 1.4m as being a safe working compromise that would take you most places: it gives a good grip on the water while avoiding all but the worst of depth problems. All the same, with a draught of 1.4m, I would advise a moderate deadrise (that is, have the sides a fair bit shallower than the centre of the boat.) This is to facilitate mooring to the bank, for canal depth seldom extends right across the canal. The figure 1.4m for draught is 'safe'. Deeper-draughted boats cruise successfully (they quickly learn how to refloat themselves when they touch ground), but some waters are closed to them.

We said that the Canal du Centre has little commercial traffic these days, but there is still a chance of coming head to head with a big barge rounding a sharp bend, of which there are many on this canal, most having a narrow bridge opening just round the corner, especially in the southern, hillier parts. Empty barges, known as *vides*, draw little water and use this route to avoid heavier traffic.

The bridge clearance (air draught) specified should not be taken too literally as local amendments are caused by 40-tonne lorries that persist in crossing bridges clearly marked with a 7-tonne weight limit, and in one or two of the smaller canals with tunnels, the air-draught has been lowered to accommodate electricity conductors attached to the roof. Check your route carefully, referring to the waterway guides. Don't stand up suddenly in tunnels.

There are canals in France outside the *Gabarit Freycinet*. In the north there are the *Grand Gabarit* canals, most notably the Canal du Nord. Their dimensions should not worry the pleasure sailor.

Canal du Midi

This title is officially apt for only a portion of the journey from Sète to Bordeaux, but is often used to describe the whole experience. *Hosanna* was too big to navigate the canal in the 1980s so we have not sailed it. This was not due to length or breadth, but to arched bridges.

Nevertheless, depth and lengths of locks are being increased and we have been unable to ascertain whether the work is complete. The idea is to improve the length of locks to the Freycinet dimension and eliminate some of the complex staircases (locks in groups). Depth of water is increased and there is hope that depths may be maintained as there are now many ex-commercial barges of deep draught converted to hotel boats. These are the bane of both the pleasure and cargo-carrying navigators alike, as they are allowed absolute priority at locks which is unreasonable on very busy waterways. Some priority is reasonable, if debatable, but no vessel of whatsoever type should have to give way for more than (say) three lock workings.

Air draught for the Canal du Midi

Different guide books give different figures and do not say on what their figures are based:

Inland Waterways of France (Edwards/May)	3.30m
Cruising French Waterways (McKnight)	3.40m
Carte-Guide de Navigation Fluviale (Vergnot)	3.00m

We could go no further than the bridge at Capestang without substantial effort. We took careful measurements of this ancient arched bridge, the most obstructive on the whole navigation. We made a template and found that *Hosanna* could have got through but for a triangular bit either side of the top of the wheelhouse, in other words, the clearance height at 1.7m either side of the centre was 1.9m. As our wheelhouse was made of 4mm steel we decided against surgery. That would have left us with the alternative once used by a friend of ours with the same problem: buy a barrel of wine, and invite the local rugby team and their supporters for a party on board. When the difficulty was explained to them, hundreds turned up and the boat, loaded like the rugby team, got through. We heard of somebody else faced with a similar difficulty at another bridge; he got all the children from a nearby school, and gave them a practical demonstration of the Archimedes principle, a lesson they would never forget. God knows what our health and safety culture would say nowadays.

There are small branch canals off the main system which are officially Freycinet but which have deteriorated and are no longer maintained to the standard. You have to take these as you find them because VNF, (the canal authority) do not know either. VNF is organised into sections that seem to do as they please regarding operating methods and maintenance. By and large, the system works, but one area often has no idea what is happening further down the line. Check with the VNF for the area in which you are cruising.

❖ Belgium ❖

Belgium has an enormous mileage of waterways. Many are of the larger gauge and should not worry us at all, and that leaves a substantial length of canals to an approximation of the Freycinet standard. Because of taxation differences, many of the Continent's commercial barges are registered in Belgium or Luxembourg, though largely crewed and operated by Dutch or French interests. Some waterways, notably

Péniches are a perfect fit in French Gabarit Freycinet locks.

that between Brugge and Ostend, have not been fully improved for large barges, but nevertheless, large barges use them. Expect anomalies like this in Belgium, the land of shrugged shoulders.

❖ Germany ❖

The book we recommend for general information about voyaging in Germany is *Slow Boat Through Germany* by Hugh McKnight (Adlard Coles Nautical). It is a general background book rather than a navigational treatise though sadly out of print now. We voyaged through Germany down the River Danube and found the Germans and their officials perhaps the most pleasant we came across in the whole long voyage, which was a cathartic experience for Bill who has a clear memory of being machine-gunned by the Luftwaffe on his way to school – twice.

Hugh has written an entertaining book, but has dodged the question of dimensions, with good reason. Most of the canals in Germany are capable of passing large commercial barges and pleasure craft are not affected. There are some smaller canals, notably in former East Germany and round Berlin, the River Lahn, for example.

Accurate details can be obtained from the *Weska*, an annual publication in German giving details with commendable German thoroughness, obtainable to order from Stanford's in Long Acre.

❖ The Netherlands ❖

Canal dimensions vary. Much of the canal system takes large cargo carriers and should pose no problem. Dutch locks are controlled with alarming efficiency. Nevertheless, there are smaller canals, most of which conform to Freycinet dimensions. Branches abound with local peculiarities: Katwijk comes to mind for having a very low fixed bridge, 2.50m, but mostly the sensible Dutch have opening bridges for such places. Expect to pay a small sum at these. Bridges do not always (in fact, hardly ever) open on demand. For example, boats wishing to go into Amsterdam must do so after midnight in a special convoy.

So, dimensions vary enormously and one has to ascertain these for the voyage you have in mind. The *Almanak Watertoerisme*, gives dimensional limits on a place-by-place basis in alphabetical order. Beware, some places are not spelled in Dutch as you might expect. No other country, not even France, has even a small proportion of the rules and regulations that are enforced in the Netherlands with ruthless efficiency.

These two volumes contain everything you need to know about the Dutch waterways, the only difficulty is understanding it. What makes the whole legal requirement silly is that the volumes are so prolix that they would take even a Dutchman several hours to read, and we only manage a page or two in that time. There is a glossary at the back giving German and English data. The message is that the Dutch will only tolerate us on their busy waterways if we stick to the rules.

❖ Italy ❖

The Italian waterway system is unconnected to any of the other waterways in Europe. There are several stretches of canal inland from the Po delta. Once there was canal traffic to Milan, now it is built over or abandoned. Several ambitious schemes to re-open the canal have started but we found little that had been finished when we explored the region in 2004. What open waterways we found were for small craft only. Nobody could give us limiting dimensions; we estimate 16m long x 4m x 1.3m. Air draught is dubious as lots of new roads and bridges have been built.

❖ Eastern Europe ❖

An extensive system of canals in the region north of River Danube, in Serbia, is known as the Banat and runs for hundreds of kilometres. This is flat country and the canals serve also to irrigate it. The locks are large but their rise and fall is modest, they would take Danube-style barges. There are no problems with dimensions.

Serbia would like to see these canals put to tourist use but frankly tourist attractions (scenery, cuisine, entertainment etc) are not there, and the distances between settlements are great. The angling is outstanding, the fish enormous, plentiful and apparently suicidal. It is hunting country. For a self-sufficient person keen on nature and solitude, it would be a great place to explore.

We have cruised the river Tissa as far as Szeged where some tourist facilities are provided. The draught is limited to 2m, and the river is subject to sudden and severe floods. One can go further, into Transylvania, but we have no experience and data is difficult to come by. The Drava is navigable to Osiçek and further for smaller craft, no limiting dimensions are available. Reliable data is difficult in eastern Europe;

Hosanna *at Passau on the River Danube.*

everybody claims to know, and is eager to help, but all too often the information has proven 'approximate' to say the least. We have tried to filter and hope figures we quote are reliable.

On our last cruise, the tributary rivers south of the Danube were not usable owing to the risk of getting shot. Now hostilities are over, they are being developed, or ameliorated. The Sava can be navigated above Zagreb by boats up to 30m x 5m, the Kupa by similar sized boats as far as Karlovaç.

The project to connect the Danube with the Aegean Sea for large barges is in abeyance because of political difficulties connected with the internecine strife in former Jugoslavia. There is a proposal for a large canal to connect the Danube with the Adriatic. Do not hold your breath.

❖ Russia and the Ukraine ❖

Not many people have navigated in the inland waters of Russia. Miles Clark's account of a terrible voyage from Arkangel to the Black Sea gives a comprehensive analysis of the system. Dimensions are of no significance to pleasure boats. The Ukraine is more amenable, but we have personal experience only of the northern, and little used, arms of the Danube delta up to the port of Ismaila. These waters take large craft, including fast hydrofoils, and there are no dimensional problems. One boat we know who tried to navigate from the Baltic to the Black Sea, ran into the serious problem of a hydro-electric power station with associated dam which had

Milan's Treff, Bratislava, on the Danube.

been built across the river since the information that they had relied on was out of date. Their 18m boat (a Viking long-boat replica) had to be portaged round the dam. They also had their kit stolen, but that's another story.

There is talk of the route being re-opened. If so, it will debouch at Odessa, which is a yachting port (of sorts).

❖ USA ❖

The Intracoastal Waterway is a popular pleasure navigation and with its offshoots has thousands of miles of safe inland cruising. Relevant dimensions (given here in Imperial only) are only those of depth: boats' draughts should be less than 6ft 6in, and preferably less than 6ft. In our ketch *Fare Well* drawing 6ft 9in, we twice navigated this waterway and only had problems at low water in certain Florida inlets. Parts of the waterway close to sea inlets are tidal. The northern part (from Delaware to New Jersey) was too shallow altogether. We were told that 4ft was the maximum there so we went round by sea.

Another canal that is well used is the New York State Barge Canal, which accommodates all sizes of pleasure boats with no difficulties.

The Mississippi offers no dimensional problems to small craft. The locks are enormous, and above Cairo (one can get confused by place names in the USA) one can carry 9ft all the way through to the Great Lakes.

Other canals in the USA are mostly restored in short lengths for 'heritage' purposes and do not concern us. On the west coast there are busy pleasure canals on the Snake River delta but it seems there are no locks and that reasonable pleasure boat dimensions are not critical.

❖ Canada ❖

Not many people think of Canada for canal cruising, but their canals are busy. They are now called Heritage canals and are administered by Parks Canada. The principal waterway is the confusingly (for the English) named Severn-Trent waterway. When we were there, boat size was limited to 50 x 13 x 4ft. There is plenty of air-draught. This was because of a boat lift, which has since been improved to take 20 boats (yes 20) together, each of about 60ft in length. There are other pleasure navigations at the Rideau which has two locks of pleasure-boat size. The old Grenville Canal has been modernised with a lock taking vessels up to 200ft long. The Canadian government has committed itself to maintaining the Trent-Severn and Rideau systems for recreational use.

❖ Egypt ❖

The problem with pleasure boat navigation on the Nile is getting there. Apart from obstructionism by the authorities, the local population are helpful, but there is not enough navigable depth of water. The delta thins out and most channels are virtually non-navigable in part. A friend had to have his Wayfarer dinghy transported over a short distance during which it was damaged by well-meaning but over-enthusiastic helpers. Above the delta, most pleasure boats of the non-keel variety should be fine.

❖ Africa ❖

Most of the big rivers in Africa, and they are *big* (the Nile is 17 times the length of the Thames and the Congo and Niger 14 times the size) were once used as main arteries for the carriage of goods and people, and are navigable often for considerable distances. There are few locks and boat size is considerable except for draught; often the rivers run short of water. Consider 1.3m (4.5ft) as a generalisation. Even that would be too deep for some of the rivers I have navigated. This cruising area is not very safe at the moment, but it could be marvellous, and I hope it will become so during the life of this book. There are some longish stretches of canal in Madagascar, too.

❖ China ❖

We have mentioned this because the country is opening up and before the life of this book is over, we confidently expect private boating in China will be permitted. China has 74,000 kilometres of navigable waters including canalised rivers. On the only two 'navigations' we have seen, dimensions would be no problem.

I am sure we have missed some canals somewhere and I apologise. I do not expect we will ever navigate the lot.

Waterway interludes:

The Intracoastal Waterway of the USA (ICW)

Now that it is possible to shift one's boat across oceans as deck cargo, this canal system is worth considering because it is extensive, interesting and one of the world's best cruising areas. We got there the hard way, crossing the Atlantic in a sailing yacht, in the days before the ARC made it less of a challenge.

There are more than a thousand miles of this waterway, running down the east coast of the United States. Man-made canals link rivers and estuaries, and cut through peninsulas to form a protected route from Cape Cod to the Florida Keys. The Okeechobee Waterway crosses Florida from Stuart to Fort Myers on the Gulf of Mexico and the Gulf section of the ICW continues for 1000 miles to Brownsville, Texas, and enables entry to the Mississippi through a lock at New Orleans.

The east coast of the USA is mostly low-lying and swampy with many islands, rivers and creeks. Rivers do not run at right-angles to the coast but meander about. Someone, George Washington perhaps, got the idea of connecting up these assorted creeks, rivers and inlets, and with comparatively little effort had a canal system running from New York to Georgia, so that small craft could pass without having to go to sea (where they risked the Royal Naval blockade). Later, when Florida was added to the States, the waterway went down to the Keys, and eventually across the peninsula to the Gulf of Mexico where it found its way among the swamps to the Mexican border. It was almost all swamp. (In our part of the world we call it marshland.) There you have the Norfolk Broads on a grand scale: birds, fish, oyster and reed-beds and alligators. The names of villages are familiar to East Anglians, and one of the main centres of activity is at Norfolk, Virginia, close to the mouth of the Chesapeake, not far from a canal called the Dismal Swamp Canal.

The excellent guide to its navigation, *The Waterway Guide* in three volumes published annually, nowadays kicks off at Eastport on the Canadian border with New Brunswick just across Passamaquoddy Bay. However, this near-Canadian area with its tidal range of 25ft has little to do with inland waterways, so we'll miss that bit out and start further south, as we did, from Rhode Island.

We had been at John Hall's boatyard in Avondale for three months, during which *Fare Well* had 'convalesced' from damage sustained by being struck by lightning during a hurricane north of Bermuda in June. The kindness and hospitality we had received there had been heartwarming, but our friends were reminding us that winter was coming, everything would freeze, and if we wished to keep moving, it was time to go south.

We left on 20 September, after several wonderful leave-taking parties. It was a grey wet day presaging autumn, as we headed down the Pawcatuck River, past Watch Hill and out to sea, albeit mostly in the lee of Fisher's Island. After sailing for seven hours, we anchored in a strong tide just inside the Connecticut River at Old Saybrook – a hop of 26 miles.

We did only ten miles each of the next two days, as we put into Clinton to look up an old friend whom we had last seen in the West Indies in his yacht *Clarity*. A social week followed with visits back and forth, and the loan of a car for shopping. Then we stitched our way down Long Island Sound to New York, arriving on the eighth day after leaving Rhode Island, which was a distance of 150 miles.

We count Long Island Sound as being inland waters of the estuary type. It has good shelter, and plenty of good harbours, though most of them have few facilities for visitors. At the south-western end you can go into the East River to New York, through Hell Gate, down past the UN headquarters, and moor in downtown New York at Skyport Marina on the East River. We spent some days exploring, as it was much cheaper than a hotel would have been. However, we are not sure whether the facility is still available. It was pretty impressive, coming in to New York through Hell Gate. The skyline was unmistakable (the twin towers were then in place).

The New Jersey part of the ICW actually starts some 22 miles south of Sandy Hook, the southern entrance point to New York Harbour at a place called Manasquan Inlet. It will take you past Atlantic City and down to the Delaware River, but only if you draw less than 4ft, and even then you need to watch the tide. You would be crazy to attempt it without the latest guides. It is an area of shifting shoals, even inland.

As our boat *Fare Well* was too deep a draught to attempt this, we went round by sea. This short sea hop is not difficult and one can wait for good weather. We left New York in mid-morning, giving our salute to the Statue of Liberty as we passed Liberty Island, and were at Manasquan inlet by evening. The distance from New York to Cape May is 160 miles, but there are plenty of places to break your journey. We went on overnight out in the Atlantic Ocean, motor sailing with light winds, reaching Cape May on the following afternoon. We anchored under the watchful eye of the US Coastguard Academy which has apparently unlimited phalanxes of life-jacketed teen-aged personnel eager to advise you, with exaggerated courtesy, on safety matters.

An official-looking craft approached us containing several very young uniformed 'Coastguards', one of whom greeted us politely, asked us our draught (6ft 9in) and requested us to move and anchor nearer the shore. Always obliging, we hauled up the anchor and moved to the space indicated, where we ran hard aground. When we'd got ourselves off, we went back to the spot we'd first thought of, and heard no more. Let us hope the young gentlemen paid attention in the next class on chart reading.

From Cape May inlet, you can make another sea trip round the point or take a short cut through the Cape May Canal with its opening rail bridge. Then you are in the Delaware River where big ships go, but it is genuine inland waters. You motor up-river for 68 nautical miles. (In this book, miles means nautical miles. While in the USA we will use their idiosyncratic version of the Imperial measurement system because that is what Uncle Sam uses.)

We left early in the morning of 6 October, passing through some vicious tide-rips, and after a misty run up the Delaware, not seeing the shore, and keeping a good lookout as this is a big-ship channel, we entered the Chesapeake/Delaware canal (a genuine canal cut through to Chesapeake Bay, 14 miles long) by mid afternoon. We were through it in 2½ hours, and anchored near to a yacht in the Bohemia River. We rafted up for drinks.

Whether Chesapeake Bay can be considered inland waters or not is a moot point. Like the Great Lakes, it is an inland sea, well over 100 miles long. A strong wind blowing its length can raise high waves, but when the weather is good it becomes a wonderful cruising area, especially for sailing yachts. Round Chesapeake, there are country fishing harbours, especially on the Delaware side, where almost every place is named after English towns like Oxford, Cambridge, and Deale. Others are named after people, or with names of native American origin. Further along the Potomac River is Washington.

We spent the next three weeks in the Chesapeake. The sailing was wonderful, and sometimes the weather was too. Everyone in Rhode Island had told us that the fall is the time to see this area; the flaming colours of the trees were reflected in the waters, and the skeins of geese flying south were something we shall never forget. Travelling at this time also avoids the mosquitoes.

We did not hurry. At Baltimore we made friends and visited the inner harbour where we lay next to the schooner *Pride of Baltimore*. Some years later, we were keenly sorry to hear of her loss. We had Naval friends to visit both in Annapolis and St Michael's on the northern shore, and revelled in crab cakes, oysters, chowders, lobsters and fresh fish, a diet we never tire of.

At the southern end of Chesapeake Bay, just inside Cape Henry (the scene of naval battles long ago), we passed the big navy yard of Norfolk on our left. After a couple of days socialising with the Navy, we made a majestic day's run back into the Waterway with two admirals and their houseguests on board. Some of them had never travelled the Intracoastal before. We took in the Great Bridge lock (the only one on the whole system – it serves as a sort of equaliser of levels which would otherwise cause some sharp tidal streams) plus a lifting bridge or two, and it was an interesting as well as a lovely day out. We arrived at Pungo ferry at teatime, our guests left to return to Norfolk, and we spent the night (Halloween, as it happened) gazing at an astonishing full moon.

The next few days we passed many bridges where it was necessary to wait for opening. Sometimes there was a broadening of the canal, or a sound to anchor in, often we berthed at small family marinas, a wooden jetty with a few berths. These marinas were too small to have shops or restaurants but there was always a 'courtesy car' you could borrow to do your shopping – one of these was an ancient jeep with the door handle tied with string and no brakes, but it got us there and back.

NAVIGATION ON THE CANALISED PARTS OF THE ICW

If you draw more than 6ft you must expect to touch bottom on occasions. This should cause little problem (the bottom is generally mud or soft sand) apart from close to the inlets in Florida where one can get stranded if aground at high water. We ran aground in the Little Choptank river, where the depths were 3ft less than charted, but that's what happens.

One memorable experience was a visit to Tony's Sanitary Fish Restaurant in Morehead City. Reputed to serve an astronomical number of fish dinners daily, it was severely disapproving. Notices outside proclaimed 'No drinking, No drunks served.' Inside was a notice 'No fishing out the window' (which looked straight out onto the sound). We had good company, and enjoyed our fish and soft drinks, but Laurel was rebuked by the trap-faced waitress for not finishing all her hush puppies. The chairs were stacked on the tables as we finished, and when the door slammed behind us, they chanted 'Y'all come back again!' It was not yet 7.30pm.

In mid-November we arrived at Hazzard's Marina in Georgetown, South Carolina. We loved it there; the small family marina was very friendly, and we were given the use of the washing machine in the family kitchen and the loan of any of the four cars. We asked young Hap to move their new car so we could get at the older one behind it: 'Hell, take the Lincoln – it's only a car', he said. We hauled out for some repair work and stayed for two months, till late January. We had covered 965 miles since leaving Rhode Island.

Incidentally, Georgetown is named not after George Washington, but after Prince George of England. The local, very old church appears to be dedicated to him rather than to a saint.

The first week of our resumed travelling was freezing, but the weather did not stop us launching the dinghy at Caper's Island, just short of Charleston, and collecting two bucketsful of oysters from the public park. The weather was still chilly when we reached Florida a week later. The girl in the Welcome to Florida kiosk was blue with cold in her summer shorts and T-shirt. She gave us literature and a glass of free orange juice, and we noticed the glowing bar of an electric fire hidden behind her desk.

We cruised down the Florida waterway for the next few weeks, getting gradually into warmer weather, though there were thunderstorms and even a small tornado. Florida is crowded; anchoring is often forbidden at the behest of local riparian residents who wish to avoid having water-gypsies overstaying their welcome too close to their backyard. Every riverside property has a boat at the bottom of the garden, and after experiencing wash from some of the speed-hogs we realised why they were all hoisted well clear of the water on davits when not in use.

Indispensable advice paraphrased from the *Waterways Guide*: 'On the waterways a "fast" boat (> 10 knots) is bound to pass many a "slow" boat (< 10 knots). Yet the simple art of passing and being passed courteously and without unnecessary rolling of the overtaken boat is an area of ignorance for too many ...'

It goes on to say that if the slow boat continues at full speed the overtaking boat is bound to pass at high speed and make waves. So the answer for the slow boat is to ease speed and let the faster boat get past easily and quickly and hope that he will do so at a moderate speed differential. Good theory.

By mid-march we left Kay Biscayne for the Bahamas. We had done 600 miles since Georgetown and had run aground countless times but since the bottom is soft mud not much time was wasted. Our masts gave us no problems as bridges have a minimum clearance of 65ft (except for one near Miami which clears 56ft; they open on demand and very efficiently too.

All-in-all, this is one of the world's best cruising grounds and it has its share of live-aboards, though these are not popular in Florida. As ever, the live-aboard life is inexpensive, and even dirt cheap if one neglects the boat and dodges obligations to pay your way. It is the water-gypsy syndrome that makes the live-aboard unpopular. The last thing we want is regulation, but it is coming in popular parts of Florida where influential people with waterside homes oblige the police to crack down.

The most popular types of boat on the Intracoastal Waterway are fast semi-planers and motor cruisers of the so-called trawler type. There are many small sailing boats that cluster near the wide, well-buoyed estuaries, but we have met few boats of barge-like dimensions, and certainly the little marinas were built for smaller boats than these. There is a shortage of charter boats, so probably the best way that Europeans can enjoy this wonderful area is to ship their boat over; it is not that difficult or expensive (see page 186).

· 17 ·
Locks

Locks are the essence of canal navigation. Canal engineers design canals to follow the natural contours of the land as far as possible and so minimise changes in water level and the need for locks – it is impossible for the constructors to avoid them altogether. One major canal with no locks is the Suez Canal, cut specifically for ships, though small craft are permitted to use it provided they take pilots. It is not recommended for pleasure navigation.

❖ A brief history of locks ❖

Historians are vague on who invented the lock. Claims are tinged with chauvinism. We have tried to sort out the facts from the legends.

We can find no evidence that the Chinese developed a working lock. Certainly they had canals and there is evidence of a change in water level. This appears to have been solved by a simple dam, over which barges would be dragged up to float on the higher level. We cannot be certain as translation is not straightforward, even though we have an educated and obliging Chinese lady sailor in the family.

The lock does not appear to be a Dutch invention either, though they like to think so. Perhaps this is because Holland is a flat country, much of it at, or even below, sea-level, from which it was re-claimed the hard way. The saying goes 'God made the world, but the Dutch made Holland.' There is a record of a tidal barrage passable by ships at the town of Damme in the 11th century. It is not clear what form this took, but it appears to have worked on the same principle as the Chinese one, helped by co-tidal equivalences which occur twice a day. This interpretation of the situation at Damme is bolstered by the fact that it is probably the origin of the English word 'dam'. We get many of our words from the Dutch, and if you know the East Anglian dialect, you can read a Dutch newspaper. These dams and sea-gates are not locks as we know them nowadays.

The next development was the single-gate lock or sluice gate. A good example of the single gate is still working at the small French port of Gravelines, where the 'lock' into the river Aa has only one gate which opens for a short time when the water levels coincide, near high water.

Our research indicates that the first reliable historic mention of a working lock with double mitred gates was one built near Milan in 1438 by two Italian engineers, Signori degli Organi and di Bologna. Italy was a great centre of learning and engineering at that time. Leonardo da Vinci followed their example by building six more round Milan in the 1490s.

The first British lock was at Exeter in 1564. We do not know who designed it, or if he was inspired by the Italian experience on some Grand Tour.

The first French lock is uncertain, but the best candidate is on the Canal de Briare connecting the Rivers Loire and the Seine. This dates from about 1640.

Countries with large navigable rivers turned to locks comparatively late. Britain, which led the industrial revolution, had urgent need of bulk transport and no large navigable rivers close to industrial centres, and therefore took up canals and locks quite early. The pioneer was the Duke of Bridgewater in the 17th century, who could claim to have financed the first canal which was not part of a river system, though it had no locks. For a brief time, England was the leading country for canals. You could say we were too early, because the standard then set for canal width turned out to be too narrow as time went on, and well-nigh impossible to rectify. So often Britain, the initiator, gets left behind, as other countries take the idea and run with it. In addition, Britain invented railways, and the financially stronger rail companies bought up vulnerable canal companies and allowed the canals to deteriorate, thus removing competition.

❖ Dimensions for locks ❖

For Continental cruising it is advisable to keep within the dimensions of the standard Freycinet lock (39m by 5.05m by 1.80m/95ft by 17ft by 6ft) and that range holds for many other Continental systems except the Dutch. Even in Holland the standard barge (often called a *spitz*) can get to most places. Pity about the English system, but we've always been different to the Continent except in railways, where almost all countries have astoundingly adopted the English gauge of 4ft 8½in (1.3m approx). If only we had returned the compliment by adopting the Freycinet dimensions for our canals.

❖ How locks work ❖

Locks transform a canal, in which, by definition, water levels would be constant, into a wet staircase, by a series of *pounds*. Boats can both climb or descend, as well as move horizontally. The lock is the riser in the staircase construction, and enables boats to undertake the apparently impossible feat of climbing over a range of hills without appreciable effort. Once this would have done with horse or manpower.

A boat in the lower pound enters the lock chamber via the lower watertight gates which are then shut behind it. Water enters the chamber through valves in the upper lock gates. The water level in the lock rises, and the boat with it, until

The lock filling at Sereaucourt, Canal de St Quentin.

the level is equal to that of the canal in the upper pound. At this point the upper gates open and the barge leaves the lock, having been raised several metres without expenditure of any energy – surely the greenest way of transport ever.

A unit of work is defined as the energy required to raise a given weight by a given vertical distance. The lock then, is perpetual motion. Ah, you will say, but the water in the upper pound will gradually disappear downhill and be lost. Yes, but it evaporates, makes the air moist and then falls as rain which indirectly replenishes the upper pound without any deliberate interference from man or the expenditure of fuel; no energy input needed.

❖ The essentials of locking ❖

The process of locking that causes most damage to boats is going uphill on rising water levels. *Montant* in French, *bergfart* in German (it means 'towards the mountain'). I have never found out the Dutch word; they seem to use German perhaps because mountains are a rarity in the Netherlands. We'll concentrate on the French set-up because that is where most of our readers will go sooner or later, and because it is a good, if somewhat aged, system. The words for descending are *avalant* and *talfart*.

Travelling upstream, after you have made fast in a manned lock, and sometimes even before (depending on how soon before the lunch hour it is) the gates will slam shut behind you and the lock-keeper will open wide the *vannes* (the valves or paddles) on the upstream lock gates. The lock will fill gently and your boat will rise with it, or (worst-case scenario) a wall of water will sweep down the lock chamber and subject your boat to random harmonic variations as the wave sweeps back and forth between the lock gates. If you did not make fast properly it will carry your unfortunate boat with it. There are *éclusiers* (lock keepers) who delight in doing this to boatmen of unpopular nationalities that have irritated them with their disdain for La Belle France. We have been regaled by them with stories of what 'I did to a boat that had the nerve to ....' (insert your own sin). 'Why, I had him hit the gates at both ends of the lock and his dog fell in the water.' It is best to laugh heartily at these stories; the *éclusier* is in charge of powerful forces. Large notices tell you to wear lifejackets and make fast properly. If you don't, and ignore the lock-keeper's advice, he may consider you fair game.

This contretemps has eased now that most locks are automated and the entry of water has been adjusted to a moderate rate, more forgiving to incompetent tourists and amateur boatmen. This sort of fun and games never happened to professional *mariniers*. The full-sized 'Freycinet' *péniche* fits the lock so exactly that there is little room for water at all. Her weight gives her such inertia that she barely moves and if she did, an irate *batelier* (barge skipper) would probably push the *éclusier* into his own lock. The professionals of the *batellerie* are not to be trifled with.

If your boat is properly made fast, tended and fendered while locking, she is not likely to suffer damage unless she has marked flare in the hull or some sort of overhang such as a rubbing strake. When descending in a lock, it is essential to make sure nothing catches on the lock edge, and hangs that side of the boat up. This is **serious**, so any projections on the side of the boat are to be avoided, or carefully monitored during descent. Even fenders can be a hazard if they over-ride and catch in some lock-side fitting. This is the reason why the motor cruiser does not fare so well in canals.

Locking is not normally dangerous if approached with care and diligence. Accidents occur, such as the collapse of a lower lock gate on the Canal de l'Est while an *avalant* was entering a lock. The rush of water carried the *péniche* through the downstream gates, wrecking them. The *péniche* was severely damaged and there was a fatality. This is a very rare event, though one worries about little-used canals where there are signs of maintenance economies. A less dramatic case occurred recently on the Canal de la Marne a la Saône, fortunately without casualties.

Whether rising or descending, ropes *must* be watched and adjusted with care. It is most important to avoid a riding turn which jams the rope onto the cleat or bitts. As the strain on the rope increases, the jam will be ever tighter and in theory one could capsize the boat in the lock. If the lock is automatic there is a 'panic stop' lever which halts everything until an *éclusier* arrives and sorts you out. If the *éclusier* is not paying attention, you have a problem. The only solution is to cut the rope.

Stand well back as you do so because it will spring back and will hurt if it whips you. *Péniches*, which tend to use wire rope, and pleasure barges over 24m (46ft), are obliged to carry an axe ready for instant use for this or other mishaps; even they make mistakes. Smaller boats with modest-sized cordage should keep a sharp knife handy. Watch out for back-lash. Yes, we have had to do this. We are still using the two resulting short ropes.

❖ How to make fast in a lock ❖

The authorities like you to moor both fore and aft, and this is fine if the lock-side bollards are conveniently spaced and there are more than two persons in the boat, because each rope *must be attended*. In the smaller Freycinet locks, barges make fast with a short spring forward, and leave their engine trundling slow ahead with the rudder hard over pressing her quarter against the lock side. It is vital when doing this to tend the spring-rope expertly. You may have to transfer it from one lock-wall bollard to another one, higher or lower while the engine is still going ahead and it must be done smartly with no fumbling as the water rises or sinks. You might have to share a lock and the water-flow from a barge's screw may disturb a smaller boat. This does not much matter if your boat is about the same breadth as the lock for she won't go far, but it might trouble a narrowboat or a yacht, for example.

It pays to have a boat with straight sides. Boats in plan that have an elongated point at one end and elegant curves to the other are difficult to keep docile. Imagine coping with an over-excited greyhound in a mini and you'll get what I mean. You can graunch the boat into the lockside much more securely if you are a straight boat resting against a straight lockside. Some locks have curved or sloping-back sides. These are difficult and need care.

PRIORITY AT LOCKS

If you have to wait while the lock gates open for you, try to ascertain whether there is a boat leaving the lock (sortant). If so, keep well back but on no account allow that party of holidaymakers in the boat behind you, who do not know the etiquette, to push past and snitch your place.

1 Passenger and hotel boats have priority, which can be irritating on picturesque canals such as the Canal du Midi where there are far too many of them.

2 Commercial craft that are loaded (chargé) come next.

3 Commerce that is empty (vide).

4 Pleasure boats (plaisanciers) come last. No doubt about that.

If you wait too close near the lock you can impede the *sortant* (the leaving barge). One has to remember that a boat changes course by swinging her stern with the rudder. Until the whole boat has left the lock she cannot do this, and her protruding bows are subject to side winds and those irritating drain-off *louvres* known as *diversoirs*, which cause fierce cross currents. No *marinier* likes to run down a *plaisancier*; it causes paper-work. So if the way is not clear for him, at least two of his boat's lengths from the lock, you will get some vitriolic French interspersed with sarcastic and bitter references to your ancestry. (A typical epithet is '*mon petit lapin*'. Though 'my little rabbit' sounds fairly harmless it would not be wise to use it back.) The only exception to standing off patiently is when there is a waiting quay (*quai d'attente*) close to the lock and you make fast to it, firmly, clear of the channel. To make fast firmly is important because of interaction (see Chapter 19) between vessels as the barge leaves the lock.

❖ Ascending locks ❖

Locking through uphill is *montant* in French and *bergfart* in German.

On deck, a *gilet de sauvetage* (buoyancy aid) is obligatory. It is worth investing in one of those waistcoats that have inherent buoyancy if you are going to spend much time in canals. They are easier to put on and take off and more comfortable than a sea-going life jacket. (See also Chapter 20.)

Be sure that you have rope(s) clear and ready for use both sides if you do not know in advance where the lockside bitts are situated. These ropes get far more wear than mooring ropes in other craft so the tendency is to avoid expensive nylon and settle for cheap polypropylene which floats, giving an added safety precaution. It is not as strong as nylon, so go up a size, which also makes it easier to handle; thinner ropes cut your hands.

Enter the lock chamber (*sass*) at slow speed and if there are other boats astern of you, move up to the front of the lock. If you are the only boat in the lock, hang back if you can; the water disturbance will be less there.

Ideally, make fast fore-and-aft, but if there are no convenient bitts on the lock wall then it is most important to make fast forward. Do it swiftly, the lock-keeper will not hang about.

The most protective fenders on the canals are motor tyres, but their use is forbidden in locks. The *péniches* fit the locks so exactly that there is no room for motor tyres, but you are unlikely to fit so neatly. Once, nobody bothered with enforcing this rule but the increased amateur use of the canals has made the authorities sharpen up a bit. If a tyre comes adrift in a lock it sinks and could end up jamming the lock gates which is then difficult to dislodge. Advice about fenders is given later in this chapter.

When *montant* (rising) be ready for the surge of water as the *éclusier* opens the *vannes*. The flow of water can be forceful and put great strain on your rope.

Don't let turns jam on the cleat or bitts. For a temporary halt such as this, avoid the half-hitch to finish. Strains can be great so in a lock, keep the tail of the rope always in hand, ready to haul in or slacken as needed. *Never make it fast*, a loop round the bollard is the best solution.

Take down the slack in the rope as the boat rises. If the total rise is large, it may be necessary to change the bitt on the lock wall. Do this smartly; don't fumble. This manoeuvre is best rehearsed, and rehearsed again before your first lock. It is not difficult if you have learned what to do and do it swiftly. On some locks where the difference in height of successive bollards is large, it may be best to change over with two persons or perhaps even two ropes. Get the drill right for you and *do it fast*.

At the upper level, do not cast off your rope until the gate is open (official rules) or substantially so (in practice). Opening gates can cause currents in the chamber. A green light, not always present, is a positive signal that you can leave.

Leave the lock slowly, especially if you are deep-draughted. Your propeller wash can disturb all sorts of junk on the lock floor which is best left there. Be prepared for craft waiting outside.

If you are in a broad, deep boat (over 4.5m (15ft) beam and over 1.5m (5ft) draught), though we say do it slowly, you may need extra power to enter or leave a lock. This is because the water in the lock has nowhere to go, other than to squeeze through the narrow gap round or under your boat. It's like drawing or inserting a cork in a bottle.

Watch out as the stern passes the gates on your way out; she will suddenly make an unrestrained leap forward and take some stopping. This is dangerous if there is another vessel in the way. (The word 'leap' is comparative.) The kinetic energy of a barge moving at all is great. If the barge's speed increases from 1 kph to 2 kph, then her kinetic energy will increase fourfold.

❖ Descending locks ❖

Locking through downwards is *avalant* in French and *talfart* in German.

In the sequence for a descent you will be entering with a water level almost up to the lock edge. This makes it hard to see from the steering position, and it pays to go out to the edge of the boat and steer from there, lining up the boat's side with the lock chamber (parallel sided boats only).

If you are in a barge, it is possible that the water you push ahead of your boat while entering the lock will raise the level until the lock edge is awash for a moment or two when you arrive. If your boat has a high freeboard (ie the deck is a long way above the waterline) it can be difficult to get a rope on a bollard. As we have already said, low freeboard is best for the canals.

This question of getting a rope onto a low bollard or bitt often occurs. The skipper must allow for reluctance on the crew's part to leap into space with a rope. Years ago, I caused Laurel to be deposited, after dark, into a blackberry bush at Ardres, and she has never forgotten it. We also carry with us a cartoon of a skipper saying to his dubious-looking wife: 'When I say GO, lasso that tree.' Laurel gets it out now and then to remind me that she once had to do something similar on the Danube.

With descending locks it pays to have a strong midships cleat or bitts. However, there is not usually much water movement in the lock chamber. The water drains out much more smoothly than it fills. One merely has to wait until the levels equalise, permitting the gates to open.

We've said this already, but we'll say it again: *if descending in a lock, it is crucial to make sure nothing gets hung up on the lock-side.* Boats with rubbing strakes need especial care. If you do hang up, use the emergency stop. A boat that is seriously hung up and slides off the lock-side can cause itself considerable damage.

❖ Types of lock ❖

We have described the procedure for the basic, simple, manned lock. Some locks are automatically operated with nobody about at all, and others are operated by the barge skipper himself. It is impossible to describe all these in detail because different regions have adopted different practices. But here are some variations:

- Some locks have big vertical handles alongside the lock wall, and bells ring and the lock operates when the handle is lifted. There is another handle, usually red, for an emergency stop.
- Various locks are operated by turning a pole that hangs down from a wire stretched across the canal. Don't miss it!
- You may find that some locks have a form of tele-command and the skipper is given the remote control at the start of the chain of locks.
- There are locks that are completely automatic and the process starts with flashing lights etc as you pass the lock gate on entry. This type can cause problems for a smallish boat because it has been designed to be worked by barges and there can be a steel arm at the entry gate that has to be pushed back against the wall. This requires a strong push and a small boat is likely to find that the force necessary will push them away before the steel arm turns (Newton's First Law).

The long chain of locks on the Canal des Ardennes is entirely automatic, one lock preparing itself as you leave the lock precedent. In our experience, it is unusual to do all 30 locks without help having to be summoned, often because water gets into the shoreside electrical system at some point.

All the above have an emergency alarm. Sometimes you end up talking to a French *éclusier* over a loudspeaker garblespeak system. If he cannot solve the problem over the wires, and cannot understand you anyway, you will hear a heartrending Gallic sigh, and he will come in his little van. Best avoid calling him at lunch-time, he won't come till 2.30pm. Nothing drags a Frenchman from his lunch. We find that, in recent years, the *éclusiers* have learnt some English. (Including 'I come at 'alf past two – aprés mon lunch-break.') Try to speak the local language, though. It shows willing, and it helps. French is simple; it is pronouncing it that causes problems for the Anglo-Saxons. We apparently have a differently shaped mouth and throat. Continentals are much better at learning English than we are at learning French. Dutch and German we find more difficult, but do try, it makes friends and increases pleasure all round.

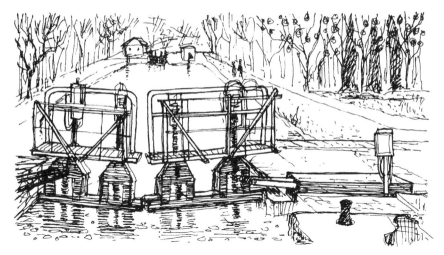

Part of the flight of 26 locks at Montgon on the Canal des Ardennes, France.

The big canals have bigger locks, where a pleasure craft may have to share the lock with commercial craft. As we have already said, the latter have priority on entering and leaving. In Dutch and German locks, the lock-keeper calls boats in as he deems fit. After he has got the commerce fitted in, he usually has some small spaces and calls in any pleasure boat that fits. '*Komm gleich!*' Do as he says and come quickly.

Do not expect German lock-keepers to speak English. In our experience they do not. Dutch lock-keepers on the other hand usually do. 'Come in the Little Englander'. This is the only time we found it acceptable to be called a little Englander. In Belgium, lock-keepers often seem to have little control over what is happening. We have already commented on Evergem. In Belgian locks one usually has to take the 'papers' to the office. One can occasionally get into difficulties because of the bi-lingual nature of Belgian administration. Just inside the border with France we presented our papers. There was a French barge ahead of us. The Frenchman did not or would not speak Flemish. The lock-keeper would not speak French. Impatiently, the keeper brushed the Frenchman to one side and attended to me. This caused bad tempered exchanges over my head. My papers were stamped and a small fee extracted. Such contretemps enliven things from time to time. As *plaisanciers*, it is better to act the innocent and say the minimum.

On another occasion, at Passau at the border controls between Germany and Austria, we had the same scenario. The Austrian official declined to speak English or French. As a whole room full of German and Dutch barge skippers waited impatiently while the Austrian sighed and filled in interminable forms, one German skipper told me in English: 'Here you leave Europe. You enter the Balkans.'

Sometimes I feel lucky that I am a sort of neutral in this wonderful area of European mutual respect, though it is galling to pretend that one is ignorant. Perhaps we do not have to pretend. The English are not noticeably good at languages.

This is one advantage of having a barge. One becomes an honorary bargeman, provided there are not many amateurs about. It is a great advantage, for the barge people are helpful and kind, though not to motor cruisers who get in their way. Amateur barges are mostly too slow to cause them problems.

❖ Large locks ❖

The big locks seem forbidding, but as they usually have floating bollards they are easier than smaller ones. The deep lock at Bollêne, on the Rhône, is not the deepest in Europe. That honour goes to one on the Danube. Entering La Bollêne at low level is like going into a great cathedral with an open roof, 26m (85ft) above you. The bollards on this and similar locks are on floating tanks which rise and fall in niches in the lock walls, squealing like stuck pigs. For small pleasure boats they can be daunting because the bollards are too far apart to enable you to make fast fore-and-aft. The best way of making fast is with one rope from amidships, looped round the bollard, and if your craft has parallel sides so much the better: you will lie there peacefully.

If a small lock with a mere 3m (10ft) rise can cause uncomfortable water disturbance that throws your boat about, you would expect even worse from these big locks, but fortunately they are better designed, with water coming in or going out through holes in the bottom of the lock chamber, no waves or disturbances, only whirlpools of swirling water. Don't fall in! You will never be seen again. It is best to keep pets below while locking.

Locks on the new Rhein-Main-Donau Kanal have an interesting water-saving feature. One of the major problems in canal design arises from the fact that as the locks are used, the water flows from the upper pounds to the lower. It is therefore necessary to have a large reservoir at the summit pound, otherwise there would

In the lock at Bachhausen, Danube, Germany.

be no water to replace the volume that goes down the lock staircase. In France, where the locks on the Canal du Centre are much used in summer, water is often used up and the canal has to be closed.

The R-M-D Kanal which goes from the Rhine at Mainz to the Danube at Kelheim, has an enormous amount of traffic and huge locks. To minimise water-loss, these are designed with side tanks. As the top part of the lock is drained, the water flows into a storage tank beside the lock. Later when filling the lock, they use this stored water to help the re-fill, another way in which locks are one of the greenest mechanisms we have.

FREQUENT LOCKS

With one or two special exceptions, all locks work on the same principle.

Approach frequent locks with a philosophical attitude, as the maximum rate of advance has little to do with your boat's capabilities. If only one barge can lock through at a time, there is no point in going faster than the barge ahead of you. You start off a good 20 minutes astern of him and even if you catch him up, you cannot get past him unless he makes a positive effort to allow you to do so (which is unlikely as he would lose time waiting for the next locking) so all that happens is that you have to slow down and tuck in astern of him. Then you are navigating in disturbed water from his propeller thrust; which makes life more difficult for you, the boat following. If you are astern and the lead boat is going slowly, then grin and bear it. Moor up for a cup of tea or drop to dead slow. Canals teach patience, whether you like it or not.

A variation on the above occurs if a pleasure craft finds a faster commercial barge coming up astern. This is unlikely to be a loaded barge, which generally have difficulty going fast in a typical canal, but it can occur in the larger canals such as the Canal du Nord. To nip in ahead of a commercial barge is rather worse than bad form. It heightens differences between professional and amateur. Pleasure boats *must* yield to commerce.

❖ Fenders for locks ❖

We have demonstrated the need for a canal boat to be built in a different way to a sea-going boat. It's not essential; just prudent because it is likely that she will be at close quarters with other, bigger craft, and that sooner or later she will take a hard knock.

This gives rise to the need for substantial rubbing strakes and preferably one at water-line level as well as under the gunwale. This is because the knuckle edge of a full lock, which you enter in order to descend, is often only an inch or two above water level and almost impossible to fender except with motor tyres which are prohibited. In addition, lock gates, which cannot always be relied upon to open to the full extent because of floating garbage (old tyres perhaps), often have nuts or bolt heads or other bits of battered metal sticking out. The same is true of narrow aqueducts and tunnels. It can be difficult to protect the boat.

Protective fendering can be obtained by a visit to a commercial port where you might find a length of abandoned plaited polypropylene rope about 10cm (4in) in diameter. A few metres of this will take the knocks quite well but it has several disadvantages. Firstly, to cut off a few metres (and it is very heavy) you will need the sort of equipment you would use to amputate a leg; secondly your cut section will tend to ride up out of the water and onto the quay edge unless one end is weighted down and thirdly, being junk it will tend to shed nasty little fibres everywhere. One solution to this latter is to encase the old rope in a length of old engine exhaust hose or fireman's hose; it is getting complicated but this solution is cheaper and more durable than fendersox. Neither fendersox nor plastic fenders survive canal cruising for long. Either can be ruined in a few weeks of busy cruising.

For boats that are so broad that there is little room either side in the lock, it is possible to buy fenders made specially for narrowboats on the English canals where it is vital to have thin fenders. The suppliers are a firm called Aquafax; they are to be found in Luton, and have a catalogue of interesting barge equipment, among other things.

LOCK ENTRY LIGHTS

Books offering general guidance on canal navigation show the entry light system that applies to locks (and also some opening bridges). As the light sequences vary greatly from place to place, we think it best to give a generalisation and give you the fun of discovering the system in force in the local area.

- Generally, a single red light (or two reds): lock closed, or a long wait.
- Red and green lights: the lock is being made ready for you.
- A green light means you can go in, but these vary. Sometimes there is a yellow light, sometimes there are two reds. The green means GO, and only a demonstrable equivalent hand signal replaces the green as permission to enter.

Officially, if in the lock, you should not cast off after the lock has either risen or fallen. You should wait for the green departure light. Sometimes you might wait all day. In these circumstances, we usually call the *éclusier* on VHF and say Thank you, which reminds him to give you a green light. We have never had any problems that way.

On any lock fitted with green and red lights controlling entry into or departure from the chamber, it is important to obey the lights. The way in or out may look clear to you, but there may be reasons to be cautious. (We describe one such in *Watersteps Round Europe*, involving the rescue of a pigeon.) Some *éclusiers* just wave you in or out.

In any event, it makes for a pleasant existence if you take the trouble to express thanks, either on VHF or a friendly wave as you go.

❖ VHF ❖

Many locks now have VHF. On the rivers, the VHF channel is given in the guides. If you know the language, call while a few kilometres away to tell him you are on the way.

'Ecluse de xxx, ici plaisancier montant, douze metres, a KP yyy, a vous', for example. It helps both of you because he can plan his lock use and knows when to put the kettle on. On the smaller canals, barges call to each other on channel 10. This is to give each other warning that they are entering a difficult stretch and avoid being taken by surprise. Sometimes they just click the microphone a few times indicating that 'there is a barge about'. An amateur in a barge should keep watch on channel 10 and announce his position at delicate stretches. Even if he is not fully understood, he

alerts the neighbourhood to his existence, and possible problems. On the Danube, the upper reaches of which are sinuous and tricky for big barges, they use channel 16. When we first started out downstream we were unaware of the importance of this procedure and after a hairy encounter with a 1000 tonne barge on a sharp bend, we got an '*engueulade*' (a telling off).

❖ General advice on locks ❖

Many locks have a short quay close by, which can make a good mooring for the night while the lock is closed. Get the consent of the *éclusier* if you can. Never moor for the night very close up to a lock unless you are prepared to move off as soon as the locks open, and even then be prepared to shift aside to let in early-bird commercial barges.

All locks are a potential hazard to your boat. They need care because if you fall in your chances are not good. The water in a lock chamber is usually disturbed with wild currents, vertical as well as horizontal. Our barge *Hosanna* which is 27m (88ft) long and weighs almost 100 tonnes fully laden may look big (see photo on page 88), but sharing the lock at Gabçikovo in Slovakia on the River Danube with one 1000-tonne Dutch barge and a tow of six 2000-tonne barges towed by a Romanian tug, removed any illusions of grandeur. In spite of its size, this lock caused no significant water disturbance.

Hosanna shows the scale of this huge lock on the Danube at Gabçikovo in Slovakia.

These big river locks work all night but may not accept pleasure craft unless you can contrive to fit into a space. The locking cycle can take a long time so be prepared for a prolonged wait. It is only when you have seen a towing tug sort out and push eight barges into a lock, two at a time, that you realise what hard work it is. He will have to re-make his tow on the other side before leaving. A locking sequence for such a professional can take several hours, even if there is no wait. Fortunately, locks are further apart on rivers.

It may sometimes be necessary to pay a fee at a lock. We found this in eastern Europe; this is probably an illegal racket, but difficult to resist because the lock-keeper keeps the keys.

In France, during the summer holidays, the locks may be in the temporary charge of a student. One sunny day, we arrived quietly at a lock in France, and there was nobody to be seen. Bill called but no response. He went in search of an éclusier. Round the back of the lock cottage, on a grassy bank, he found a reclining young lady of considerable charm, fast asleep. She had no clothes on, but was not the least dismayed when woken. She was reading philosophy at university, lock-keeping was her summer job.

❖ Water loss from locks ❖

People argue about how much water is 'lost' with each lock working. This cannot be measured by considering the passage of one barge in either direction. One must consider a complete cycle and we will use the envelope principle of logical analysis: that is, consider two extreme cases; then all others must lie between these two.

Here is an example: using metric measurement, in this case the lock is designed to fit exactly a maximum vessel of 20m long and 5m breadth, and drawing 1m of water.

The boat's volume is thus 20 x 5 x 1 = 100 cubic metres. The normal lock rise is 2m.

The empty lock chamber would hold 100 cubic metres of water but when the boat is within it, there will be only a negligible amount of water.

The lock waits for a rising barge. As the barge enters the lock, she displaces the water that was in the chamber. All of it remains in the low canal (100 cubic metres).

Now, we let in sufficient water to raise the barge 2m to the higher level. The amount of water let in from the high canal is 20 x 5 x 2 cubic metres which is 200 cubic metres. This is the amount taken from the high canal. As the barge quits the lock at the high level, then her own volume of water, 100 cubic metres, enters the lock chamber from the high canal to replace her.

Another similar barge waits to go down. As she enters, she will displace 100 cubic metres of water back into the high canal. When the gates close, there will be in the lock a total of the 200 cubic metres taken from the high level to raise the first barge.

As the second barge descends, 200 cubic metres passes from the lock chamber into the low canal. Thus 200 cubic metres of water has passed from the high canal to the low canal. As the barge leaves she draws into the lock the same volume of water as the first barge pushed out as she entered the lock. Thus the amount of water that has passed from the high canal to the low in one locking sequence is the difference between lock full and lock empty, ie 200 cubic metres.

Now let us look at the same sequence with a little boat, that displaces almost nothing. As she enters the lock at the low level, no water is displaced. The amount of water needed for the lock level to rise to high canal level is still 200 cubic metres and that comes from the high canal. The little boat leaves the lock at the high level without there being any water movement. The sequence is similar for a little boat descending.

Clearly, there is a more economical use of water if the lock workings can alternate, that is to have boats rising and descending alternately. In times of water shortage, a conscientious lock-keeper will make pleasure boats wait until he can achieve this.

❖ *Ecluses de Control* and stoppages ❖

There are a few locks which are '... *de controle*' where you disembark and take your papers for mild bureaucracy. Take the opportunity to read the *avis a la battellerie* (notices to mariniers) which may contain important information regarding temporary closures (interruptions) caused by urgent work needs. Longer closures for planned maintenance usually take place in the winter, but can be at any time, usually when you want to go that way. These are published on the internet, usually in February, in the annual *liste des chomages*. In our experience one cannot rely on individual *éclusiers* knowing circumstances, problems or conditions outside their own 'section'. This can even extend to the next lock if it is across the boundary. Once at the lock at St Omer we were told there were no problems on the Canal de Calais only to find the lock closed at the very start of the canal, only a few kilometres away. A commercial barge had the same experience. The difference was that while I fumed, he just shrugged and went below for a tot. I hadn't got used to the canal life then, he had. He knew! *C'est la vie des bateaux.*

One last thing. If you carry a heavy load on deck such as a motor car, and have no crane, you stand a chance of inducing an *éclusier* to help you embark or disembark, especially if the lock is not busy. When the deck level of your boat is the same as the lock-side, he will suspend the water entry or discharge and you can easily roll off the car or other heavy gear. This would deserve a *pourboire*, which literally means 'enough to drink your health'.

· 18 ·

Barge handling

I f you are buying your first barge, you will find this information helpful. We bargees need all the help we can get. The advice will also help those with smaller boats.

❖ Weight ❖

One significant difference between barges and other, smaller pleasure craft on the waterways is weight. Weight affects the way a boat moves through the water, and the force required to move her – and the force required to stop her. This is of the utmost importance and people new to barges must exercise great caution. You, unaided by engines, can by sustained effort set a barge in motion in still water: are there any other circumstances where one person given a little time can easily move over 300 tons of artefact? But it is a different matter trying to stop that weight, whether it is coming at you or under your feet.

Never try to stop a moving barge with any part of your body.

Fortunately for we barge-handlers, it is possible to use the barge's weight and horse-power to do the work for us, using ropes with a skill which it is important to acquire. We will cover more of this later.

Because the weight of a barge affects the way she moves through the water, she takes longer to slow down and accelerate. (Acceleration = force divided by mass.) This applies not only to straight line acceleration, but also to angular acceleration, that is, turning. Barges take longer to start turning when the rudder is put over, and they turn more slowly, which means they will have a larger turning circle. And when, at the end of your planned turn, you return the rudder to amidships, the barge will not stop turning straight away; her angular momentum carries her on. She will need a few degrees of opposite rudder for a moment or two to stop the turn. On the other hand, when pointed in a given direction and steadied on that course, barges tend to keep to a straight line.

Nobody should have difficulty with a boat moving in a straight line. Only an occasional tweak of the helm is needed to correct any tendency to wander off course, due to wind perhaps, but once trundling along, the barge will keep her course much more reliably than a small boat. Where people need tips is in manoeuvring, especially

Laurel, well wrapped up, drives through a hailstorm on the River Shannon in Ireland.

in tight circumstances. 'Tight' refers to the amount of room, not the amount of vino. It is best not to drink and drive.

❖ Propellers ❖

Most barges are single-screw. Because their rate of acceleration is slow, they need large propellers that exert much force while turning slowly. Their gear-boxes usually have a large reduction gear, say 3:1. This means that for every three revolutions of the engine, the propeller goes round once, with three times the torque. Barges have diesel engines that develop power at low revs at the expense of high revs at full power. A barge engine will drive the barge at a suitable speed for a narrow canal while still barely ticking over. Make sure, therefore, that the belt-driven alternator that charges your batteries has pulleys that enable the alternator to turn fast at low engine speeds. The maximum revs of a barge engine is unlikely to affect a modern alternator that is designed to accommodate fast-reving engines.

Being a stick-in-the-mud I do not advise turbo-charged engines; it's just another thing to go wrong and reputed to shorten the life of the engine. The engine suitable for an amateur is 'fit and forget'. Well, you can't quite do that; you must maintain it to some extent but it should not need cooing over like a baby.

❖ Bow thrusters ❖

A bow thruster makes close-quarters handling of boats of all types infinitely easier, not only for barges but for any boat over, say, 12 metres in length. It consists of an electrically-driven (for smaller craft) propeller, fitted in a transverse tube close to the bows. The reversible propeller pushes the bows to port or starboard; the direction is selected by using a joystick. See also page 130.

❖ Power steering ❖

If you have hydraulic power-steering have a dedicated pump for it. I had a cross-connection for emergency use but in 22 years never had to use it. Fit hydraulic steering pumps and rams larger than the books say; a margin of error is advisable in boats. I wish those fanatics that yacht-race around the world would realise this.

❖ Bitts ❖

If your barge has been in commerce, she will have bitts (pairs of posts for use in mooring) in the right places, but if you are buying a replica this may not be the case, depending on the parsimony of the builder. There should be bitts either side at the boat's shoulders, raised high enough so that you do not need fairleads, which are never wholly satisfactory. They should be in pairs, about 8in (20cm) diameter and about 12in (30cm) high with a 1in (25mm) diameter bar through about a couple of inches (50mm) from the top. If you do a lot of cruising, they are best left unpainted and clean, your ropes will keep them scoured. Paint on the bollards invariably comes off on your ropes.

A second pair of bitts should be sited aft. In traditional barges, these are usually abreast of the wheel-house on the side deck, ahead of the after cabin. It is usual to have a single bitt right aft on the centre-line, and I like a lighter, smaller one on the stem-head forward. Lastly, a valuable manoeuvring aid is a single bitt amidships on either side. Quite apart from manoeuvring considerations, we have found that with moorings getting ever more crowded, the shore-side bollards are seldom placed just where you need them, and the flexibility on board is valuable.

Turning up on a bitt

There are several ways of turning up a rope on bitts and, whatever I advise, some dockside expert will suck his teeth and shake his head.

My way works. For mooring, take three or four turns round the bitt drum and *then* finish with a figure of eight half-hitch on the cross bar. If you are using the ropes for springing or locking, then two round turns will do – hold the rope across the bar, and don't let go. It is then ready to shift or adjust, while holding the ship against all normal strains.

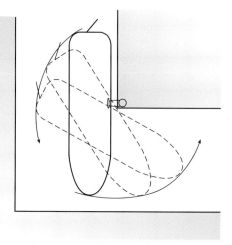

Using a short spring from a midships bollard to turn short round the knuckle of a quay while in a restricted space.

❖ Ropes ❖

On the canals, polypropylene ropes are best. They float, and are unlikely to wrap themselves round your propeller if you allow them to drop overboard. They are cheaper than nylon (best for use in sea-going craft) and this matters, for they will get rough usage on the canals; in locks it's particularly brutal. We have used 12mm (½in) diameter (ESFSWR) wire rope as the professionals do, but you have to know how to handle wire. It is not as easy as rope, and needs care and attention, otherwise it is a limb amputator. Also, individual strands occasionally stick up and can cut severely. Use leather gloves to handle wires. The following piece of advice is so important that it is virtually an order (the only one in this book, we hope).

NEVER STAND IN THE BIGHT OF A ROPE OR WIRE

This is especially important if the rope could come under strain. A bight is the curve in the way a rope is lying, and the danger is that sudden strains can cause the rope to straighten with great force, cutting like a cheese-wire. This also applies to fibre cordage. A barge has a lot of kinetic energy, remember to allow for it. Keep arms and legs clear of danger and watch what you are doing. Don't mess about when handling ropes under strain – concentrate.

❖ Paddlewheel effect ❖

Unlike many smaller craft, a barge can usually be steered when making a sternboard, that is while going steadily astern under power. If she is stopped and the engine is engaged 'astern', then her stern will kick to one side or the other depending on the rotation of the screw, and this varies from boat to boat. If you view your barge from astern and the screw, when going astern, revolves anti-clockwise, then the stern will swing to port, and vice versa.

This, known as paddle-wheel effect, is caused by the lower blades of the screw gripping the deeper and denser water, and thus having more effect than the upper blades in lighter water. It happens while going ahead as well, but the effect is much reduced because the thrust race of the propeller is directed onto the rudder.

Paddle-wheel effect is a useful tool when manoeuvring, so understand which way your boat moves. Turn in the direction that would be assisted by a touch astern while turning, and don't forget to watch both ends. Be reassured that even the most experienced professionals occasionally screw up, so to speak. If you do get in a mess, try not to use too much engine power. That way you minimise the damage.

You need to keep your nerve when a large barge approaches as close as this!

❖ The use of springs ❖

You soon get tired when pushing and pulling a barge about by main force. Let the barge do her own work by using 'springs' intelligently. Springs are ropes that can be used to move the barge in a particular way. They are particularly useful when berthing or unberthing in a tight spot. If you can recall an understanding of 'statics and moments' from your schoolboy mechanics, it helps, but it is not essential. Plenty of brilliant seamen never learned to read and write, but understood springs, relying on their powers of observation and natural intelligence.

I've used springs to great advantage berthing *Hosanna*. When mooring in a marina at Southampton there was only one berth alongside, with boats moored close at either end of it. We hove-to in parallel to, and alongside, the berth and sighted across from stem and stern to see if there was enough room for us. There was less than a metre to spare. I backed off and prepared a long spring at the port shoulder and then approached the berth at an angle, putting my bows up to the quay close to the boat ahead. The man ashore wanted to put the rope on as a headrope, but I asked him to take it well aft and when that had been done, we motored slow ahead with the rope taut and the stern still out in the stream. Slowly, Laurel let out the rope as the bows slid along the quay while I used the rudder to keep the stern clear of the boat at our other end. When our stem was but a few inches from the boat in front Laurel stopped all forward movement with her rope (I didn't have to tell her), and a change of rudder brought our stern in without touching either boat. To have tried to place *Hosanna* alongside in such a short gap without a spring would have been irresponsible. Note that Laurel was the key to this successful berthing (See diagram below.).

Another time when a spring was vital was when we were pinned against a stone quay by a mistral blowing at a good force 10, and wanted to leave the quay. We describe this hairy episode in *Watersteps Through France*.

Another use is when leaving a berth in a narrow side-cut to turn into a narrow canal which is probably less wide than the ship is long. Then the amidships bitt does its stuff. Pass a short spring from this bitt to a bollard on the knuckle of the quay, and she will swivel round beautifully with the engine in slow ahead.

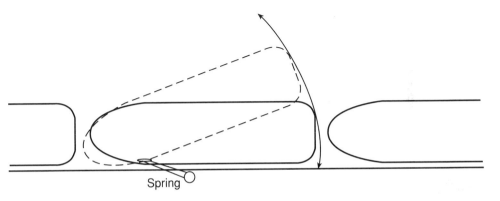

Spring

Using a spring to berth in or unberth from a tight situation.

❖ Entering a lock ❖

This is daunting if you have only an inch or two either side so here are tips for successful manoeuvring:

- Approach in line with the lock.
- Go out to the side of the barge and sight along her straight side and line it up with the lock wall while going slow ahead.
- Keep the engine going and make your approach. You will be surprised at how well even a touch of rudder will align her bows to the opening, but contrive to keep the line of the lock.
- Go slow ahead until the bows are inside because the turning screw pushes water on to the rudder, making it more effective than it would be with a stopped engine. While manoeuvring into a lock, little rudder is needed to make fine adjustments. *Hosanna* was steered by joystick and the unit of rudder I used was a sort of 'flick'. When using the wheel, turning it one spoke was usually enough. It is a common mistake to use too much rudder.

❖ **Man overboard** ❖

Clearly, the problems of coping with a man overboard in a narrow canal are quite different from the equivalent situation at sea or in open water. We will deal fully with this problem in Chapter 20 Coping with Risks and Dangers.

DON'T STOP BOATS WITH YOUR FEET

If you are berthing in a gusty wind, it is quite possible that you will bump against the quay. Persuade willing helpers on the quay *not to try to stop the barge with their feet, legs, hands or any other parts of their anatomy.* Fenders are required; failing that, let her bump.

❖ **Running aground** ❖

Eventually, your barge will touch bottom, run aground, or even do some mountain climbing up the bank. What do you do?

The first thing is be careful. Barges have enormous kinetic energy and do not come to a total stop instantly when the canal bottom comes up near the surface. They go on, slowly decelerating as the bows climb up the hill. When this happened to *Hosanna* once, I thought that we had found a hump in the bottom and gave her full power so that she would be able to ride over it and come down the other side. This was an error. The hump was much bigger than I had thought and *Hosanna* ended up on top of the hump with her waterline two feet higher than normal, giving Skipper a red face. We had to get help to shift her.

The best advice is to stop engine and go full astern straight away. If she will not back off readily, then go astern while wiggling the rudder from side to side.

Still aground? Sound round the boat. That is, check the depth of water all round. Then use the quant pole to shove sideways whichever end of the boat is still floating the most. By moving her sideways and/or rotating her you can widen the groove she is lying in.

Still stuck? If you have a dinghy, or there is another boat nearby willing to help, run a hefty rope across the canal to a tree or some other substantial device, and heave that in on your crab winch while also going astern.

Still no go? You are in a mess, aren't you? Take heart, we've all been there. The best plan now is to go along to the next lock upstream and ask the *éclusier* to release some extra water. They are usually agreeable, but if you are in a long pound (*bief*) it won't help much. Then it is a matter of collaring passing boats until you have put a team together willing to help. Afterwards have a party.

· 19 ·

Canal effect, interaction or squat

At this point we will explain the way a moving boat reacts with another boat, whether moving or still, or even with the canal bottom and sides. This is known as canal effect, interaction (a term used by pseudo-scientists) or 'squat'. Failure to understand this phenomenon can cause grief.

A loaded barge occupies a substantial part of the cross-section of the canal. Typically, the central, navigable cross-section of a canal has about five times the block coefficient of a barge. Canals that are under-utilised silt up, and this ratio decreases. Another cause of decrease is that barges carry lighter loads than they did when the canals were dug. They can no longer carry their designed load because of serious silting, so my figure of five times (above) is seldom achieved on older canals.

In France, canals are nominally navigable by barges that are 1.8m (metric measures only given here) draught, which indicates a dredged depth of 2m or more. That is generally no longer the case, and if it is, that depth would be only in the centre. There is a flat-bottomed area in the centre of most Freycinet canals that is about 7m wide. On each side of this there is typically a width of another 10m and in this the canal bottom slopes up, often until it is quite shallow. A barge which would be 5m broad and loaded to about 350 tonnes, would draw about 1.8m. Canals' depths are maintained by the craft that use them; they are seldom dredged. This means that the typical loaded barge is about 10cm clear of the bottom when she is stationary; imagine the drag. Think about the effect of this drag on her manoeuvrability.

When any craft moves through the water, she interacts with the water which flows past her. Though this interaction occurs with a ship in the open sea, it is unnoticed because she is not close to anything that matters or to which her movement can relate. The interaction only becomes significant when the moving ship or barge is close to something else, such as another ship, the bottom of the sea, or the bottom and sides of a canal. It only becomes serious when speeds rise.

It did not matter in the old days when ships were small and slow, but times have changed. In the Suez Canal I learned that if you went too fast in the canal you lost control of the ship, a major matter if the ship weighed 30,000 tonnes. In those days the canal was dredged to 36ft (11m) feet, and ships up to 33ft (10m) draught could pass.

A drained section of the Canal de Roanne à Digoin, France. PHOTO: SALLY ANDREW

It was found that if big ships tried to pass each other in opposite directions at any speed, they would inevitably be sucked sideways into each other and collide dramatically. Ships passing through the canal were accordingly marshalled into convoys. One convoy would stop and make fast while the opposite convoy would creep past, very, very slowly. Otherwise, if clear of other craft, one could order power for 8 knots and achieve 6.

❖ Canal effect in French canals ❖

In the French canals, as a loaded barge advances, her screw propeller sucks the water from under her and pushes it out behind her in a flurry (*le gerbe*). The lack of water underneath her lowers her down until she is just gliding over the muddy bottom of the canal and thus maintaining canal depth. Her screw can no longer draw water from underneath and instead draws it from either side, so the water level alongside her drops. All this slows her down considerably.

At the same time she is pushing ahead of her, like a piston in a cylinder, a wall of water in the form of a long wave. It is often possible to detect this wave a kilometre ahead of the barge. If moored, you notice a sudden fidget in the water, your mooring ropes twang. Look out! A barge is on its way. Set taut your moorings!

Close in front of the barge, this long wave increases in height. The water level at her stem may be half a metre more than normal and the final rise of that wave is steep. The plan of the crest of that wave is crescent shaped, curling back on either side of the barge's bows like a Victorian walrus moustache.

Consider a boat going in the opposite direction and wishing to get past. Given sufficient time and good facilities, one might moor up securely and wait, but you are out in the countryside. The only things at the canal side are those little steps placed there by nature-lovers to help ducks and wild life get out of the water, no good to you unless you are a duck. Mooring stakes are not adequate.

One's inclination, seeing a barge approaching at constant speed and remaining in the centre of the canal, or only just off-centre, would be to pull right over to starboard and generously leave the monster plenty of room. You might regret that because the forward-facing slope of the crescent-shaped bow-wave of the barge will push you sideways with some force, probably into, or in extreme cases, right onto, the bank. Which is a horror story.

So you get to the top of this wave, having hit the bank sideways. You now cascade down the reverse side of the wave into the hollow alongside the middle of the barge in shallower water, having just bashed your starboard topsides against the piling. You now drop like a stone and bounce on the bottom of the canal. Your teeth and assorted china mugs rattle but you have no time to contemplate the damage, as you are now coming to the stern of the barge where its screw is pulling water in from the side (because there is no water underneath her) and where the level is beginning to rise after the trough following the big bow-wave.

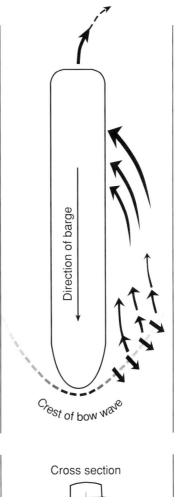

Interaction: this diagram shows the forces round a barge on a straight course in a narrow canal. The arrows show the direction of the water flow on the surface; the thickness indicates the strength of flow.

Suddenly, you are sucked violently in towards the barge's quarter, giving your port topsides a hearty bash as you graunch past, bouncing in the barge's wake. This sort of collision, for that is what it is, is common among barges.

The way to do it needs nerve. Slow down and aim just to one side of the stem of the barge, apparently intent on a near head-on collision. It is possible that you will un-nerve him, persuading him to move over a bit, but that is unlikely if you are a small boat unless he is a nice chap. If you have a big barge, he may shout, trying to frighten you into going to the side because he believes all pleasure craft are shallow-draughted. He will probably continue on inexorably. If you have judged it right, his bow-wave will throw you to one side as we described above (and as he knew it would) so you rev up and once more steer towards him until you slide down the rear slope of the wave. Ease speed while close alongside his length. Then, when you begin to feel sucked towards him by his screw, accelerate to full speed and steer outwards until the centre of your boat is level with his stern and then steer the other way to cross his wake. It is likely that the left hand cheek of your boat's backside will strike a glancing blow to the left hand cheek of the barge, a common occurrence, known to mariniers as a *coup de fesse*, or a smack on the buttocks. *Hosanna*, our barge, usually had a thick motor tyre or two, hung well aft on the port side but only between locks.

Hosanna, drawing 1.5m (5ft), was deep for a pleasure barge and we had to stand our ground. The alternative was to have our starboard bilges banged on the stony edge of the canal. We warn elsewhere that when buying old barges, pay particular attention to the starboard bilge plating. Over many years of being bashed about it may have become several millimetres thinner than the plating on the other side, and have the rivet heads worn away as well. When we bought *Hosanna* in 1985, her starboard bilge plating was down to 4mm in places, compared with 7.5mm on the port side. She had been built with 8mm plating. We re-plated the turn of the starboard bilge, doubling up with another layer, and I also fitted bilge keels to take the knocks. It's not a big job.

If I have given the impression that the *mariniers* are callously indifferent to wrecking pleasure boats, this is not the case, but remember that they have little room for manoeuvre, and the above is a worst-case scenario. If *they* touch the side, they, too, may finish up the bank, and 340 tonnes has a lot of kinetic energy and is difficult to stop, even when going up-hill. If the barge *does* mount the bank, it is a devil of a job to get her off again, so they stay as close to the centre as possible and keep as much steerage way as they dare to keep control.

What happens when two loaded barges pass each other? Normally, in a very difficult part of the canal, both slow right down to a snail's pace and 'feel their way' past each other, often with their sides rubbing together all the way.

As many mariniers think that pleasure barges are shallow-draughted, they make no allowances for us; but our problems are becoming known and the professionals have learned that most amateur barge-owners handle their boats considerately and are willing to yield priority to commercial vessels. Now that we pay canal dues, we help to maintain the canals on which their livelihoods depend. We have found that the professionals are not a bad lot at all.

If you doubt the seriousness of interaction between ships, the worst example I am aware of was reported by the Marine Accident Investigating Board concerning a container ship entering Felixstowe in the narrow, shallow approach channel and passing a 500 tonne coaster leaving, both ships going too fast. The coaster was sucked violently sideways into the side of the big ship and capsized with loss of life.

DETECTING AN ON-COMING BARGE

You will know the direction the barge is travelling by the first significant move of your moored boat which will be *away* from the on-comer. She will settle down, until just before the passing barge arrives, when she will strain away from the on-comer as if trying to escape, stretching her mooring ropes considerably. As the barge passes, the moored boat will move laterally out towards the barge, suddenly and violently. This puts enormous strain on her moorings. It is quite common for ropes to part, bollards or cleats to pull out, whether on the quay or on the boat, and feeble little stakes almost always pull out. Afterwards as the barge passes, the moored boat (if still attached) will move sharply in the opposite direction to that of the barge and often she will hit the quay with a fender-shattering bang.

❖ Cleats and ropes for canals ❖

You can now see that it is important to make sure that your cleats and ropes are well up to the job. I have seen 15m (49ft) glassfibre boats, part-built in the Far East and then completed by the importing agents, in which the fittings were criminally inadequate for any maritime use, let alone for canals. Cleats suitable for ropes of 15mm (6in) diameter were fastened to the deck without adequate backing reinforcement; they pulled out of the boat in an instant. It is vital in a canal boat that the mooring cleats can withstand a pull equal to, or greater than, the breaking strain of the rope. I go further and opine that one should be able to hang the boat on the two main cleats. The minimum rope size for a 15m (49ft) boat is 20mm (8in) in diameter. For a 12m (39ft) boat, 15mm (6in) ropes and for smaller boats at least 12mm (5in) nylon or polyester. For polypropylene (which makes sense for canal craft because it floats and is less likely to end up round the propeller), increase the rope size one notch because it is not so strong. Nylon ropes cope with snatch loads better than others because nylon stretches. This has disadvantages because the mooring then becomes slack and the boat can move about and damage itself. I have seen nylon ropes that were subject to a sudden snatch load stretch to twice their normal length before parting, though under those conditions the rope was ruined because the intense friction in the fibres had melted the nylon and fused the rope into a solid bar.

One manifestation of canal effect or interaction is the way that vessels of any size become difficult to manage when going too fast in shallow water. Technically, if the speed of the vessel in knots exceeds 75 per cent of the square root of her waterline length in feet, and is navigating in water that is less than one and a half times her draught, she will have steering and manoeuvring problems. (An example was the car ferry *Herald of Free Enterprise* where interaction did not cause the accident, but made it far worse once the ship had lost directional stability.)

If the depth (of water) is less than $1\frac{1}{2}$ times the draught, $(D < 3d/2)$ the critical speed is reduced by roughly the same proportion. All this is an approximation because much depends on the ship and her block co-efficient, which is to say

This bargee got it slightly wrong and got stuck under the bridge.

roughly her cross-sectional form. If you are inclined to be a 'press on regardless' type of navigator (not advisable in canals, they are not suitable sites for displays of machismo), it might pay to spend a little time doing some experiments.

Amateur boat drivers do not need to worry about interaction in wide channels or the open sea, nor in deep waters. It only becomes a problem when there is barely enough water to move about in, and you are going too fast.

I hope I have not worried you too much. People with sensible boats who behave prudently seldom get badly affected by this phenomenon, and I have only discussed it because minor manifestations occur in canals even at lowish speed, and it is advisable to recognise the effect if or when it starts to become apparent. If you suspect that it is happening to you, slow down gently. Not too quickly, do it gently. Do not ballast your boat down too much. I think 1.5m (5ft) is the maximum for a pleasure barge, and some care is required even then. Once again, if you have to slow down, do so gently if you have the room. Best make sure you always have the room.

Waterway interludes:

River Rhône

In an ice cave nearly three miles up in the Swiss Alps, the River Rhône is born. It tumbles westwards down from this tremendous altitude, over glaciers, rocks and occasional high valleys till it spreads out into Lake Geneva, at this point 375m (1230ft) above sea level. It leaves Lake Geneva and descends through further mountainous terrain, is joined by another turbulent river cascading down from Mont Blanc (the Arve). After more heights and gorges, collecting more glacial tributaries on the way, it widens and calms down, as it approaches the Lyonnais. When it encounters the Massif Centrale, it turns south, with 175m (574ft) still to descend before reaching the Mediterranean.

Nowadays, partly tamed by locks and hydroelectric barrages, the river is not the terror it once was, though still a formidable descent, enough to produce one fifteenth of France's total electric power. In the 18th century, no engine existed to drag boats against the torrent. The ride down from Lyon to the river's mouth (or more likely to Avignon where for a time the popes were installed; or Beaucaire where a stupendous annual fair was held) was fast and dangerous; the tow back upstream was slow, arduous and just as dangerous. In his *Poème du Rhône* Frederic Mistral tells of the *mariniers* embarking 80 horses to drag the barges upstream, a journey that could take 30 days. In cases of extreme difficulty, bullocks and mules would be hired from local farmers, and the *mariniers* themselves would put on the *bretelles*, or chest harnesses, and add their brawn to the tow.

The contemporary vessel most like those engaged today in *tourism fluviale* was the *coche*, a small comfortable craft rather like an Admiral's barge. This was used by wealthy merchants and doughty voyagers such as a certain Madame Cradock, who had to hire 32 horses to tow her off when her boat ran aground on a sandbank in the winter of 1784. Lyon to Avignon could be done by *coche* in 42 comfortable hours, which compared favourably with the 35 hours it took in a *diligence*, when you allowed for bad roads, accidents, robbery and appalling discomfort.

Lyon

The Rhône becomes officially navigable at Le Parc, about 95 miles from Lyon, with a depth of about a metre. Most of us, however, start our navigation of this once ungovernable river at Lyon, a delightful place to stop for a day or two. In the River Saône, just north of the point where it meets the Rhône, you will find moorings at a tree-lined quay below the busy traffic at Quai du Maréchal Joffre. From here you can browse fashionable shops in Rue Victor Hugo, walk north to the riverside open air market on the Quai des Celestins, or take your ease in the Place Bellecour, bordered with cafés where watching the passers-by is a delight.

You will not want to miss the rich (and copious) cuisine of the Lyonnais, whether you buy meals at a *traiteur* to take home, or go to one of the restaurants. The more adventurous will try one of the renowned *bouchons* close to the Mairie. These are ancient bistros where, in times gone by, the redoubtable *méres cuisiniers* cooked for 40 workmen in a space like an under-the-stairs cupboard, and the dining room was not much bigger. You will need some French, and an ebullient sense of humour to get the best out of these. On one of our nights out we studied the menu on the blackboard and decided against the *tablier de sapeur* (Fireman's apron – a dish of succulent sheets of tripe). Bill went for the *tête de veau* (calf's head). A huge plate was solemnly placed in front of him with a morsel the size of a postage stamp centred between two stalks of chive. Puzzled, Bill ate it, and looked around for more. There was an expectant silence from the watching waiters, then a burst of laughter. 'It is because we just heard that London has been awarded the Olympic Games, and not Paris', they said, bringing him the rest of his dish in a generously sized casserole. 'You are not offended? No?' No. The portions are generous; expect nothing dainty, share if you like.

If you are in Lyon on a Sunday in late May you will see rows of barges at the Quai Rambaud, gay with flags and music, clustered round the Chapel barge *Le Lien* for the *Pardon*. It is a religious festival for the barge folk, but they welcome anyone travelling on the river and it is well worth joining in and paying a small sum for the al fresco food on offer. There is usually a band, and you can even get a blessing for your boat.

At La Muletière you enter the Rhône proper, and your boat is pitched into a broth of spirits, legends and mythical creatures. The *drac*, a water dragon who as the *tarasque* gave his name to Tarascon, the *lerts*, evil entities up to no good underwater, all waiting for the unwary *marinier* to fall in, while the *oulourgues*, unshriven spirits who haunt the tombs of Arles, stalk the strand at night. Many stories are told as you go down-river. That huge rock at Pierrelatte was shaken out of the giant Gargantua's shoe; Pontius Pilate, once governor of Vienne, threw himself into the Rhône in a fit of remorse; the King's Table, just after St Vallier, is a flat rock in mid-river so named because Louis IX, King and

Saint, stopped to have lunch there on the way to the Crusades – these are just a few of the canon.

The names of the vineyards you pass in the Côtes du Rhône will make you thirsty if you are a lover of wine: Hermitage, Gigondas, Chateauneuf du Pape, and the less assuming but ever popular (especially in summer) Rosé de Tavel.

Your progress down the Rhône will be fast. While in the canals, 30km (18M) a day is good progress, in the Rhône you can do 80km (50M) a day. It is theoretically possible to get to the Mediterranean from Lyon in four days, but it needs long hours of daylight and luck at the locks. Good stopping places are spaced fairly well apart; some are worth a leisurely visit, some merely an overnight stop. Among these are:

- Condrieu KP 41: base nautique, should you need such a thing.
- Tournon KP 91: an awkward little mooring for a big boat, but worthwhile for shopping and restaurants.
- Valence, Port de l'Epervière KP 112: base nautique
- Viviers KP 166: Base Nautique for smaller craft
- You then pass the Defile Donzère Mondragon, through a magnificent gorge, where the highest lock in France, that of Bollène KP 186, awaits you. As it has floating bollards you should have no trouble descending 26m (85ft) in about seven minutes.
- There are useful stops at St Etienne des Sorts KP 204, Roquemaure KP 225 and Vallabregue KP 261.
- Avignon KP 242: is of course a lovely town, and there is much to see. The base nautique is not safe in some conditions, be aware that here, and at Arles, flooding of the river can cause much anguish – watch the weather in the upper reaches of the River Durance. Melting snow and thunderstorms can lead to serious flooding that carries away pontoons. In these conditions you are better off riding up and down the Ducs d'Albe downstream of a lock.
- Arles KP 283: Another beautiful Provencale town, but see note above on flooding. The *sapeurs pompiers* (fire fighters) will make you leave your boat if there is any risk.
- The last port of call is Port St Louis du Rhône KP 323. Although not at first sight so attractive as some towns, it has its points, good fresh fish, mussels from the *étangs* (lakes), a supermarket within walking distance, and an excellent street market.
- From Port St Louis, the Mediterranean is just at the end of the *canale maritime*, a few short kilometres away. It's nautical miles from then on.

· 20 ·
Coping with risks and dangers

While not fans of the Health and Safety Executive, we would not be alive today if we had been imprudent. There are aspects of life aboard a boat which demand different thinking compared to life ashore. There is not only a risk of falling overboard, but the cruising life demands precautions against other elemental but rare problems.

❖ Risks on the domestic scene ❖

Starting with domestics, it is likely that cooking, water heating, and domestic heating will all be different to methods in use ashore. It is possible to have an all-electric boat with 230 volt AC supply throughout, but that supposes a powerful generator, running for many hours a day as would happen in a big ship. Running generators semi-continuously risks incurring the wrath of boats unfortunate enough to be berthed alongside you. Generators are comparatively quiet during the ambient noise of daylight, but in the still of night they intrude. Even if the exhaust noise is negligible, the trickle of cooling water can be highly irritating. We recall an Italian motor yacht running a generator all night for its air-conditioning (which uses a great deal of power). The trickle of water so irritated one yachtsman that he turned out in his nightwear and hammered a plug into his neighbour's outlet. Avoiding confrontation is a safety measure.

The etiquette of air-conditioning is that it is run at night only when connected to shore power or when in an isolated mooring, and that begs thought because, as we said above, most inland waterway moorings have only limited supply of electric power, usually 15 or 16 amps, or even as little as 5. We counsel against the all-electric boat for your own convenience.

❖ Safety with gas ❖

Gas is the most widely used system for cooking and providing water heating and domestic heating in winter.

For a full-sized domestic cooker, you can manage on Camping Gaz. It comes in 3kg blue bottles of butane. In France at the moment (June 2009) a full bottle costs €27, which is €9 per kg. An advantage of Camping Gaz is that it is widely available, except in Germany, where you only find it in caravan suppliers. This matters because big gas bottles are heavy, and difficult to lug about if you do not have transport. Better value are the 13kg bottles costing €26 (€2 per kg), but these are hernia potential when lowering them into an appropriately constructed locker. Consider installing a hoisting point or sky-hook above the locker so that you can easily lift cylinders out or in. Of course Continental gas bottles have a different thread from British ones.

For use in winter, propane is better than butane as it evaporates better.

We have found that when used only for cooking, (oven and three burners) a 13kg bottle will last over two months. With two bottles you have plenty of chance to find a nearby supplier when one is emptied.

You can get a device that connects to two gas bottles at the same time. It draws off one bottle until it is empty and then automatically changes to the other. The point of change-over is hard to detect, but there is an indicator, which avoids the risk of half-cooked meals. You can get this device with tubes (known as pig-tails) with French threads, but it needs some persistence to get them in UK and they are rarely found in France. Going back and forth, we have several sets of pig-tails as every country seems to have its unique threads. We get the impression that there is not much demand for these 'foreign' pig-tails because when we ordered a set, they sent us one with time-expired tubing, though the error was due to culture difference. The English put the date of manufacture on the tubing and specify a use-by date separately. The French put an expiry date on their tubing with the legend, for example '*A remplacer avant 2010*' (Replace before 2010). The English supplier did not speak French.

Regulations

Check your tubing is in date – it could invalidate insurance. It is important to change flexible tubing at the right time.

Have your gas locker constructed according to legal requirements with adequate ventilation to the exterior of the boat and no ventilation to the interior. A top loading hatchway is best. There must also be a substantial $5cm^2$ hole to vent the base of the locker to the outside. These rules are liable to be enforced. The locker, with its isolating cock must be clearly labelled.

In France, there are intermediate-sized gas containers called cubes. These are recommended for smaller boats for which the size and weight of the 13kg cylinders are too much.

We use a portable radiant gas heater mounted on top of a 3kg Camping Gaz cylinder for emergency heating, or localised heating for a job on deck in deep mid-winter. Used like this as a stand-by, one is prepared for the high cost. It is not advisable for use below, but we have occasionally done so, mostly while working on the partially completed boat.

Other forms of cooking and heating do not come within safety headings other than plain commonsense,

❖ Safety with electricity ❖

The draconian regulations for houses do not apply to boats. In a boat you are allowed to electrocute yourself if you wish to.

Check that your electrical circuits are safe. Not just initially, but also at intervals. It is nice to have the reassurance.

In steel boats it is advisable to have galvanic isolation between your electrical circuits and the shore. Even if *your* circuits are above reproach, your boat may suffer severely if moored close to another boat with current leakage. This risk of galvanic corrosion is a serious matter in a steel or aluminium boat. Having suffered from this (our anodes were eaten away in less than six months), we spent the money and fitted an isolating transformer which weighs a ton, costs the earth, but gives peace of mind. Galvanic corrosion is likely to be less significant in fresh water, but not absent altogether.

❖ Safety with hot water ❖

If you draw hot water from the engine cooling (an economical method) and pipe it through your calorifier, you run the risk of scalds, so be careful. Fit a temperature limiting valve on the calorifier outlet; they do not cost much.

❖ Physical effort ❖

It's unnecessary to stress the dangers of awkward lifting. It is important, particularly for older people unused to arduous work, to learn how to lift heavy objects safely: back straight, knees bent; best of all use a tackle. It is such a useful skill, why don't they teach it in school? Once you get a bad back you seem to have it for ever.

❖ Buoyancy aids ❖

If conditions warrant it, wear a buoyancy aid of the waistcoat type. We wear one under certain hazardous conditions but not as a normal course. There are many occasions when to be impeded by awkward clothing is a danger in itself, and this certainly applies to life jackets with their tapes and exterior lungs. These should be carried as an important safety measure if required to abandon ship, no matter where, but they are not ideal as a precautionary measure. When tootling along a canal, the light-weight waistcoat buoyancy aid that fastens in a way that does not snag on things is far best. It will keep you afloat long enough for your mate(s) to come to your assistance. Which leads us neatly on to:

❖ Man overboard ❖

There are innumerable books giving advice on what to do at sea. Bill has, himself been overboard at sea without a lifejacket but, luckily, he was wearing a commodious oilskin smock which trapped air. He is a mediocre swimmer but he survived. For

MOB at sea, unless you are experienced, use the officially approved methods from official sources.

MOB on inland waters is a different matter. While navigating a canal or narrow river, especially in a boat which is longer than the navigable channel is wide, the Williamson turn is out of the question, so is any other form of navigational turn. Here is how I would go about the manoeuvre:

A boat that cannot turn in the narrow canal

- Don't panic.
- If someone falls over from the bows, stop the engine instantly, but do not go astern. You do not want him to face problems with a turning screw, these can be lethal.
- Let the boat's momentum carry her ahead and throw him a life belt as he passes, then let him get astern of you. When you can see he is well clear, put the engine full astern to stop the boat. Then reduce engine speed as soon as the way comes off the boat.
- Carefully keep her slow astern – very slow – and patiently back up towards him.
- Stop engine while still some distance off, 10m (33ft) say, and let the boat's momentum carry her back towards him. KEEP ENGINE STOPPED. Now see Retrieving the casualty below.

A boat short enough to turn back

- Don't' panic.
- Stop the propeller instantly because, in canals, there is an increased tendency for anything – including a human being – to be sucked into the screw race. See Chapter 19 on Canal effect for an explanation. As soon as the MOB is clear aft of the stern, turn the boat round. Turning at rest is easy with twin-screw boats but presents difficulty with larger single-screw boats. I recommend putting the boats stem gently against one bank (depending on the direction of rotation of your propeller) and then motoring ahead at half speed with the rudder hard over. Ease up as the stern swings past the 90 degree point and back off at 135 degrees. Complete the turn going ahead again and approach the MOB slowly with plenty of room to stop before the MOB is alongside.

Retrieving the casualty

Now (in both cases given above), try to reach him by throwing a coil of floating rope while hanging on to one end of it. If he can grab it, pull him gently towards you. A 15m (49ft) coil of orange-coloured floating rope, preferably about 10mm in diameter, is essential safety equipment and MUST be carried. (Orange to distinguish it and discourage people from using it for inappropriate purposes; plaited because it is less likely to kink. It is no good heaving a rope which kinks and turns itself into a triple Matthew Walker knot and drops into the water like a lead balloon.)

If you can get the casualty close to the boat, use a boathook carefully. If the MOB is unconscious, use the hook end to grapple clothing or whatever, carefully so as not to injure him. If he is conscious, do not use the hook end because that is dangerous. Instead offer him the handle end to hold on to. I have seen several cases where the hook end of a boathook has injured someone. NEVER poke the business end of a boathook at anyone, and this applies with extra emphasis to those criminally dangerous boathooks which actually have a spike as well as a hook. These are not a navigation aid, they are a *weapon*. Chuck them out. (It is noteworthy that professionals never bear off with the hook end anyway, they use the haft.) Use a boathook with two hooks (rounded M-shaped) at the business end.

The MOB will need help to climb aboard, especially if he is hurt. There are too many variables in all this, so be prepared to think clearly. Getting a body, alive or dead, out of the water and into a boat is difficult unless the boat has low freeboard or a swimming platform. Watch out! Swimming platforms tend to be close to the propellers. We keep a lightweight swimming ladder long enough so that the bottom rung is 1m (3ft) under water. You can stand on that while helping the MOB. Be continually aware of the danger of using your engine while the stern of the boat is anywhere near the MOB. DO NOT leave your boat to aid the casualty by doing a heroic dive in; this is the best way to end up with two casualties. If anybody falls even part way overboard between the boat and the quay, that is a serious matter. In this case, the instant insertion of a large pudding fender (every boat should have one) between boat and quay is essential (see page 89).

One last thing. Keep a usable lifebuoy handy, a lightweight one that is not likely to hit the MOB on the head and knock him out – it has been known.

It is doubly difficult if the person in the water represents half of the total crew. The need arises so seldom that one cannot reasonably go around with a special davit for the purpose. It is significant that the builders of the 'Caribbean' class of inland cruisers opted for low freeboard because they had noticed that fatalities among boat hirers who had fallen overboard on the Norfolk Broads were greatly increased by the inability of the boat's crew (who may or may not have been sober) to get their mate out of the water even if they got hold of him. The low freeboard of the 'Caribbean' class was an important safety feature, bearing in mind that most hirers had little or no boating experience.

> On inland waters, more people fall in from a moored boat than from boats under way; a major cause being alcohol.

For ease of recovering a MOB, the conventional motor cruisers have the advantage over barges, but only those who have a bathing platform aft. If you have stern davits for a dinghy it still is not easy. Solving this problem can be difficult for barges, you could use the car crane if you have one. We recommend for new-build barges (and even retro-fitted if possible) a set of toe-hold foot steps let into the side, and let's hope you never use them.

❖ Safety with ropes ❖

There are some safety measures to be taken when handling ropes, especially in large boats when the strain can be great. For preference have panama (closed) fairleads rather than open topped ones. Ropes cannot jump out of a panama.

Never stand inside a coil of rope if any part of it is under strain, even if the coil you stand in is on the slack side of the bollards. When ropes are running, never stand in a bight, which means to say, do not stand on the inside of a curve in the rope.

Keep your fingers well clear of bollards, bitts or cleats especially when veering rope or when the strain is about to come on. Professionals have a technique of controlling ropes using mainly the palms of their hands instead of their fingers.

Never let a rope run through your fingers: it will burn them in seconds.

❖ Moving and working safely ❖

- Wear non-slip footwear.
- Use non-slip paint or treadstrips on steel or GRP decks.
- Bare feet on boats are a menace.
- Flip-flops are dangerous.
- If handling wire ropes, wear leather gloves.
- Have strong handholds in strategic places, such as the bathroom and galley.
- Think carefully about steps, ladders and stairs. Well designed and positioned they give you exercise, badly thought out and with no handrails, they cause trips and falls.

❖ Anchors ❖

The law obliges inland waters craft to have an anchor ready. Most boats have an anchor, but how many have it ready for letting go?

Have a big anchor, because, if you ever need it, it is an emergency. A typical scenario might be that your engine fails when just above a weir, especially one on a big river with a hydro-electric power station attached. (See our book *Back Door to Byzantium* for a real-life description of this event, though in that case an anchor would not have been a solution.) If you are moored above a weir in a fast running current, then lower an anchor with three times the water-depth of chain as a precaution against criminally irresponsible passers-by.

❖ Being cast off ❖

Jokers cast boats off. Foil them by mooring with a length of 4mm chain at the up-stream end of your boat. Make it fast tightly twice round the shore bollard and padlock the two closest links together. Paranoia? You might say that, but we have been cast adrift by jokers or vandals three times and on two of those occasions, we were in fast-flowing rivers; these could have been total disasters. In the peace of canals or marinas, you should be all right, but in towns and cities people have awoken in the morning to find they are no longer alongside a quay.

❖ Fire ❖

Bill is professionally qualified as a ship-firefighter and has had several practical experiences during his service in a salvage tug. In our other cruising book, *Sell Up and Sail*, there is a serious chapter on fire in boats, so get hold of a copy and read it. Because Bill qualified a long time ago he got two current fire officers to give the chapter the once-over and received endorsements from the then Chief Fire Officer at Liverpool (who is a yachtsman) and a Deputy Fire Officer in Kent – a brigade which has great experience of civilian ship fires. The chapter is too long and detailed to reproduce.

We advise having (rule of thumb) one quality extinguisher for each 5m (16ft) of ship's length. Don't keep them in cupboards – they need to be conspicuous.

We avoid chemical powder extinguishers because a serious principle of dealing with fires is to use the extinguisher *immediately*, and the chemical ones do more damage than an early-stage fire.

Halon extinguishers were best but are now illegal except in certain volatile spirit environments. That dubious decision should be reviewed. Nobody at sea uses an expensive fire extinguisher except in an emergency. In those circumstances, 'greenery' should take second place to life saving.

After halon, carbon dioxide is the best material for fighting fires in boats though I am surprised that it is still permitted. In large boats, a fine high-pressure fresh water spray (the sort that produces a mist rather than a drenching) works well. One must be careful about using water as a fire-fighting medium aboard boats, owing to the danger of sinking or capsizing due to free surface. Can anyone remember the *Empress of Canada*? She was capsized in her berth by the over-enthusiastic use of water by the Bootle Fire Brigade.

Fire-fighting aboard ships and boats is a completely different skill to fire-fighting ashore because you cannot walk away. It is a serious life-saving matter, and I feel strongly that it should not be regulated by environmentalists who neither go to sea nor understand technical dangers.

Ordinary smoke detectors are of limited use in ships and boats. They are triggered too easily. There are smells and odours in a boat that are not harmful or even objectionable – an inevitable consequence of boat living, and these can trigger cheap smoke alarms. We have come across dozens of cases where fitted smoke alarms have been turned off because they repeatedly gave false alarms. One factor is that boats are ventilated from on top, whereas a house gets low level ventilation every time an outside door is opened.

❖ Ice ❖

See Chapter 13 Over-wintering in icy conditions.

❖ Leaks ❖

Openings in the ship's skin should be kept to a minimum, and all those below the waterline should have a proper seacock. We use 316 stainless steel ball valves which need lubrication with lanolin each time the boat is slipped. There are requirements under safety schemes that even outlets above the waterline should be fitted in this way – so they should for sea-going craft. My view is that, provided there is an unbroken fall of 2ft (0.6m) of rigid (galvanised or stainless) piping before reaching the skin, a ball valve is not necessary, but it costs little extra when building so why not do it? An important point with seacocks is to make sure that they are accessible. The backs of low cupboards behind boxes of disused Christmas presents are not good enough.

❖ Be aware ❖

Finally, we write in the chapter about a sea crossing that boats are only dangerous when you forget that they are dangerous. Life itself is risky, but by taking care we can enjoy living it. The same with living aboard a boat. In total, it is probably no more dangerous than living in London, but the dangers are different. Learn and understand them and you will cope easily.

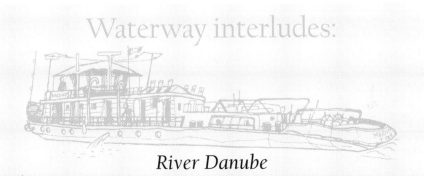

Waterway interludes:

River Danube

The Danube is the Mount Everest of European inland waters. It is tempestuous in its upper reaches, where we once experienced a flow of 21 kilometres per hour (12 knots) during a flood. It is treacherous in the middle where, in former times, before it was comparatively tamed by the locks at the iron Gates, it raced over dangerous rocks through the narrow Kazan Gorge. In the Delta it is deceptive; shifting channels and shallows can strand the unwary craft. The Danube is never blue, some say; others say that it is if you are in love.

The river begins in the Black Forest of Bavaria, where two little rivers, the Breg and the Brigach, join together at Donaueschingen, where an attractive spring is allowed to represent the actual source. Crystal bright and brook-sized, you can jump across until it goes underground and surfaces at Ulm. This is where northerly navigation on the Danube began, with a depth of about 1m (3ft). In the 18th century, craft known as Ulm crates went down river with passengers and cargo. They were simple wooden boxes, with a rough shelter aft. They drifted downstream guided by steering oars and most became firewood at journey's end, because of the near impossibility of going back up-river.

The Danube, descending 678m (2224ft) from source to sea-level over 2850km (1770M) was mainly a one-way route, particularly the first 700km (435M), where the downstream current could be unmanageable. From a southerly direction the delta was more approachable.

For practical purposes today, navigation on the Danube begins at Kelheim, 2414km (1499M) from the sea (and from where the kilometre posts commence). Navigators can get there by traversing the Rhine–Main–Donau canal, opened in 1992. To get to the beginning of this canal, you can come down the Rhine from Strasbourg, as we did, or you could come up the Rhine from Holland, probably a more difficult journey against strong currents.

The German section

Downhill from Strasbourg to the river Main was a swift and hairy run: 202km (125M), which we did in one long day on 21 May. The rules are strict. Being over 15m (49ft) in length, we had to take a pilot, and were glad we did; the river was flowing fast after considerable flooding, the barge traffic was intense, and it was a relief for us to hand over to an experienced holder of the *Rheinpatent* (barge skipper's licence for the Rhine). Thereafter we were on our own, travelling the great W shape of the river Main, where one is astonished to find, between Wertheim and Lohr, and Ochsenfurt and Schweinfurt, that one is travelling due north, before finally turning southeast at Schweinfurt. Having had to reroute in France because of intense spring flooding along the Belgian border (our voyage had started close to Calais), the TV news showed us pictures of the Danube in flood. We hoped it would subside before we got there.

We reached the junction of the River Main with the RMD canal three weeks after leaving Strasbourg, and the beginning of the Danube proper at Kelheim by the middle of June. Here we had to take refuge in the commercial haven, as the Danube was still in flood and all navigation was suspended. The forced interval brought us into contact with barge skippers of all nationalities, whose advice on the difficulties to be encountered lower down was invaluable.

Close to Kelheim is Saal Marina, the only marina on the Danube that most yachtsmen would recognise as such. It has all facilities.

If Germany by river was new to us, we were new to the Water Police, who had nothing in their rules to cover a pleasure barge of 27m (88ft), all pleasure craft being in their experience less than 20m (65ft), and most of them less than half that. They got round it by good-humouredly reclassifying us as an *arbeitschiffe* (workboat), when they discovered that we wrote books.

This did not help us with moorings. Marinas were invariably too small to take our length, and we would have been in trouble were it not for the friendly reception of commercial craft, dredgers, crane-barges and hotel boats who let us lie alongside them for a night, and our inability to read notices that told pleasure craft to keep off certain inviting (and empty) stretches of quay. As we have already mentioned, in Germany, practically everything you want to do is *verboten*.

The towns we passed were full of interest and history, we particularly enjoyed Bamberg and Regensburg. Shopping was not a problem, except that credit cards were little used, and we learnt to take cash everywhere. Helpings in restaurants were huge, one copious plateful (considered by the Germans a mere snack), was often enough for two elderly Brits.

We reached Passau, the border with Austria at the end of June.

The Austrian section

At Passau, the last German town before the border we learnt why a German skipper told us 'After here the Balkans begin.' To get our papers to enter Austria (go by car and it's no trouble, but by boat!) Bill queued for hours, and there was none of the friendly rule tweaking that the German police had evinced. Here was bureaucracy hard and relentless.

At Linz we found a mooring on the small pontoon of a yacht club. A member of the club came down in the afternoon and angrily told us to leave at once – we were far too big; but we had been beckoned in by a club official, and in recognition of our size, had made fast to the shore rather than the pontoon, so that our weight would not damage it. We left when we were good and ready.

The Danube is picturesque in Austria. At Grein begin 20km (12M) of steep and rocky narrows, a place feared by mariners till the course of the river was modified in the 18th and 19th centuries, and almost tamed by the Ybbs barrage in 1959. The area known as the Wachau is popular with tourists, rightly so as the villages bordering the river are charmingly pretty, each with its painted church topped by an onion dome. Austria is a small country, however, its share of the Danube is only 233km (145M) long, and we were through it in a week. There was no mooring in Vienna for a boat our size, alas, we had hoped to stop there for a rest and a bit of tourism.

The Slovakian section

Slovakia rules the Danube on both sides for only 33km (20M), but we spent longer there than we did in Austria. This was because we found our longed for haven in Bratislava, rather unexpectedly in the old Bassin Petroliu, off the hurly-burly of the main river. Not a marina, but a place with staithes and pontoons to moor among trees, and a welcoming restaurant barge, Milan's Tref, which had water and power for the hordes of little boats that arrived from Vienna every weekend to take advantage of good food and beer at half the price of Austria. We found a mooring close by the Tref, and our cable was long enough for Milan to plug us in. We had a long rest in warm summer weather.

Bureaucracy was relaxed. On paper we should have 'booked in' to Slovakia. We hadn't? It didn't matter. Our expert was a customs officer who brought us, on a Saturday, a parcel marked 'Spares', because he thought we might be needing it. 'Yes, there was some duty to pay. No cash? Just call by the office on Monday.' That really was a first.

The Hungarian section

For another 140km (87M) the Danube is Slovakian on the left bank, and Hungarian on the right. The town of Komarno/Komarom straddles the river, and the two countries are connected by a bridge. Here you must check into Hungary, and the bureaucracy is massive, it will probably take all day.

The people were friendly, but we were regarded as fair game by a variety of spivs. It is as well to beware, not only of officials, but of some taxi drivers and *garagistes*, to whom capitalism now means the ripping off of those seen as mugs, rather than an exchange of services for a reasonable sum. Fortunately, we met mostly those of the latter persuasion. Food and restaurants were cheap, except for the centre of Budapest. Marinas were rare, the one in Budapest had room for us, otherwise we laid alongside derelict barges, or the pontoons for boat trips and ferries, and on one occasion a disco barge.

The Serbian section

Mohacs is the border with Jugoslavia. We were there at a bad time, the fighting in Serbia had flared up again, so when we had finally overcome the mass of red tape, both Hungarian and that of the UN sanctions team, our only thought was to pass through to Romania as quickly as we could. We spent only two nights in war-torn Jugoslavia, both at anchor. It would be unfair to comment on bureaucracy in a country at war, suffice it to say that the Serb officials, and their military, treated us correctly, and with far more courtesy than the Hungarians had.

The Romanian section

Here the scenery was spectacular, as we went through the Iron Gates and the gorge of Kazan to Orsova, where we arrived too late to get visas (good heavens it was after four o' clock), and not only were forbidden to go ashore, but given two armed guards to ensure that two unarmed pensioners and their cats did not invade Romania during the night.

We checked into Romania the following day. Here the bureaucracy went into a hitherto undreamed of dimension, where the port captain held Bill in virtual captivity in his office all day, perusing our papers and tsk-tsking, playing some diplomatic game of which only he knew the rules, until Laurel realised what the problem was and arrived with a bottle of whisky. That said, the people were wonderfully friendly, and anything that was available in the shops, (not a lot – nothing imported or out of season) was heartbreakingly cheap.

The southern bank of the river is Bulgarian until Silistra. We did not attempt to visit because at that time the Bulgarians were charging every boat a swingeing cruising tax (purporting to be an entry visa) every time they entered a Bulgarian port, or moored to a pontoon. We stuck to the Romanian side.

As the Danube spreads and becomes shallow, the channels alter unexpectedly, and we ran hard aground near the Isle Bellene. A Romanian patrol boat came to our aid, but as they could not shift us, they called for their opposite number in Bulgaria to come and help. The two of them finally got us off, and waved away our attempts to pay for the service, though a couple of bottles of wine were happily accepted. Best of all, nobody involved asked to see our papers.

The last bridge was at Giurgeni, and at the next anchorage (KP 212) we put up the masts for the first time since leaving the North Sea. It was 25 August.

The Delta

This is another country altogether. The Danube divides into a mass of waterways and islands, some very remote. The few towns have no roads to anywhere else, the river is the road, and ferries ply in the navigable channel as water-buses. This means that there are regular pontoons, a barge with two huts built on it. One is a waiting room, and the other houses the guardian. You can spend the night at one of these 'bus stops' as long as you square it with the occupant (probably $1 and fresh fish thrown in), and leave room for the ferry.

This region is a wildlife paradise. The land is wooded to a great extent, there are also marshes and reed beds: different habitats for the many bird species. The local fishermen have used their traditional methods for centuries; the river teems with fish, which they catch from narrow tarred skiffs. We towed one for 7km (4M) against wind and current (they were trying to row the distance) and were rewarded with a bucketful of beautiful pike-perch.

There are several ways out to the Black Sea. For the 60km (37M) Danube–Black Sea Canal that begins at Çernavoda you might have to take a pilot. The way out through Sulina is another 300km (186M), but a much more interesting journey, and was the one we took – after an abortive attempt to exit via the Ukraine, where we were politely turned back as we had no visas. Any visa we could have got at Budapest would have expired by the time we got there. We could get them from Odessa, there was a train, they said proudly, but we could not catch it as we had no visas. A Gilbertian impasse.

So we sailed out through a minefield into the Black Sea via Sulina, on the 3 September, ending a voyage that had begun in northern France on 5 April.

· 21 ·

Sea crossings

An important feature of our attitude to the cruising life is that one should be able to change from one inland cruising area to another. A sea crossing should be as short as possible, as your boat is probably not ideal for sea-going. It can also entail a journey overland. Neither should cause you alarm. Moving safely and comfortably is the essence of cruising.

❖ Transport over land to or across Europe ❖

Road transport is not so heavily regulated as it once was. (Things get easier for vehicles as they get worse for boats.) If your vehicle and load is less than 4.5m (15ft) wide you can proceed on ordinary roads provided you have an escort vehicle properly marked, inform the police in advance, and do not travel after dark. Undoubtedly there are other requirements too, but if you get an experienced company such as Abbey, who shift many of the huge craft you see at the London Boat Show, they know all the details. They are expert and reasonable in price. They loaded, shifted and launched our new boat *Faraway*, with a beam of 4.6m (15ft) for a surprisingly modest sum, and they did it with impressive and reassuring care.

It is possible to ship boats over the channel by truck on a ferry. Given the beam of a narrowboat, one could load two side by side and still be within the maximum width allowed. The lowest total cost that we have been quoted from the Midlands to Calais was £2,000 for a single narrowboat, including craning out and in, and though this might seem high, the crossing afloat is not going to be cheap if you take proper precautions and do it correctly.

❖ Sea crossings as cargo ❖

Getting a boat across seas or oceans is not that big a deal nowadays. If you do not fancy the sea voyage, you can ship the boat as cargo.

For ages, the only means of cruising the inland waters of other parts of the world was to charter locally. In the last ten years or so, cruising your own very special boat in many parts of the world has become feasible. How do we go about solving the problem of getting boats from one continent to another without getting seasick? Our American cousins may wish to take their own boats to the French canals, and Europeans should consider the joys of the American Intracoastal Waterway.

The Americans could always charter in France, but that is expensive especially in summer, if you want to cover a large part of the system. If you live in a boat you will probably want to explore in your own boat surrounded by familiar things. So ship the boat over. The equivalent applies to Europeans wishing to have an extended cruise in America because chartering in the USA is not that simple.

Thirty years ago, shipping a boat as cargo was rare. Nowadays it is common and cheaper. Efficient agents arrange to use ships running a specialised regular service taking new boats for delivery; they often have spare places. Some have submersible after-decks onto which your yacht can be floated, and then the ship pumps ballast while the yacht settles into a pre-prepared cradle. By this method, sailing yachts can be carried with their masts stepped, which saves hassle and expense at both ends. On less well trodden routes, your boat can be carried as deck cargo. Steel barge-type boats might be welded to the deck for the voyage which isn't a problem.

If possible, arrange to travel in the same ship as your boat. Boats arriving in a foreign country as cargo are often treated differently to those which arrive on their own bottoms, there is a possibility of acres of paperwork. The agents should know all about this; it's their job.

Ships' cargoes are almost exclusively negotiated by an agent, we recommend that you consult one. For illustrative purposes, I asked Peters and May for ball-park figures to give an idea of the sums we are talking about. For a 12m (40ft) boat with 4.3m (14ft) beam and weighing up to 20 tonnes, one could ship from Miami to Southampton, water to water, for $18,000.

Crossing from Southampton to Palma (Mallorca) would cost £8,650. (Of course one could do Miami to Palma direct, or choose different termini.) Both these quotes would include cradling. Compare these prices with the cost of making an ocean passage which, done properly and prudently, would not be peanuts, let alone the time and planning it would take. Factor in the extra security equipment, repatriation fares for crew and a month's (say) loss of earnings for them. Extra insurance might be needed and a mountain of stores. For a powerboat, the fuel costs would be substantial. Many power boats cannot carry enough fuel.

For inland waterway boats, and for those which are coastal-passage capable only, this represents the only way of crossing oceans. I think it is cheap for what you get, especially if you make it a once in a lifetime adventure.

We have made eight ocean crossings in a yacht and quite frankly, after the first excitement it becomes boring – rolling like a pea on a drum for about three weeks. The best parts of any voyage are the departure fix and the landfall. Not a lot happens in between. Well, maybe the odd hurricane, but what is that between friends?

❖ Crossing the Dover Straits in an inland waters boat ❖

People in England contemplate the Straits of Dover and think, 'It's only 21 miles. People swim it. We can do that on a calm day, can't we?' Such a crossing is possible. It can be done; and it has been done, but it is not an enterprise to be lightly undertaken.

The English are adventurous sailors. They hate being told what to do, but we, ourselves, have crossed from England to France many times in small boats and can offer some generalised advice on how best to make this significant voyage safely in an inland waterway boat. Understand that despite the advice, it is you who make the decision. Only you know your boat, only you know your capabilities and like the captain of any ship, it is you, and only you, who are responsible for everything. It is not necessarily incautious to take an Inland Waterway Boat (IWB) to sea. It might be, but that depends on the skipper and his judgement.

Before going any further, go on line if you can and Google *Unorthodox Crossings*. Pay attention. Though the site seems a bit obsessed with people swimming the channel, it contains relevant advice, and quotes regulations which you need to know. My experience tells me that many novices have made this crossing successfully in unsuitable boats, but perhaps they were lucky. We have to remove the element of luck from sea-going, and recognise that people who are not skilled in seamanship can cause problems for those driving big ships who know what to expect of other professionals. If no problems occur, OK, but given the enormous difficulty of manoeuvring a big ship in confined waters, unexpected and unconventional manoeuvres of small boats can result in memorial services in Dover Church. So think carefully.

This chapter, though written with typical inland water craft such as narrowboats at the back of our minds, is relevant to all boats not designed as serious all-weather sea-going craft, and not skippered by experienced sailors.

I have navigated many seas in a variety of vessels: some of these voyages were in unsuitable craft (usually at the behest of the Queen), and I have arrived safely by tempering bravado with prudence. I shall tell you how I make the voyage, and if you follow this advice, you should do well, providing you also take sensible precautions. The sea is only dangerous when you forget that it is dangerous, and there is nothing wrong with caution.

Bear in mind that some of the regulations governing small-boat crossings carry the force of law. If all goes well, OK, but if you unknowingly cause an accident, you could face not only criminal proceedings, but could be held liable for the financial consequences. You must therefore get adequate insurance cover. This is obtainable – which tells you that marine insurance underwriters, who are specialists in assessing maritime risks, hold the voyage to be feasible under reasonable conditions.

Make sure your boat carries reasonable safety equipment for such a voyage and, apart from the special requirements of the Dover Separation Scheme, conforms to the bureaucratic norms printed in the publications of the Boat Safety Scheme, or some such. Most of those norms are somewhat over the top but, if you were to be in an incident and some official found deficiencies, it would be used as evidence not only against you, but against us all.

If you do the voyage on your own bottom, I suggest you will need the following gear on board, in addition to what is considered essential for canal or inland river use.

❖ Crossing in a narrowboat ❖

A narrowboat must take special precautions against sea movements even on a flat calm day, for you may well have to cope with wash from a big ship. We recommend completely closing in the open well that most narrow boats (and some wider ones too) have right forward. This need not be a matter of beautiful joinery; use 20mm (approx ³/₄in) shuttering plywood. Make sure you do this - the typical well in a narrowboat would hold about 2¹/₂ tonnes of water and that could be a serious problem. You would need also to reinforce the door from the well into the accommodation and make it substantially watertight. Install a good submersible pump and take a spare battery to help with it.

Some narrowboats have very little aft to protect the helmsman. We have no recommendations except that you should think seriously about it. It is possible to slip on a wet deck and slide under a waist-high rail.

Narrowboats are built to diverse standards; be sure that yours is structurally sound and suitable for the passage. Narrowboats (and similar small barges) must be professionally surveyed and any recommended adjustments done.

❖ Equipment needed for a sea crossing ❖

- *A compass*, preferably a gyro-stabilised electronic one. Don't forget to go through the installation procedure. If it is a conventional magnetic compass, then have it adjusted for the magnetic influence of your boat.

- *A GPS* that will track progress towards a waypoint, and even better, one that will take you on a pre-set 'route' of successive waypoints. The cheaper sort of GPS sold for use in motor cars will probably be unsuitable. Take expert advice if you are not sure, as this is a very important piece of kit for the inexperienced Channel crosser.

- *A book of standard waypoints*, especially if you have trouble coping with latitude and longitude. If you are inexperienced, these books help and there is nothing shameful about their use.

- *Medium scale paper charts of the voyage* (1:70,000 to 1:150,000) for use in planning and if the electronics go awry. There is strong evidence that wind-farms interfere with some electronic navigation aids and I have twice had the experience of having GPS turned off by Uncle Sam without notice.

- *Navigational large-scale plan of the intended arrival port*, plus alternative refuge points en route.

- *Tidal charts* which give the tidal streams at times relating to High Water at Dover. They are usually in a booklet or an almanac.

- *A 2B pencil, sharpener and a ruler.*

- *An up-to-date copy of a coastal almanac such as Reeds Nautical Almanac.* If you can read French use the *Livre de Bord.* Make sure the one you choose has full details of the Dover Separation Scheme.

- *A Marine VHF with DSC* (Digital Selective Calling). This is now obligatory. Hand-held low-power sets are NOT good enough. Set it to the correct channel, currently 11 for the British service (callsign 'Dover Coastguard'), and channel 13 for the French, (callsign *Gris Nez Trafic* – pronounce it Greenay Traffic, but they speak good English). You will probably be called by the Coastguard and must be able to respond in a proper manner as the radio channels are busy and nobody wants to waste time. Some Continental authorities require ATIS facilities on your VHF. This is because Britain did not join the RAINWAT scheme adopted by the Continental countries. Check with the supplier of your VHF set and get him to install it if necessary. It should cost nothing.

- *Foul weather gear for the helmsman at least,* for you must expect exposure to spray in the unprotected steering position of a typical narrow boat.

- *A liferaft* that will take all on board, equipped with a coastal survival pack. This can be hired.

- *A sea-going standard life jacket* for everyone on board.

- *An in-date coastal pack of emergency pyrotechnics.* This can be hired.

- *Navigation lights* appropriate to the size of your boat. They must be proper electric ones, not improvised torch-lights with coloured cellophane. You might hope, but cannot guarantee, to complete the voyage in daylight, and you would be an unacceptable menace in the busiest waterway in the world if you were not properly lit, and you must have lights in the event of unexpected fog. It might be possible to borrow a set of four, but make sure they are properly mounted.

- *A radar reflector* which the rules say you should have. It is arguable that poor echo detection is due to inadequate watchkeeping. That may be so, but you are the one in danger so look after yourself.

- *Proper ship's papers*: registration certificate, VAT certificate, radio certificate for the ship, certificate of third party insurance, Crew's papers. One person on board should have an appropriate licence to drive. One person should have a VHF (DSC) operating licence, preferably translated into French.

- *First aid kit*, including seasickness tablets. Hyoscine hydro-bromide is what the Royal Navy found the best for most people. Take care: almost all seasick pills induce drowsiness so don't fall into the trap of thinking that a heavy dose is more effective than that recommended. The trip takes time and demands prolonged concentration.

- *Pre-cooked food that is easy to prepare and eat.* Hot food cheers you up if you get tired and/or over-anxious. If you have a microwave, take some things that can be heated, then nobody has to go below for long periods. High carbohydrate snack food such as cereal bars are useful. Fizzy drinks (notably dry ginger ale) help to stave off seasickness.

❖ Passage planning ❖

You *must* know the rules for the Traffic Separation Scheme (TSS). These provisions carry the force of law. Associated with them are other special rules. I recommend buying Admiralty Chart Number 5500, which is entitled *Mariners' routeing guide to the English Channel and Southern North Sea*. This will tell you far more than you need to know, but a good read before setting out will put difficulties into perspective and help you appreciate just why such a traffic separation scheme is necessary. Make notes of those parts which affect you directly. This may involve consulting somebody knowledgeable, but you should do that anyway.

I shall neither quote the rules nor recommend any particular track; because that depends on you and your boat, but *do your homework*.

IS MY BOAT SEAWORTHY?

Good strong hand-holds are advisable. Your boat will roll and even if you stay within the boat, you can get thrown about and suffer bruises or worse. Even if (as you absolutely must), you choose a good weather window, your boat can be badly tossed about in a big ship's wash.

Take comfort from the fact that the British Expeditionary Force would never have been embarked from the Dunkirk beaches, not far from where you are going, if it had not been for a myriad of small boats mostly unsuited for the sea, and certainly lacking the prudent gear I have recommended. It was a case of 'needs must ...' but we hope the devil is not driving you.

Lastly, boats or skippers that are dubiously seaworthy should cross in company with a boat that is sea-kindly and properly equipped and qualified. Do all that is possible to minimise risk. This trip is not a picnic, though with good weather and no problems it may seem so afterwards.

See the advice given on coping with waves on page 196.

❖ Timing ❖

Whether you are heading for Dunkerque, Gravelines or Calais, it is *strongly recommended* that you arrive in daylight and with a margin for error especially if you lack practical experience of night navigation. The entry to Gravelines is tricky in the dark, and unless you are familiar with Calais, the system of traffic lights that govern entry and departure can be confusing. (Consult the pilot book.) Dunkerque is a busy cargo and passenger port and finding your way around inside the port is confusing if you are a stranger to the harbour. It is easier now there is a separate entrance for big ships.

At all three ports, time your arrival for the interval between High Water minus 90 minutes - and High Water. As the tidal streams flow parallel to the coast, this needs careful judgement. In neither port is slack water coincidental with High Water. Hence the need for a good tidal atlas. The tidal stream flows across the entrance; don't be set on to the downtide pierhead. It is always advisable to arrive at a strange port in the period before High Water; this allows for errors in estimating tidal heights which can vary with wind direction and atmospheric pressure. You may have to moor at the edge of the channel.

CHECK LIST

- Engine function
- Filters fuel, coolant, oil.
- Navigation lights fitted and working.
- Marine VHF radio.
- Ship's papers, passports, Certificates of Competence, insurance certificate, VAT evidence, Radio certificate, Radio Operator's Certificate.
- Charts and pilot book/almanac.
- GPS function, waypoints entered along route, waypoints entered for alternative port of entry. Stand-by way points for 'bolt-hole' ports if obliged to abort the passage.
- Food and drink for passage. Seasickness pills.
- Serious protective clothing for two, and weather-proof gear for remainder.
- First aid kit.
- Life raft, fireworks, plus emergency equipment embarked.
- Inform Coastguard of voyage details, crew list and contact details.
- Use the loo before departure, then close the seacock.
- Keep morale high. Bon voyage.

❖ Departure ❖

To achieve the right departure time, you must plot backwards from the destination and decide on the port of departure. This decision depends to some extent on the distance to be travelled.

The Straits of Dover, with their elaborate separation scheme, is not a doddle. There are some very fast, very large ships about and, assuming your vessel is less than 20m (65ft) long, you will be bound by Rules 9 and 10 not to impede their passage. Even if you are over 20m (65ft), you can be in a tricky situation because the other ship has no way of telling your size. Care is needed even if technically you have right of way. In these circumstances when doubt can arise, as I know from experience, *Hosanna* being 27m (88ft) overall, you may be in more danger than at any other time on the crossing.

Here lies the body of Mike O'Day
Who died preserving his right of way.
He was right, so right as he sped along,
But he's just as dead as if he were wrong.

Big ships take a long time to react. One big ship I sailed in did not start turning until half a minute after wheel-over, and then turned at only about 20 degrees a minute. Tugs with long tows are difficult to turn at short notice. For a small vessel, the best method of yielding right of way and making it obvious you are doing so, is to make a 360° turn to starboard.

❖ Departure and arrival ports ❖

To my mind, the only two departure ports I recommend are Ramsgate and Sheerness. Ramsgate has a well-sheltered marina with fuel available. However, their charges are crippling, so it does not pay to be trapped there for days by adverse weather in a narrowboat, when the mooring fees depend on length. However, if the forecast is 'set fair' (essential for this voyage) you should be OK and Ramsgate is a nice town.

My own preference is to cross in late June or July. I like to spend the night at Stangate Creek in the Medway estuary during spring tides when High Water is at about 0430. You can lie at anchor in a well-protected creek where the holding ground is excellent. Set the alarm for dawn or about half an hour before High Water and get started straight away, passing out of the Thames estuary down the main big ship channel on the ebb tide and carrying the favourable strong tide all the way past North Foreland until the Goodwins are abeam to starboard. Keep well over to the southern side of the channel in the presence of big ships. There is a shorter route via the Spaniard Channel, but it requires greater concentration and I have found that one cannot rely on all the channel marking buoys being on station. You would not lose much time by taking the deep channel because the ebb stream is stronger there.

Depending on speed (*Hosanna* cruised at 6 knots under power and this is a voyage that should only be done under power) we were north of the Goodwin Sands at slack Low Water and set off to cross the separation channels with the southwest-going tidal stream on the beam. You will have travelled about 40 miles and the tide will start setting southward. If you cross the main southwest-bound channel and then the deep-water channel (heading at right angles to these channels), you should be set down a bit by the tide and be off the Sandettie. There is no reason why you should not cross over the Sandettie Bank and every reason why you should; there is plenty of water to float a barge, and there you would be out of the reach of big ships. Your heading now should carry you to a point somewhere between Calais and Gravelines. Adjust your heading to cross the remaining (northeast-bound) traffic lanes.

You are obliged to cross the TSS channels at right angles, and this means that the boat should be *pointing* across at right-angles. The result is that the tide will oblige you to take a slanting geographical track across. Once clear of the northeast-bound channel, you can alter course along the French coast for either Calais or Gravelines, arriving at either in a desirable state of tide.

There is a sandbank parallel to the French coast, and ferries approach Calais inside this bank, which is well buoyed. I recommend keeping to the seaward side of this channel and thus to the landward side of the bank. The tide will be on the flood so that a small shoal draught boat can navigate safely just outside the channel and be safe from big ships. At high water, a barge should be able to cross this bank without trouble

Now, Calais or Gravelines?

Calais

Here the pleasure boat harbour is in a side basin to the west, once accessible only through a sea lock and bridge which opened for a short time at High Water. The sea lock has given way to a cill, but you would still have to wait for the road bridge to open so little has changed in practice. You would have to find a temporary mooring in the outer harbour if you do not arrive absolutely at the right moment which is unlikely, however good you are, because another factor governing the bridge opening is ferry movement. In Calais, everything takes second place to ferries. Small boats can find a swinging moor, but larger ones such as barges make fast to the high wall under the lighthouse, this is safe because you have arrived just before High Water, haven't you? Don't stay there long with a falling tide.

When the bridge opens, the boats within the basin waiting to get out have priority and come through the gap like the start of the Grand National; there can be dozens of them. This lot threading their way through all the boats who have slipped their mooring and are milling about waiting to enter the yacht basin, turn the inner harbour into a fairground and the Port Officers do not like that to happen unless the ferries are tucked up in their berths. We were there once when a mistake was made and the yachts got the starter's flag just as a big ferry was entering the port, tooting like the devil on her siren. It sorted itself out, but it was a close-run thing.

The unfortunate thing about Calais is that the Port Authorities do not normally want pleasure boats mooring in the Bassin Carnot which is on the way to the canal. I do not know why. When I asked I got a Gallic shrug. The *bassin* is almost always near empty. To access the *bassin* requires passing a road bridge and lock gates and these are normally closed and open only on demand. Even if you find them open and dash into the *bassin*, whistles will blow and men come dashing to bid you nay. (This may be changing soon.)

There is a fat fee for mooring in the crowded yacht harbour, where there is an excellent club-house, a fuelling berth and a crane. You normally stay there while negotiating the opening of the Bassin Carnot lock and the bridge and lock which lets you into the Bassin de la Batellerie, which connects to the Canal de Calais. This lock is usually efficiently run; call on VHF channel 17. During this waiting time you will be expected to get your *vignette* from the offices of VNF for which payment is exacted according to the ship's footprint (overall length x overall breadth) with a maximum value that is quite reasonable. Each year the system changes and you will have a choice of period. In my view it is better to get the *vignette* over the internet, which is devised to be intelligible to foreigners and very nearly is. Thank the DBA for negotiating this; the RYA do not bother about inland waters boats.

Close to the Calais Yacht Club, are many good restaurants. We like Calais, but unfortunately the Bassin de la Batellerie, where there are good pontoons for mooring is inhospitable as the pontoons are fenced off behind impenetrable gates and fencing. Whether this is due to boats suffering interference from illegal immigrants (of whom there are many) or drug addicts and/or delinquent youth, depends on whom you ask. Best not to use these berths at all, but to pass the lock early and go on up the canal without further ado. We describe our experience of this canal in *Watersteps Round Europe*.

Once in the Canal de Calais, you will find several bridges that will open if you are lucky. Sometimes the canal is covered by a green carpet of pond weed, and those with keel cooling for their engines will feel very relieved. There is one lock before joining the river Aa. It is best to get somebody to phone the lock in advance to make sure it is attended.

Calais is a more convenient port if you have crew joining or leaving.

Gravelines

This port is entered at the extremities of two long break waters sited at right-angles to the coast. At High Water the tide runs sharply across the pier heads and some aim-off is needed when entering but it is not difficult and you can keep the long straight channel in view to guide you. This channel dries out at Low Water.

At the inner end of this channel you turn sharp right and then through a bridge and lock gates, which are usually open, into a basin. There are marina-like moorings and a visitors' pontoon close right on entry. The people here are hospitable and we never had any problem with *Hosanna*, though the facilities in the basin have changed and it is now more amenable to boats less than 18m (59ft). Flat bottoms are best, but the mud is so soft and deep that keel boats stay upright when on the bottom at low water. There is a supermarket almost on the quay and the small town is close. There is a crane and Leffe on draught. The marina restaurant/bar offers cheap and cheerful nosh There is also the Michelin Restaurant le Turbot, which is worth the effort to find. Gravelines is noted for its fish; at one time their sailing trawlers went up to Iceland for cod and halibut.

To pass into the River Aa from Gravelines, you need to give notice to the port captain. It is a single gate lock. You will have to stand by close to the gates while the water levels equalise and then the gates open and you dash through, with the gates slamming shut close under your stern. It is exciting but safe if you do as you are told. There is a free mooring just above the lock, which is little used, and a railway swing bridge and you can head for the canalised river further on. Alternatively you can turn sharp left, enter a conventional lock and pass down a sleepy narrow canal to Bourbourg which has a municipal pontoon, set among the trees, where you can rest.

Otherwise you join the Canal du Nord, a big one (grand Gabarit) and go on your way to Arques and the south.

If you enter at Gravelines, get your *vignette* in advance. There is no local office of the VNF there; the first you come across en route southward is at Béthune which is the head office of VNF. In spite of a notice on the canalside, the office is miles away from the canal in a modernistic building; the people there are courteous.

Other French ports

Those with more seaworthy boats have the option of a larger choice of departure and arrival ports. Just down from Calais, is the delightful small port of St Valery-sur-Somme.This is a fine place to enter the canal system via the Canal de la Somme, but the entry to St Valery demands above-average navigational skills, for the bay has a bar across the entry and the channel is long and confusing to the inexperienced. Those coming from the west country might consider entry at Le Havre. If so I recommend not stopping at Le Havre, a busy port. You would be lucky to find a berth at the charming little harbour of Honfleur on the opposite side of the river. Go to the latter if you can, but be prepared to go on up river towards Rouen. The tidal stream in the river can be strong at spring tides so try to arrive at low water.

HOW TO COPE WITH WAVES

As we have already said, it is essential to select a weather window of reliable calm for the crossing. Getting into the wash of a fast big ship is bad enough but to have to roll your guts out for hours on end in a boat not designed for it is a penance. We are doing this for pleasure.

If you find yourself having to cope with waves, take them almost head on. Trawlers faced with serious seas use a technique they call 'dodging' which puts the direction of the waves at about 15 degrees on the starboard bow, allowing the wind to vary a bit without going round the bows. They find this safer and more comfortable than keeping the sea right ahead. The most serious situation in a narrowboat would be with a sea on the beam. A barge has a large positive GM, a technical term which measures initial stability and indicates a propensity to roll with a fast period. This is uncomfortable and dangerous because crew can get thrown about badly and in such a boat something is bound to come adrift. You can only reduce rolling by putting the sea either fore or aft.

Waves from astern are fine provided the wavelength (distance between crests) is short. If the wave length is long, over half a barge length, say, then you get two serious problems. The first is that the boat will alternate between being balanced about her mid-point like a see-saw (called *hogging*), and being supported at either end and having no support in the middle (called *sagging*). A boat needs to be designed to cope with these strains; few inland waters boats are. The second danger is that as waves pass, her stern will occasionally lift and the engine will start racing for a few seconds. It won't like this.

❖ A Dutch crossing ❖

To cross to the Netherlands, the best departure is from the northern shore of the Thames Estuary, Levington Marina, Pin Mill or Woodbridge perhaps. The voyage is about 100 miles and needs careful planning. Watch out for the entrance to Felixstowe harbour. Here are big merchant ships driven by impatient local pilots, though I have always found them correct and appreciative of co-operation. The ferry captains are almost criminally unco-operative with small craft (unlike those on the Dover/Calais run) and the fast ferries make an enormous wash in shallow water. They are supposed to slow down when approaching the port, but there is little evidence that they do so. The question of a vessel of 21m (69ft) insisting on her rights under Rules 9 or 10 in a narrow channel, is a black comedy. If the land based extra-masters who wrote the Colregs knew their job properly, they would never have let such a farce get into the book. If you are in this position, then please yield. Inform the Port Control in concise clear terms that you will do so and do it before any confrontation can develop. Big ship drivers only hate amateurs who screw them up: they appreciate co-operation. If you wish to pause to allow a commercial vessel to cross ahead, it is better to turn 360 degrees to starboard than to remain at rest. The turn makes your intentions clear.

Suddenly, it is the end of the voyage. We have not said it all; at times we have hardly covered the ground – it is a very big subject and a book has limited space – as our editor keeps reminding us.

We hope we have all reached a destination. We fervently hope that there will be many more voyages for all of us and that they are as satisfying for you as ours have always been, even the tough ones.

We wish you *Bon voyage*, *Tot ziens*, *Gute reise* and leave you with the following story:

A Thames barge was trying to berth under power in the tideway at Yarmouth. She was making a mess of it – backing and filling repeatedly. Finally, the bows got near enough to the quay for the mate to throw a line to the shore and see it made fast. He then stomped aft and went below, saying 'Do what you b....y well like with your end. My end's made fast.'

Appendix

❖ Further reading and websites ❖

Blue Flag The journal of the DBA (The Barge Association), is the best up-to-date reading, available free to members of the DBA.

Fluvial This French magazine is a source of much up-to-date information.

La Vie Batelière This is a journal for the professional batelier (French barge skipper).

Code Vagnon Fluvial is a comprehensive guide for French speakers. Marian Martin's version (less comprehensive) is in English, published by Adlard Coles Nautical.

Croyances et Coutumes des Gens de Rivières et de Canaux by Anette Pinchedez. (Beliefs and customs of river and canal folk.) This fascinating book deals with the folk-lore of the rivers.

Rheinschiffahrtspolizeiverordnung This is the rule book for the River Rhine, published in German.

De Schuttevaar A journal publishing professional boat news in the Netherlands.

Histoire des canaux, fleuves, et rivières de France (History of the Canals and Rivers of France), a classic work by Pierre Miquel, well worth looking for it if you are interested in history.

Cruising French Waterways, 4th edition by Hugh McKnight (Adlard Coles Nautical).

The Ups and Downs of a Lockkeeper by Jake Kavanagh (Adlard Coles Nautical).

The British magazines covering the British waterways are:

    Canal Boat
    Canals and Rivers
    Waterways World
    Motor Boat and Yachting and *Motor Boats Monthly* both have regular articles on cruising inland waters.

❖ Clubs and associations ❖

The Barge Association (DBA) offers coverage of the whole inland waters scene, both British and European. Its *Blue Flag* journal features technical articles about barges and canals in general, news about canal navigation, and some cruising yarns. Its website is a good source of information: www.barges.org

    Inland Waterways Association www.waterways.org.uk
    Historic Narrowboat Owners Club www.hnboc.org.uk
    Association of Waterway Cruising Clubs (AWCC) www.awcc.org.uk
    The latter three organisations are good sources of information on the British canal system.

❖ Books recommended for inexperienced boaters ❖

The Boater's Handbook published by the Environment Agency in conjunction with British Waterways. It is nice to give a pat on the back to a government agency, and this little book is excellent for what it does. Obtainable at the London Boat Show, otherwise try www.environment-agency.gov.uk/navigation or 01454 624 376.
The Barge-buyer's Handbook published by the DBA. The title is self-explanatory.
How to Buy a Boat for Canal or River published jointly by the British Marine Federation and the Canal Boatbuilders' Association. It gives information on how to find a builder and about the many aspects of British 'red tape'. Bureaucracy rules but don't be put off. It's all worth it.

❖ Other useful websites ❖

Internet browsing needs a caution. Nobody can possibly 'know' the whole scene, and many sources are of doubtful reliability. Forums are only as good as the questions they ask, and the answers they get.

Apart from the ones listed above, here are three we have found useful:

Boat shippers: Peters and May: www.petersandmay.com

Cruising in Ireland: www.carrickcraft.com

Taking pets abroad: www.defra.gov.uk

❖ Driving licences ❖

The rules of navigation on Europe's waterways differ in each country. Things are improving. Most countries, except the Netherlands, adopt a commonsense attitude to foreigners on their waters.

The rules have just changed again in France, ostensibly towards standardisation. Here is the situation in 2009 as we understand it:

Permis rivière (river licence) This is obligatory for anyone steering a boat on a canal or river (except for hire-boats).

Permis plaisance côtière (coastal licence) A licence valid for up to 6 miles off-shore.

Permis plaisance en eaux intérieures For vessels less than 20 metres.

Permis grande plaisance en eaux intérieures For vessels over 20 metres; the maximum is unclear.

- International certificates remain valid.
- Existing certificates remain in force, including the PP (*péniche de plaisance*).
- You can get a restricted VHF licence for inland waters. See www.anfr.fr

How to qualify for a permit

Members of the DBA should consult that organisation; they are the best informed. Non-members should try the RYA, who may be involved in issuing some minor certificates. It is likely that serious bargees will want a GP licence (best obtained in France) they should get in touch www.bargehandling.com

In Britain, there are barge (including narrowboat) courses at Marlow, Buckinghamshire. Try www.bishamabbeysailing.co.uk Tel 01628 474960.

The technical rules for barges and other craft in European waters are likewise still not yet ratified. They are called the *Technical Regulations for Inland Waters Vessels* (TRIWV). Again, the DBA is the best source of reliable information but the RYA might also help if you can find the right person to ask.

A recreational licence or cruising permit (*vignette*) is needed for cruising French waterways. These can be obtained on line at www.vnf.fr/vignettesVNF/accueil.do

❖ Maps, guides and charts ❖

We have discussed these in the various chapters. Charts are available from Stanfords in Long Acre in London, but but your may find them cheaper in your local chandlery.

The best electronic inland waterways chart is PC-Navigo which is a route planner programme which contains all the data you need for the navigable waterways of Europe. All countries are required to produce Electronic Navigation Charts (ENCs). The northern countries have complied. France has only done so for the *grand gabarit* (larger) canals so it is of limited use in France. Many people have experimented with Google Earth mixed with GPS with encouraging results. This would require mobile broadband which is not good in France.

Index